Donald Trump,
Made in the U.S.A.

Other Books by Jon Huer

Labor Avoidance (2015)

Call from the Cave (2013)

Auschwitz, USA (2010)

American Paradise (2010; Arabic Language edition 2017)

The Green Palmers (Fiction 2007)

The Post-Human Society (2004)

The Wages of Sin (1991)

Tenure for Socrates (1991)

The Great Art Hoax (1990)

The Fallacies of Social Science (1990)

Marching Orders (1989)

Art, Beauty and Pornography (1987)

Ideology and Social Character (1978)

Society and Social Science (1978)

The Dead End (1977)

Our Savage Nation ("jonhuer.com" 2016)

Donald Trump, Made in the U.S.A.

A Study in Consumer Capitalism, Mental Trash and the Privatization of White America

Jon Huer

Hamilton Books

Lanham • Boulder • New York • Toronto • Plymouth, UK

Copyright © 2017 by Hamilton Books
4501 Forbes Boulevard, Suite 200, Lanham, Maryland 20706
Hamilton Books Acquisitions Department (301) 459-3366

Unit A, Whitacre Mews, 26-34 Stannary Street,
London SE11 4AB, United Kingdom

Library of Congress Control Number: 2017938898
ISBN: 978-0-7618-6927-6 (pbk : alk. paper)—ISBN: 978-0-7618-6928-3 (electronic)

∞™ The paper used in this publication meets the minimum requirements of American
National Standard for Information Sciences Permanence of Paper for Printed Library
Materials, ANSI/NISO Z39.48-1992.

To Terry and Jonathan Huer,
and our beloved Aunt Sue

Contents

Foreword   ix

Introduction: In Donald Trump, America Reaps What It Sows   1

1 The (White) Children's Crusade   7

2 Trump's America We Hardly Knew   15

3 The Day of Revelation   25

4 The Child with a Loaded Gun   31

5 Trump's "Moral Immunity"   41

6 Who Created the Monster?   49

7 The Nature of "White Anger"   57

8 Trump between Capitalism and Fascism   63

9 The Nation Divided, Once Again   75

10 The End of a Demagogue   85

11 The American Character   95

12 Trump's Conquest of America   105

13 Mental Trash   115

14 The Lost Mind   129

15 Capitalism Triumphant   141

16 Capitalism Eternal   157

17 How Money Buys the Law   167

18 The Ten Reminders   179

Bibliography   187

Index   189

Foreword

For the better part of my academic career at the University of Maryland, I have been teaching social science subjects at the U.S. military bases, including Camp Humphreys of the movie *World War Z* fame. At every military base, large or small, there is a "food court" where flat-screen TV sets, strategically spaced, show their programs, mostly sports and news, while customers eat their lunch. Soldiers munch on their food and occasionally and unconsciously look up at the TV screens. What's striking about these TV screens is that nobody pays any real attention to what's shown on the screen. They glance at the screen, without any particular meaning or purpose, while eating their food. Their faces are totally devoid of expression, lifeless and vacuous, although their eyes seem to be fixated on the screen for a stretch at a time. This blank, no-reaction to the TV screen is quite in contrast to the animated, excited and colorful actions that they are watching. On the flat-screen TV, everything is so seriously and elaborately presented that you cannot tell if the program you are watching on the screen is about World War III or Game III of the World Series. Why is there no sign of reactive intelligence or human feeling in the eaters' faces while they are watching such extravagant and expensive presentations on TV? (A similarly lifeless expression is also observed when they are engaged in smart-phone browsing). The answer is not complex: *Because the stuff they are watching on the screen is garbage*, utterly meaningless whether they watch it with attention or in half-sleep. If all the screens went blank the whole day or didn't exist in the first place, nobody would miss anything that is significant enough in one's life! To paraphrase Marshall McLuhan: It's made up of nothing that has become something only because it has become part of our daily routines. What kind of people would we become if we were fed this garbage for decades by our Consumer Capitalism?

What does a typical American, who has had nothing but mental garbage all his life, think or feel as a human being? The 2016 presidential election gave us a chance to see a first-hand manifestation of this phenomenon that the world had never seen before. Just prior to election day, The *Nation Magazine* undertook a study in order to understand the so-called "Trump Whites" because it was wholly unthinkable that such a person as Trump had so many supporters. In the study, they located a quintessential "Trump White" in the person of Patty Dwyer, a divorced respiratory therapist in New York, who could be anyone in the crowd at a typical Trump rally. In 2008 she had voted for Obama. But this year, after a radical downturn in her family, marriage and job situations, and thus feeling frustrated and angry, she found a savior in Trump. She tells the reporter how she felt about him: "I just can't believe that this man, with all his money and all that he could be doing right now. . . that he'd want to make a difference here. The experience (of encountering Trump) totally blew me away—I left there crying and, you know, choking up." Her vision of Donald Trump is quite similar to a spiritual experience, or a sinner at the moment of sudden religious conversion. But, like the millions of people who voted for Trump, she was easily mixing the personal with the public. Whether you are religious or not, this act of confusing public events (election and presidency) with deep personal awakening is normally found among the intellectually idiotized and emotionally confused, not among the smart horse-traders of the bygone-era Yankees. Patty Dwyer is a miniature version of most, if not all, White Americans who have been shaped and molded by the flat-screen TV or smart-phones all their lives. She happens to be the voter version of all the blank faces staring at the TV sets at Camp Humphreys as well as in most American living rooms.

In the daily lives of both Humphreys residents and Patty Dwyers all over America, the consumption of meaningless garbage, here today and gone today, has become their religion and pilgrimage. Garbage in and Garbage out, their thoughts and feelings are processed from nothing to nothing, today like yesterday, and to continue tomorrow, leaving nothing meaningful to show that they have lived a day as human beings and as members of a social community. To give us a clearer perspective on American society and its character, we are told at this writing, that an Internet poster-child called *Snapchat* has gone public. Its anticipated initial investment exceed 25 billion dollars, one of "the largest ever." What is *Snapchat* that is the rage of the Millennials, the Humphreys residents and the Dwyers, that attracts so much capital interest as a sure thing? It is the Internet's first *nothing* invention, in which the images you send or receive are programmed to "disappear" as soon as you see them, and it is deemed to be the future of life in America in general and on the Internet in particular. Its premise, and promise, is that everything in American life is going to become a temporary, ephemeral and meaningless daily repetition. The blank faces that stare at the TV screens and the voter who cries at a Trump rally, as if she were at a revival meeting, are the consumers of *Snapchat* which is made up of *nothing*, as what you glance at once is unlikely to be retained in your memory after it vanishes into thin air as if it never existed. Billions of dollars would be invested in *Snapchat* because smart money is betting on America spinning surely into generations of intellectual dummies and emotional children in the coming years. Not surprisingly, *Snapchat* is not shaping America; it is merely confirming it, in the same way Trump's election confirms this Garbage-In, Garbage-Out America, not creates it. In essence, Snapchat's America is Trump's America, as much as it is the America of those blank faces and minds gone dead.

If you are not angry or worried about America, it's because you are a happy American who has been fed garbage for decades now. It is not just that Consumer Capitalism—particularly in its digital form—makes Americans dumb intellectually and childish emotionally in their consumer routines, which is beyond dispute, that should anger and worry us. It is that the American Masses are manipulated into the dumbness and childishness by Corporate America and its Best and Brightest, with the help of technology and psychology, that should properly alarm the citizenry. In short, there is no way the garbage-fed American Masses can stay immune from the powers of those at the top who profit from their dollars and, as we have seen in the election, from their votes. The common Americans possess two prized items that Corporate America covets and wants to take from them, the dollar and the vote: The American Masses, now as garbage-fed children, are smart enough to protect neither.

We in the U.S. have *deserved* someone like Donald Trump as our president for some time. Until now, by a string of luck, we had mostly centrist presidents, both Republican and Democratic, some with only a modicum of intelligence and humanity. Even with the visibly low-brow occupants of the White House in the past, we still had presidents better than what we as Americans as a whole deserved. With Donald Trump, however, we finally ran out of luck: When you raise a child on nothing but garbage, you end up with a sick child. When you feed Americans mental garbage day after day for decades, you get sick Americans. Only the insane would expect a different result.

Undoubtedly, Donald Trump is the most disputed and divisive president ever to occupy the White House, and it is natural for the reader to wonder if *anyone* can write a book about him that is both objective and enlightening. Of course, it is impossible to be both objective and enlightening on a social-cultural-political phenomenon, especially on a sitting president who is as controversial as Trump is. However, we can be less subjective and less un-enlightening if we look at the larger framework of society and history in which Donald Trump made his appearance. But even on that high level, the writer assumes certain things about society, history and humanity. My own assumptions are embedded in the book's title and subtitle, which are described below:

DONALD TRUMP, MADE IN THE U.S.A.: In spite of all the attention that the person of Donald Trump gets in the media, he is after all a product of his own society. As a billionaire, as an entertainer, and now as president, he is by and large what American Society has created. America has created Donald Trump by way of creating Trump supporters. Famous or anonymous, we are all products of our society and nobody can buck this principle of social life: Society giveth and society taketh away. Trump's rise to power is reminiscent of the rise of Adolf Hitler to power, in that both owe their ascent to prominence to their social-historical circumstances, Hitler to WWI and the Great Depression, and Trump to Consumer Capitalism.

CONSUMER CAPITALISM: Consumer Capitalism is different from its predecessor, Industrial Capitalism, which produced goods and services we needed; in that economic system we consumed to live. In Consumer Capitalism today, however, we live to consume as what we consume is largely made up of what makes us feel good, happy and powerful, but not serving any practical ends required in our everyday life. Television and smart-phone entertainment is particularly prominent in our present-day list of things we cannot live without but serving little or no practical purpose. Trump's rise to power owes itself to our consumption of daily Mental Trash which, day and night, feeds Americans garbage and, as a result, creates garbage Americans.

MENTAL TRASH: Mental Trash is the "mind garbage" we feed ourselves daily and in great quantities. It is garbage because we cannot retain any of what we are fed every hour and every minute on so many channels and screens that we click, and must throw it out constantly. Unlike the things we used to consume, such as shoes and automobiles, Mental Trash affects the way our minds work: It makes us selfish, childish and solitary human beings who live only to process trash; and, on the flip side, such minds are easily affected by anxiety, anger and vengefulness. On television and computers and other media of mass circulation, we have become trash cans--Mental Trash Cans--that exist just to process trash that comes into our minds and goes out of our minds almost at the same time. Mental Trash, devised by the best and brightest in America, keeps us away from everybody else as we become *privatized* as citizens and neighbors.

PRIVATIZATION OF WHITE AMERICA: The worst part of democracy and consumer capitalism is that we must *assume* voters and consumers can do no wrong. All political and economic analyses in America begin with this assumption, which is morally wrong and analytically fruitless. Germans were wrong to support the Nazis and Americans are stupid to consume what they consume, but nobody can say this out loud. The end result of our Mental Trash consumption in America is that it privatizes our moral and intellectual citizenship ever deeply into our private cocoons in which we live, play and die a solitary, unconnected life. We used to find "privatized" people only among the idiots and mentally ill, who could not connect to "others" in society. In America today, after decades of Mental Trash garbage pumped into our bloodstreams, we (especially Whites among us because they are among the most-affluent and most-consuming segments of America) have all become unconnected citizens and neighbors: In short, non-humans who are completely useless in a democratic society which survives only if its citizens remain alert and fighting--together.

The following pages will elaborate, explain and clarify all that is condensed in the few words above.

Jon Huer
U.S. Army Garrison Humphreys
South Korea

Introduction

In Donald Trump, America Reaps What It Sows

With Donald Trump as the 45th President of the United States now as a given fact, there is a quiet desperation in intellectual America to distance itself from Trump's persona and presidency. The prevailing mood in the intellectual community is that "American Society" is somehow *better* than Donald Trump in civility and social justice and does not deserve him as its president. The badge of honor in the learned circle today is to declare that you didn't vote for him and that he is a terrible human being. The intent here is to establish that you are a good American and Trump is not. The main difficulty in this effort is how to explain the very fact that Trump is *the legitimately elected president of the nation.* The cold historical fact staring in the face of intellectual America is that, whether you like it or not, America *created* the persona (now the president) of Donald Trump, first as its chief agitator and now as its chief executive. As a nation, culture and society, we sowed the seed of Donald Trump and nurtured him along to fruition, and we must now reap what we sowed. Donald Trump *is* us, the quintessential American of our time, the product of all that is the United States of America, good or evil. Simply put, he represents what America yearns for: Success, flamboyance, machismo, swagger, fame, fortune and, perhaps most pronounced, power to be wholly selfish (that we call "freedom").

For many of us, Trump is a bitter pill to swallow but swallow it we must. By relying on some old-school sociological analysis, this book attempts to help us with our self-admission and -confession—yes, *we are more like Donald Trump* than we would ever want to admit or even imagine. Three quick examples should dispel any doubts about how quintessentially "American" Trump really is and how we are like him:

1

One, "I WON!" president-elect Donald Trump emphatically declared at the pre-inauguration press conference (the media reported it with capital letters) in response to the questions about why he refused to release his tax information. Trump's answer: *Winning* the election resolved all the questions about him, and people who voted for him obviously didn't care about it. This claim is hard to dispute, given America's system of competition. In America, every child knows that winning is *everything*. It is so American that our most-celebrated game, the Super Bowl, is played for the "Vince Lombardi Trophy" in honor of the coach who famously said, "Winning is not every-thing—it is the only thing." In America, lacking in tribal tradition, Feudal experience or subconsciously-connected community, life is a game played according to the established rules. Trump won it fair and square and that's all that matters. We celebrate the two of the most famous winners in America, Lombardi and Trump, in the grandest manner possible as if to confirm their American-ness.

Two, prior to his inauguration the media widely reported that the Russian government, under the instructions from its president, interfered with America's election in favor of Donald Trump. The media referred to this news as a "bombshell." Trump's reaction to it as he tweeted it: "FAKE NEWS – A TOTAL POLITICAL WITCH HUNT!" (Caps are original). This pattern of bombastic, sweeping and *non sequitur* statements is rather typical of the Trump Style. The media topic of the moment was fairly serious: That the Russians have some "compromising" material that they could use to "black-mail" Trump the American president, and this was a part of the larger report submitted jointly by the four top intelligence agency chiefs in the American government. Why does Trump's totally vacuous, unconnected response style—more fitting for a Roman Emperor than the Leader of the Free World—work so well with the American public? Because the American Masses, especially those who voted for him, live a vacuous and unconnected lifestyle themselves: In short, the public doesn't care about public issues like Russia, "compromising" material, potential "blackmail," or anything of that sort unless it comes out as entertainment or it affects their lives directly and immediately, which is to say, only fleetingly if at all. Donald Trump has proven this point time and time again, perhaps better than anyone, all the way from the chief entertainer to the commander in chief.

Three, on the same topic of Russian influence on the American electoral process that distinctly favored a Trump win, he was asked whether that was a matter of importance in America's future dealings with Russia. His answer, given at the same pre-inaugural press conference was very typical: "If Putin likes Donald Trump, guess what folks, that's called an asset, not a liability." Trump's perspective is uniquely "American" in that interpersonal percep-tions and relations are judged in strict calculus of assets and liabilities, or gains and losses. There is neither a sense of intellectual balance nor political propriety in his response, a crudeness that borders on stupidity, not normally expected at a presidential press conference. But this is remarkably "American," a concept of gains and losses based strictly on the Benefit Calculus of self-interest and self-aggrandizement. Popularly known as "not what you know but who you know," favorite connections are a part of America's game of life. We have a pre-Trump example in young entrepreneur George W. Bush, the son of a sitting president in George W.H. Bush at the time, explaining his business acumen in attracting Saudi money for his oil-drilling business in Texas: "When you are the president's son, and you've got unlimited access (to the president). . .people kinda respect that." Its lack of finesse aside, Trump's, and Bush's, perspective and philosophy are perfectly part of American lore of self-interest. Trump is keenly attuned to the essence of Consumer Capitalism, learned from years of casino and show business, where the American Mind is almost exclusively geared to the self-centered calculus of assets and liabilities that says, if we don't like it we just click to the next, but do what's best for you.

All in all, no one approximates America's Masses—especially the White Masses--more closely than Donald Trump, who, in turn, is the most "American" of all products created by America's social and cultural system. In short, to be famous, to get elected president, is to be part of the society in which the process of fame and public approval takes place. Much of what we call Life in American Society, collectively and individually, consists of doing what we don't want to do, should not do, or need not do, day after day, only because we are persuaded, tempted or seduced, by America's best and brightest, to give up our dollars or votes. Someone who is wholly unrelated to this style of life in America, say, Jesus or Henry David Thoreau, could never imitate Donald Trump's success.

Now that we have seen how closely we as Americans resemble Donald Trump, and vice versa, we need to take the next step in order to recognize the larger relationship between American society and the persona of Donald Trump.

II.

In 1927 a 25-year-old pilot named Charles Lindbergh became an overnight celebrity in America after his solo trans-Atlantic flight. Reports and stories about him were so extensive and relentless it was as if America's soul had been possessed by the man and his flight. In fact, Americans talked and read about nothing but Charles Lindbergh, for days and years. Historian Daniel Boorstin in a three-volume chronicle, entitled *The Americans*, even calculated the millions of gallons of ink that were consumed to print the stories about Lindbergh and his wife. This obsession with the new national hero was so great, especially after his son was kidnapped and murdered, that the Lindberghs secretly fled to Europe to avoid the incessant glare of publicity in America.

The Charles Lindbergh story was the greatest media event of the era. Today, we have the Donald Trump story as the greatest media event of our era.

Lindbergh and Trump. There can be no two personas who are as different from each other, both in character and in accomplishments, as these two personalities. But, they are strikingly similar in one singular aspect: *The way American Society has created them and consumed them.* In two very different eras and through two very different paths that gave them their respective fame, both Lindbergh and Trump are created by America's hunger for such stories and events: They are both *Made in the U.S.A.* Although the media in both eras has reported frenziedly on both personalities, the real subject of our study is neither Lindbergh nor Trump. It is American Society itself, the creator of all that means anything in our life and thought. Both of them happen to fit the bill.

Yet, in the incredible volumes of stories and reports on Trump, we scarcely find any reference to American Society itself, for example, why we hunger for someone like Trump and why the rise of Donald Trump seems to resemble collective madness more than an historic movement. In short, we have great details of everything about Donald Trump, his every thought and action, yet we know virtually nothing about what makes Donald Trump what he is to us and will be to our next generations.

We live our routine lives hardly giving any thoughts to what is vaguely known as "American Society," an entity somewhat powerful and large, but hard to grasp in the Big Picture. The reason for this vagueness is that we actually don't live through society but through its workhorse "institutions." Society is vague, but institutions are concrete. It is the institution—like the government, the schools, the military, the church, the media—that shapes and determines how our lives are to be lived and what bills are to be paid. Donald Trump, like Lindbergh before him, occupies our daily attention as we read about him in the newspapers, watch him on TV, and browse his stories on our smart-phones. But an institution, such as the media, connects us as individuals and in our individual interests, like the Trump stories, to the purpose of the larger society, which creates the hunger and determines how the hunger is to be satiated.

The purpose of the larger society is generally articulated as the Social System. In America, the system is known as Classic Liberalism, which puts the emphasis on individual freedom. It is this "liberal" tradition that encourages us to pursue "whatever we want" and structures the economic institution to "give us whatever we want." We should already see that such a national creed is good for neither a healthy nation nor a happy people. So, over time,

Classic Liberalism becomes a free-for-all playground now called "Neo-Liberal-Capitalism" where what people want and what the System wants meet at a place of exchange called "the Marketplace." Donald Trump is one of the products the Market sells and we, American Consumers, buy. In this way, whatever we do as individuals in our "freedom of choice" is all instructed from the Social System.

By its very own nature, the media institution cannot report on events and *analyze* them at the same time as it is too busy giving people what they want and people don't want analysis. For the media, Trump is interesting and sells; American Society is not interesting and does not sell. The media pursues stories about Trump but it avoids stories about American Society. For its own reasons, the Social System discourages too much analysis by the citizens about the System itself. It is for historians and sociologists to provide analysis about what the System does, for example, America's peculiar hunger for Donald Trump, both as a story for the consumers and as a Messiah for the supporters. Naturally, when Trump says outrageous things or Tweets mindless messages, they reveal more about his supporters for whom they are intended than Trump himself.

Admittedly, there has not been enough social nor historical space between us and the Trump Phenomenon to make an objective analysis of America's hunger for someone like him and his functions in our era. This defect would have to be overcome by our intellectual distancing, for, after all, from a historical and sociological perspective, Donald Trump is but a "type." Someone like him existed many times before and will continue to exist after him. As long as the hunger exists for someone like him, there will be many more Donald Trumps. We just want to know more about the peculiar hunger itself so that we understand the *why's* and *how's* of the Trump Phenomenon. The answers are not in Donald Trump, not any more than they were in Charles Lindbergh. They are with the larger Creator of our interests in personalities like Lindbergh and Trump, that is, American Society itself that shapes our yearnings and desires and exacts the price for our pleasure of enjoying them.

We have enjoyed the ride with Donald Trump and are now asked to pay the price of our enjoyment. That could be prohibitive, for us and for our children years later, for transforming a TV show host and businessman into the U.S. president. Before, he only had influence, but now, he has the *power* to have us all killed.

III.

When a political leader assumes his power legitimately, we look to his society for the explanation and responsibility. History holds all of Germany responsible for the rise of Adolf Hitler to power in 1933, for Hitler, like

Trump, rose to power legitimately by the process of his society. In order to understand Hitler, we must understand Germany and all its historical features. In order to understand Trump (or for that matter Lindbergh), we must turn to America, circa 20th and 21st centuries, and its peculiar sociological features that shape the minds of its main beneficiaries, mostly White Americans.

In this book, we attempt to find the answer to perhaps the most important question: *What had happened to those White Americans who found their Savior in Donald Trump?* What, indeed, made their faith in their Leader so strong that no matter what the established world threw at them to dislodge or weaken their faith in their Savior, they did not budge, as their faith grew only stronger?

Had they lost their collective minds? If so, why, how? In search of the answers, we take our sociological journey in three stages:

First, we need to react to the event of 2016 that elected Donald Trump the 45th U.S. President and speculate on what it means to live with Trump's new nationalist political power and how it may come into conflict with the established economic power of Capitalism. (Chapters 1 through 12)

Next, our journey discovers how Consumer Capitalism destroyed White Americans' intelligence and humanity in the last three decades with its relentless supply of entertainment in America, particularly of *Mental Trash*, making the White Majority extremely selfish, childish and dumb. (Chapters 13 and 14)

And finally, our journey traces the origins of Consumer Capitalism in America and describes how it is entrenched as America's Social System that will control and regulate Trump's new political power and any other social forces that may disrupt the System's progress toward greater wealth accumulation. (Chapters 15 through 18).

A *caveat*: I never met or saw Donald Trump in person, nor corresponded with him. I never had to. He is a public figure and the most-reported-on persona since Charles Lindbergh and there is enough material about him already available. Unlike other political figures in the past whose public and private spheres are generally kept separate, Trump seems to be the same person and personality whether in public or in private: In short, he is what he is described to be in the media. After the first ten days or so of Trump's flurry of executive orders, *Washington Post* columnist Christ Cillizza writes: "Trump is governing almost exactly how he said he would during a campaign that he won. No one should be surprised." The only thing we don't know and always wonder about is *what he will do next*, not out of a sense of depth or mystery about him, but out of his patented unpredictable outbursts and whims: After all, he is the Child with a Loaded Gun, and he will hold us hostage for the next four years with his unpredictability and whim. His presidency surely deserves our most thoroughgoing analysis.

Chapter One

The (White) Children's Crusade

On November 8, 2016, White America underwent massive hypnosis. Under hypnosis they told the world what had been on their minds and it shocked everyone: What *had* been on their minds kept so long and so intensely felt—the twin streams of nationalism and racism that strongly suggested Fascism—was blurted out in broad daylight by the ruling majority of the hitherto Leader-Nation of the Free World.

Everyone, both here and elsewhere, was shocked because such horrid thoughts and feelings had never been suspected to have been hidden in America for so long. The images of the "United States of America," here and the world over, would never be the same. We have seen the true face of Trump's America, and it is ugly. Could we trust and be inspired by "America" ever again? As an Old World saying goes, *once a rose fell into the sewer, even a hundred washes could not restore its original fragrance.* Toward the end of WWII, a high German Nazi lamented: "Germany will live in shame for the next thousand years!" How long would it take for the U.S. to restore the pre-Trumpian America?

Secret balloting is like hypnosis as it reveals something that normally stays deeply protected and denied by consciousness. Under the cover of absolute secrecy and privacy, the voter is told that he can do *anything* with his ballot: Cast it any way you want. Your deepest desires, your hidden yearnings, your most private longings, anything you want, can be allowed at the moment the vote is cast. The voter, like a child with money to spend at a candy store, has nothing to fear or hesitate as he is shrouded in secrecy and only God and he share how the ballot is to be cast. He has the vote and he can cast it for the Devil if he wants to, or an Adolf Hitler if he so desires. At the moment of his voting, it is the Absolute Power of God that is accorded a Common Man. No logic or reason is applicable in this voting process, any more than logic or reason is applicable to the five-year-old at a candy store: Their choice of X over Y or Z is entirely accidental. A tad more sugar taste in one candy or one candidate is all the difference one needs among all the similarly contesting merchandise.

The 2016 election, under the revelation of hypnosis and the freedom of five-year-olds at a candy store, spoke the truth about America and Americans, particularly White America and White Americans, and what the world saw as revealed in America's election is not pretty. But it was the truth about ourselves as Americans that was revealed and the world saw, and that is what has been most shocking about the whole Trump Affair. It is indeed difficult to say which one was more shocking, the state of the election or the state of American society.

Someday, future historians might divide American History into two epochs: Before Trump or BT and After Trump or AT. With his election as President, there have also emerged two types of Americans: One who supported Trump and the other, who opposed Trump. This division, and realizing its existence in our midst, identifies Americans into two enemy camps, like the Nazis and the Jews in the Third Reich, the former voting to send the latter to death-and-labor camps, and the latter suddenly losing all their civil rights. America has been divided before, once during the Revolutionary War, pitting Americans against each other over the issue of independence, and once during the Civil War, dividing Americans over states' rights and slavery. What is so shocking, so devastating, and so degrading this time, unlike the aftermath of the Revolutionary War or the Civil War in which the nobler side of freedom won, is that this time the Good Side lost: For the first time in American history, the side that represented everything that is Un-American, inhuman and savage won the contest, and the Evil Side triumphed. Those who believed in Progress got whacked in the face—by Lady Progress herself--and have not recovered from the shock.

Often such momentous events in our lives are so close to our personal and public lives that we fail to realize that something historically momentous is happening right in our faces. Only with much intellectual and emotional distance from the epicenter do we understand, even vaguely, the nature of the events we are witnessing or living through. What did the followers of Jesus think when they were witnessing His life and death? What did the generation that was witnessing the unfolding of the McCarthy Communist Scare think they were witnessing or living through? Did they realize that they were in the midst of a great historical event, or comprehend why it was such a great historical event?

How momentous is the election of Donald Trump as the President of the United States? Robert Maranto reports thusly: ". . . Professors at campuses like Yale and Penn let students skip exams to grieve the election results. Stanford actually offered students and faculty psychological counseling to help with election-induced 'uncertainty, anger, anxiety and/or fear.' At many colleges and universities, including mine, chancellors issued *de rigueur* official statements making clear that they feel the pain of Hillary Clinton voters."

Americans are now unquestionably divided into two very hostile and unbridgeable enemy camps. The very persona of Donald Trump, what he favored and what he opposed, made any other result unimaginable between the two groups. What brought him to the front and center is the promise that he would punish the Lesser Americans for the pleasure of the White Masses and he must fulfill his promise. Unlike most other presidential winners who go through the motion of reconciliation and unity among Americans, Republican and Democratic, Donald Trump cannot even pretend the reconciliation or unity. Trump brought a very different kind of, but just as intense and unbridgeable, division in America that a new war, perhaps a Cultural War, must follow his reign.

II.

To visualize what the Donald Trump presidency means to America, backtrack your mind a little, to the time when George W. Bush and Al Gore were contesting the Florida votes, the whole result hinging on the interpretation of the infamous "hanging chad." The case went through the State of Florida and eventually ended up in the U.S. Supreme Court, which pronounced Bush the winner. This process took days and supporters of both parties lined up the streets of Florida cheering for their own party: On one side were Democrats, and on the other, Republicans, both wildly cheering and shouting, but all in good spirits, as no violent or ugly incidents broke out among the opposing crowds. This was in the year 2000, sixteen years before the Trump-Clinton contest.

Now, it is the year 2016 and imagine that something similar to the Gore-Bush situation occurred again in Florida, in which the State's vote would determine the presidential winner between Trump and Clinton. Imagine the crowd lining up on opposite sidewalks across the street supporting their own candidate, one side having the Trump supporters and the other side the Clinton crowd. What kind of people would we see on each side? On the Trump side we would see predominantly *White males*, and on the Clinton side we would see the *Lesser American*s, namely, blacks, Hispanics, Asians, women, Muslims. One side is very light, the other side very dark. Both sides are ardently cheering and shouting but would they be doing that in good spirits? We are sure the media would describe this as a Race War, Whites vs. non-whites. Violence may break out, shots may be fired, and law-enforcement would surely be called. This imagined scene would simplify the stark division on which Trump's presidency is sworn in to live or die.

After each election, both parties have always made up once the election was over. As a party and as individuals, Democrats made peace, after the election, with the followers of John McCain who ran against Barack Obama; they also made peace with the followers of Mitt Romney, however reluctantly, who ran against Obama's second term. Practicality and decorum required this reconciliation. While the contests were certainly contentious and raucous, voters for both parties went back to their respective political camps, hoping that they would win the next go-around; their feelings against each other were hardly those of hostility or unbridgeable permanence. After all, if we put McCain, Romney and Obama, and their supporters, together, we would find more similarities among them, being "Americans" and all, than differences. *Neither McCain's nor Romney's policies presumed the total annihilation of their opponents.* Both camps still assumed that losers and winners would work together toward those very elusive but shared goals called "the Perfect Union" collectively and "the American Dream" individually.

III.

Prior to the rise of Donald Trump, "The United States of America" was always considered in a unified sense of one history, one body politic and one set of laws and values: In other words, one "American Nation" for all.

This "oneness" was true also of the designation "Americans" which had a definite qualifier that all those who lived in America implicitly understood. When a social observer (a professor, a politician, a man in the street) says, "American people," "American masses," "we as Americans," "most Americans," or "few Americans," and so on we of course assumed the designation meant *White Americans.* This assumption was so strongly and subconsciously held that the racial designation of "white" was never necessary to be mentioned. It was White Americans whose opinions were sought, it was White Americans whose heads were counted when it mattered, and it was White Americans whose money was eagerly solicited. When a person was White, it was deemed unnecessary to mention his race: An "American" was naturally assumed to be White. All others were specified as "Hispanic American," "black American," "Asian American," or whatever other qualifiers were needed.

The reason for this assumption was natural and convenient: It was the White population that controlled America's culture, politics, economy, education, entertainment, and general self-image. An "American," whether a scientist, a professor, an actor, a politician or a pilot, what have you, that represented a profession or an institution was assumed to be a "white" American *unless otherwise indicated.* The White Majority, either as leaders of the American nation or as consumers of the American economy, were always thought to be at the center of all that made up what we thought of "America."

Those who were not white, the non-whites--blacks, Hispanics, Asians, American Indians, new arrivals—were mentioned, if at all, only as "special" categories that served a particular purpose, such as official and academic researches and media head-counting. They formed the darker circles around the white center of American society in various shades, some closer to the white center, like Hispanics, and some farther out from the white center, like black Americans, some trying to figure out where they belonged in the expanding concentric circles, like the Muslims. In the dynamic vortex of America's liberal politics and capitalist economics, often dramatic and contentious, these marginal non-whites still believed they surely belonged and were legitimate players in this process, however tenuous their belonging and however marginal their playing field might be.

The prevailing assumption in "one America" was that the White Center was holding. And in the grand tradition of American Liberalism and Consumer Capitalism, little by little, however slowly or even reluctantly, White America was expanding its bounties to include non-whites so that this "one America" was still progressing toward the Perfect Union as conceived by the Founding Fathers, and in the practical reward of "the American Dream" to accommodate its non-white brethren. If there was any sense of division, even in the "digital divide" that separated Whites and Blacks in computer benefits, time was America's great ally that would heal the hurts and ameliorate the differences. This one-nation America was moving and moving upward as it was moving forward. There was enough for everyone in America, and all Americans, Whites and non-whites, could share the bounties of America sooner or later, sooner than later, many believed.

The Rise of Donald Trump shredded this "one America" concept to pieces. The one-America consensus of opinion, believed by everyone, professional or lay, both at home and elsewhere, was rudely thrown out by Trump's win. The world is shocked to find out how wrong they had been about "one America," which turned out to be a New-World imitation of the Old-World nationalism and racism.

There were writers and reporters at the left-leaning *Nation* and *Mother Jones* or social critics like Robert Reich and Michael Moore who were highly skeptical of the notion of "one America" and thought of it almost a hoax. Even in 1992, Andrew Hacker wrote a book entitled *Two Nations: Black and White, Separate, Hostile, Unequal* to put a damper on our illusion. Aside from the two physical Americas that Hacker identified, many saw that there were also two metaphorical Americas, one *pretended* and the other *real.* The Real America had developed, according to these few observers, for example, a more efficient police state in America than the Nazis or the Soviets ever could and an economically unequal society that would make the Founding Fathers turn over in their graves.

But the Pretended America was much too powerful to resist. It owned the media, the classroom and the law, among the tools of mind-control that shaped most Americans psychologically and molded the world at large ideologically. With the help of the burgeoning Consumer Capitalism, in Hollywood and on Madison Avenue, which supplied anything people wanted and shaped their thoughts, the United States was on its path to becoming a model nation for the world to envy and emulate.

IV.

Then came Donald Trump that turned the "one America" idea on its head. In Trump's win, everything that the intellectual community in America and the world believed fell apart. There was no such a thing as "one America" and there was no such a thing as American Progress, and there was no such a thing as the American Dream open to all. Katha Politt, writing for the *Nation*, says, "We thought Trump's misogyny would be repudiated when America elected its first female president. Then he won. . . .(W)e feminists have been in a bubble."

In spite of all the shock and awe Trump's election has inspired, we must recognize that Trump is an *American*, who won the presidency fair and square, and better than anyone. Why? Because he represents the spirit and mood of America *better than anyone*. He is more American than Hillary Clinton could ever be. America created Trump, not the other way around. Since he did not create America, America would have been the same society and nation with or without him. Hence his early death (after all, he is only several years away from the average White American male's life expectancy), natural or otherwise, would not solve the Trump Problem. He may fade away, but the America he revealed will certainly not go away or change. The Ugly America—White nationalism, xenophobia, jingoism, Narcissism, racism—that he revealed would not go away or change. If Clinton had won, instead of Trump, say with 51 percent of the Electoral College vote, the intellectual community would be busy with the impossible task of explaining away how the White Half could have voted for Trump's White nationalism, xenophobia, jingoism, Narcissism and racism. Like cancer growths nobody knew about, such horrid atavistic ideas could have grown inside America's underbelly even if Clinton had won. How could they have voted for Donald Trump? The intellectuals would be asking the same question over and over again for a long time even if Trump had lost to Clinton but still winning 49 percent of the vote.

With or without Trump, then, Ugly America will always be the same as it was before Trump, "ugly" and "America." Michelle Obama said in great despair some time after the election that Trump's win showed "what it's like to live without hope." But under Trump's alternative, Democrat Hillary Clinton, Americans would be living under "false hope." (By definition, all hope is false; what is true is never hoped.) The White Majority would be seething with anger toward non-whites, dreaming that some day a Messiah would rise up from among them to make America a "Great White America Again." Most Americans, White and non-white, would be living under *false hope* instead of *no hope* if Trump had not won the election.

Now, it is apparent that the American Masses, White or non-white, would have lived either with the Democratic false hope or with the Trumpian no hope. Why? The top One Percent would keep all of America's wealth regardless of who wins the political game. It is not strange that the Clintons and the Trumps have been friends for a long time and their daughters, Chelsea and Ivanka, are "good friends" as well. Again, it is not strange that the Clintons and the Trumps would find each other more comfortable than they would be with their respective constituents, Trump with his White supporters and Clinton with her non-white supporters. In lifestyle and elite values they have more things in common with each other than with the Common Masses they claim to represent. Both the Clintons and the Trumps (who used to be nominally a Democrat) are part of the movers-and-shakers elite of America, political and economic, respectively. Neither their lifestyle nor their circle of friends has anything to do with the Masses whose votes they court. Off stage and out of public view, they are back to their elite life and association. What would they say to each other in private, if they ran into each other even during their fierce campaign against each other?

Cardinal Dolan of New York had a chance to eavesdrop on the two rivals alone when they came to the Al Smith annual charity dinner. According to the Cardinal, Trump said to Clinton: *"You know, you are one tough and talented woman. This has been a good experience in this whole campaign, as tough as it's been."* Then Clinton responded: *"And Donald, whatever happens, we need to work together afterwards."* (The Cardinal, totally oblivious to the irony of their public-private discrepancies, thought, "This is the evening at its best" and told the media, "I was very moved by the obvious attempt on behalf of both Secretary Clinton and Mr. Trump to kind of be courteous, to get along, to say nice things privately to one another." Obviously, the Cardinal, like the rest of us in America, never thought about the oddity in which the two candidates played their public part, fiercely attacking each other, and, in private, remained friends.)

We have been told over and over that Donald Trump destroyed America's political civility and tradition of dialogue, and introduced new savagery into American life and politics. Did he really do that? The civility and dialogue in solving issues toward shared values and social progress, it turned out, have been nothing but an elite fakery and self-delusion. There was no such thing as civility or political dialogue in our midst; American society had already become a savage nation long before Donald Trump who just smoothly melded into this America while his opponent kept the "one nation" idea as her story. In spite of our "one nation" self-delusion, the election revealed that, after all, the winning half in America, is just made up of snarling dogs.

Because of the "one America" self-propaganda, we just deluded ourselves, and the world along with us, and believed in it, only to be shocked and awakened from this one-America dream: There are actually *two Americas*, White and non-white, and they are neither separate nor equal. Trump swore to his White supporters that America would be a White America. (Quite contrary to popular impression, the non-whites are actually fighting Whites, not Donald Trump in the White House, who loom large, like a typical regent-ruler in the Old World, behind the throne. It is this White America looming large behind him that gives Trump all his executive bravado and swagger.)

If this "one America" had been wrong, both as a popular image of America and as a theoretical conclusion on American History within the Western Progression toward the Enlightenment and its Perfection, *what indeed was America?* What *was* the American Nation really like, as a society and as a culture, and why did we fail to see or understand this before the Rise of Donald Trump?

Chapter Two

Trump's America We Hardly Knew

The most ironic dilemma that has befallen America is that we could never again think of America as a "Good Nation," neither to ourselves nor to the world. Anyone who is still smug enough about America would shut up at this question: If the U.S. were such a good nation, how could you have elected somebody like Trump as your president? In fact, a pre-election survey showed only *four percent* of Norwegians, perhaps one of the fairest and most intelligent tribes on earth, would have voted for Trump. (It is actually shocking that there *are* four percent of Norwegians who would vote for him).

Given this dilemma, ever since Donald Trump was elected president of the U.S., the intellectual community has been frantically trying to explain what happened. The shock they experience is due to the conviction that they (or the American Nation) *do not deserve Donald Trump as their president:* They still think Trump was a mistake in an otherwise good nation. There must be some resolution in this dilemma between a continuing bad nightmare and a visibly good life. In their effort to escape this shock and sustain their conviction, the intellectuals try different combinations to explain the so-called Trump Phenomenon:

The first attempt is that Donald Trump is actually a "good president" elected to lead a "good nation." This is a comforting thought except it cannot explain why Trump is universally condemned as a bully and a bad president. Besides, the intellectual community cannot quite stomach the idea that Donald Trump is a "good president" although a great deal of inner compromise, for the sake of career and peace of mind, is being worked out in its midst. But, still, this is a decidedly minority-held attempt at explanation.

The second attempt inherits the "good president" idea but changes the American nation from a good nation to a "bad nation." Aside from the difficulty of explaining how a bad nation can elect a good president, this alternative cannot explain all the gloom and doom about the Trump Presidency and the universally bad publicity following the Trump win. In the intellectual community, which overwhelmingly rejected Trump, this is still a minority position held among the few closet supporters of Donald Trump.

The third attempt is perhaps the most common resolution: That Donald Trump is simply a bad president who somehow managed to get elected president (here is the mental acrobatics among the intellectuals) in a (still) good nation. The difficulty is obvious and even insurmountable: This bad-president-for-good-society option cannot explain how a good nation elects a bad president. Discarding the first two options, this is the moral and intellectual refuge of all intellectuals who must somehow explain away the election result and, and at the same, extricate America, including themselves, from its moral dilemma. (This comic-tragic position has been amply demonstrated in post-Hitler Germany). But this is the most common perception in the intellectual community and the most preferred conclusion in the post-election America at present. In this conclusion, everyone is trying to convince himself that, for some *inexplicable* reason, a bad-boy president has been elected to lead the good-society of America. Since it is logically impossible for a bad president to be democratically elected president of a good society, smart people everywhere, in the media, in the classroom, in the street, are having a tough time to reconcile the two contradictory factors: The bad boy president and the good nation.

In the meantime, with the election of Donald Trump as the 45th President of the United States, much of the U.S. and the world, including Trump and his supporters themselves, has concluded that America has taken its gigantic step in a new direction few observers ever thought possible. Virtually everybody who had anticipated the result to be otherwise wondered how strange and abnormal the whole electoral process became. Typical of such a reaction was *Stars and Stripes*, the military's in-house newspaper, which headlined one of its post-election editions with "UNCHARTED TERRITORY," speculating on what kind of commander in chief the new president would be.

The consensus, according to this bad-president-for-good-America thinking, is that: Donald Trump is nothing like anyone they had ever predicted; the White Majority's choice of such a person was nothing like anyone had ever anticipated; the American Nation's unfolding political-social-cultural life under Trump would be nothing like what anyone had known and expected; what the election revealed is that American society, hitherto always stable and well-maintained, has gotten off its normal track, its routine orbit, its reliable political behavior, and so on.

Against the idea that the Donald Trump Phenomenon is something special, our "conservative inertia," the tendency to pacify our natural impulse for equilibrium, is also tempting us to harmonize Trump and all he portends with our normal social reality. So, on the one hand, we sense that Trump started a revolution; on the other, we urgently hope that Trump is merely another politician, perhaps quirkier than most, but (as many Germans had hoped when Hitler was appointed Chancellor of Germany), he will make peace with the existing American society and its culture.

These are indeed the times that try an American's soul because such easy mental acrobatics are not working and are obviously not workable. Mostly in shock and confusion and anxiety, the U.S. has been frantically trying to recover its psychological and structural balance, a state of mind with which it had almost always been familiar. Trump's win is a political equivalent of September-Eleven, shocking and terrifying and unprecedented, that prompted a frantic effort for Americans to return to their normalcy (like then president Bush urging Americans to "go shopping" while the Twin Towers were still smoldering). Ruefully, they reminisce, after both Trump and September-Eleven, what America *used to be*: Before the Event, America seemed to be the embodiment of a Good Society, peaceful, stable, orderly, and a consumer's haven where one could enjoy all the freedoms of an affluent society; it was protected by the world's strongest but just military, and maintained by an effective and efficient, if not just, law-enforcement agencies trained to protect the citizens and maintain law and order in their neighborhoods. After Trump, this is the America that most of us, who did not see the shock coming, are desperately wishing to return to, at least in the psychological part of our pre-Trump America.

Professional observers of society—intellectuals, writers, reporters, commentators—are struggling to recover their perspective and balance that was rudely disrupted by Donald Trump's electoral victory over Hillary Clinton. They are making a stupendous effort, personally and sociologically, to "rationalize" the irrationality, the unbalance, the instability that Donald Trump's win has wrought. They want American society to become "normal" again and all of Trump's supporters to become normal Americans and go back to their normal routines. But these professionals find the task of intellectually normalizing America impossible to do: At this writing, our president-elect is displaying all sorts of behavior that suggest that Citizen Trump, Candidate Trump and President-elect Trump are the same person and even President Trump will not be that much different, which is only heightening the level of uncertainty in America.

This third option obviously cannot reconcile Good America with Donald Trump as we cannot recant all that has ever been said about him during his presidential run: This option, as widely adopted by America's intellectual community as it is out of sheer desperation has us believe that America was such a nation of happiness and goodness that was rudely disrupted by this rogue president named Donald Trump.

II.

Here comes the fourth explanation for the Trump Phenomenon that we have not considered yet: *Donald Trump is a bad president elected by a bad nation.*

The following facts are collected for their ironic-sociological value. With these facts and their truthful interpretations, we will get re-acquainted with American society that existed before Trump. These ten most prominent features of America, both unsurprising and familiar, although often hidden in the shadow of glitz and fame, are so selected just so that we are not being swept away in the tidal wave of nostalgia for pre-Trump America. Now, this was America *before* Trump:

1. *The world's first and only "natural-savage" society.* Lacking tribalism or subconsciously-connected community, and as a membership-only territorial entity, the U.S. is history's first "Natural Society," created to promote one primary idea, that is, the idea of Freedom. All other ideas, such as community, society or humanity, exist in the American Consciousness only as marginal to what one's natural desire calls for. All social relations and material life serve this end of personal freedom and its yearnings: Convenience, pleasure, and power are always supreme in everything we do and value, transforming our commitment to Natural Freedom into most savage struggle against one another in American society. Capitalism, a philosophy of Natural Man doing his "natural" thing, has been adopted as the perfect system for this natural-savage nation. This Natural Society concept created the celebrated Jeffersonian free America when its economic equality ensured its political freedom for all. But today this Natural Society is asserted only according to our economic power displayed in competitive consumption. The White Majority is at once the beneficiary and victim of this naturally-free society as they have pursued to be free and, as a result, they have become self-centered children easily manipulated in their own self-centeredness, and savagery and stupidity that naturally follow their imitation of personal freedom or its vicarious expression in someone like Donald Trump.

2. *The world's largest number of prison inmates.* The U.S. has 5 percent of the world's population, yet it has 25 percent of the world's prisoners. The U.S.'s number of inmates is *six times* the average of advanced countries. (We also have the world's highest male arrest rate as close to half of American males aged 18-23 are arrested for non-traffic-related violations). Ours is the only nation that imprisons people for writing bad checks or failing to pay bills. European criminologists call the U.S. a "Rogue Nation" for its inhuman criminal justice system. Perhaps prisons are the best-fitting imagery of America, the natural-savage nation where people devour one another naturally and savagely. Norway became *more open and more liberal* after their massacre that took 77 lives, the Norwegian equivalent of September-Eleven; the U.S. has become a more repressive, police-state-like society following 9-

11. How and why did prisons become America's all-around solution for "life, liberty and the pursuit of happiness"?

3. *The world's most work-hating nation.* Americans as a whole are the world's most labor-fearing human beings and work-hating employees in spite of its vaunted Protestant-Puritan Work Ethic. Avoiding work and making somebody else do the work for them has become America's most elaborated arts and sciences in the college curriculum. Having to expend unnecessary energy in their daily living—America's fear of "inconvenience" as foreigners deride—is the national burden of grave proportions. Virtually all Americans struggle hard to be successful, rich and powerful, just so that they can avoid having to work. It's a savage, unending struggle to find ways not to have to work. Why is labor so detested in America? How does this labor avoidance affect our society and its human behavior?

4. *The world's longest television-watching time.* The U.S. has the longest average TV-watching hours in the world, at 8 hours a day, the second longest being Greece with half of the U.S.'s. TV-watching, like all other forms of entertainment, is escapism from reality: What is America trying so hard trying to escape? Why is our life's reality so unlivable? Why can't we stand ourselves? Why do we hate ourselves so much? In the fantasy world of television, we say, "you can do anything you want!" But in the real world or work, money and power, we say, "you can't do anything!" No wonder, we are driven insane, dumb and childish with the confusion.

5. *The world's longest computer time for children.* Average American kids spend 60 hours a week, per *USA TODAY* report, while Bill and Melinda Gates allow their kids only five hours of computer time a week. The executives at Google, Apple, Yahoo, and Hewlett-Packard send their kids to schools that allow *no computer access.* Like the drug dealers with drugs, these computer gurus *forbid* computers for their own kids while pushing them on American children at large. Why does the U.S. government allow such frauds on America's kids? Most ironic of all, ours may be the only one among the advanced nations to leave its children a society *worse off* than the parent generation's. Just think about what we are leaving behind: Television, computer technology, air quality, food, civility, political culture, economic equality, consumption, education, and so on, all of which would only put our children at *greater risk* of being corrupted more thoroughly than their parents. In none of these social artifacts, could we foresee our children inheriting something "better"—to make them happier and more trusting with one another--than what existed for their parents' generation.

6. *The world's largest advertising expenditure.* Advertising is always inversely related to citizen intelligence, and the U.S.'s advertising expenditure matches the next 10 advertising nations of the world combined, including China whose population is five times the U.S.'s. What does it *mean* that we advertise so much in America? That's a lot of money-power to manipu-

late people's minds. Unsurprisingly, the White Majority is most susceptible
to the effects of advertisement.

7. *The world's largest drug-taking population.* The U.S. has the largest
drug-taking population in the world, both legal and illegal: 25 percent of
American women and 17 percent of American men are on mood-altering
prescription drugs (70 million and rising), and 10 percent of American children are diagnosed with ADHD and are taking medication. The number of
ADHD kids in France is one half of one percent of the children's population.
Who is pushing these drugs on us and why? What are their effects on our
minds and society?

8. *The world's fastest-growing obesity rate.* The U.S. leads the world in
obesity as close to one-third of Americans are classified as obese. Experts are
warning that the Food Industry's increasingly processed foods are slowly
killing Americans of all races. Thanks to Monsanto and other food-industry
giants, Americans eat sugar, fat and salt as their daily diet and cannot help
but get fat and sick and die of heart and kidney diseases. In America food is
manufactured factory-style, not grown on soil. Regulatory agencies like the
DOA, EPA or FDA exchange jobs and favors with the Industry and the U.S.
has the worst foods for its school children and public.

9. *The world's largest number of lawyers.* Over 70 percent of lawyers in
the world are Americans. What does that mean? Lawyers prosper in a society
full of distrust, conflict and self-aggrandizement, and are few in number and
insignificant in status where trust, peace and harmony prevail among the
citizens. American lawyers in general represent the extent of savage relations
in their society. Donald Trump, the savage American par excellence, has
been involved in over 5000 lawsuits in his business career.

10. *The world's largest wealth gap, military expenditure, and national
debt.* Our public accounting in America also fits the reality of savagery in our
public life as we maintain the world's largest wealth gap between the rich
and the poor (second being China), the world's largest military power (larger
than the next 20 largest militaries combined), and the largest national debt
that reveals how we spend more than what we bring in as our national
revenue. Questions are inevitable: Why is our inequality in wealth the
world's largest in a nation whose Founders declared that "all men are created
equal"? Why are we maintaining the largest military in the world where
Nazism and Communism are no more? Why are we refusing to pay higher
taxes or lower our expenses to fit our national income and live within our
national means? We have spent five trillion dollars on the War on Terror,
exceeding our expenditures for Vietnam and WWII combined, fighting not
Hitler and Tojo, but those ragtag guerillas on camels with vintage rifles for
their main weapons: Our question is, where did all the money go?

These 10 most obvious and ironic facts paint America as a very strange
and abnormal nation and it has indeed been a very strange and abnormal

nation for decades. In a culture and society with such oddities pumped into our brainwaves and supplied into our bloodstreams day and night, would we not become strange and abnormal in our individual personality and behavior and in our social character? Is it so surprising that the White Majority, perhaps the most afflicted group of Americans by such strange, abnormal and odd facts around the clock, elected someone who best represents such a nation? Would it not be more surprising if the White Majority, under such an assault from their inhuman society every minute of their lives, remained normal?

III.

It stands to reason, after we encountered theoretical and practical difficulties of the first three options and had to discard them, that American society and Donald Trump were perfect for each other: America was not a very good nation, nor was Donald Trump a very good person asked to lead the nation. To paraphrase Winston Churchill, in a democratic society, people deserve the leader they have. On November 8, 2016, the democratic nation of America elected the leader that perfectly fit their nation.

As odd as it sounds, the model of a bad leader for a morally corrupt society has had its historical precedents: Mussolini and Italy where a crazy nation embraced Fascist Mussolini; and angry and depressed Germans rejoiced when Nazi leader Hitler was made Chancellor of the Third Reich. In both cases, bad societies and bad leaders coincided. In either case, you cannot condemn the leaders without condemning their nations as accomplices who brought their bad leaders to power.

For the United States, Donald Trump's supporters shocked the world but his win happened exactly in a way that perfectly fitted White Americans, with their around-the-clock entertainment that had been killing their minds slowly for decades. Why was the election result so shocking when the election campaign itself, by both sides, was the ultimate display of stupidity, childishness and abnormality? After all, Donald Trump was a popular personality on TV, in his own right, long before he became president. His bad-boy trademark of shouting at somebody, "You Are Fired!" was not only his own favorite declaration, it also delighted millions of power-starved Americans. If Trump seemed quite radical and unusually childish, American society itself had undoubtedly become radical and unusually childish.

Under the most extreme form of Consumer Capitalism, now enforced by the Digital Revolution, the White Majority in America had also become extreme in their social character. They had developed a set of character traits almost universally recognized as "American:" The distrust of one another, a pursuit of comfort, entertainment and pleasure, a hell-bent worship of money, and with social relations so savage that even Trump's wife described America as "too mean and too rough." Was it shocking that, in this frame of mind and character, that they found someone like Trump as their Savior, who typically personified all such traits?

In spite of our nostalgia about the good old America before Trump, America was not a very good society, nor were Americans, especially White Americans, very good people under Consumer Capitalism. Bad America created bad voters, and bad voters created a bad president.

It is the pre-Trumpian America we hardly knew and we will pay dearly, perhaps fatally, for our indifference to and ignorance about what had become of America. In our indifference and ignorance, Donald Trump was ushered in to lead a nation that had already been corrupted in its own moral development. Slowly but inevitably, the U.S. was becoming the kind of nation and society that was perfect for someone like Trump.

Long before Donald Trump emerged on stage, with his characteristic savagery and inhumanity, America was already a savage and inhuman nation in which the masses had already become selfish, childish and stupid under the relentless assault from Consumer Capitalism and its entertainment opioids. (Visit *jonhuer.com* for my picture book entitled "*Our Savage Nation*" for detail.) Long before Donald Trump, one needed a specially-conscious effort not to be selfish, childish or stupid in one's daily dealings with other Americans. As a neighbor, a customer, a colleague, it was not easy for an American, especially a White American, to act decent, civilized and truthful with other Americans, especially non-white.

Long before Donald Trump, Americans acted as if they were *free* citizens in a *free* society, but in truth, they were economic slaves chained to their employment and entertainment imperative; they acted as if they were *equal* with each other, with first names for everyone, but beneath such façade was a fierce competition for power to dominate the Lesser among them; they acted as if they were *happy*, but their happiness was purchased by their hard-earned wage's ransom, which made them only lonelier and more miserable; they acted as if they were *friendly* toward all, but in truth this friendliness covered up their distrust, fear and loathing toward each other, only strengthened with guns and lawsuits; they acted *pious* with God, but outside the church, did everything against the teachings of Jesus in favor of the Devil's seductions and temptations; and they were *critical* toward every nation and group on earth but tolerated no criticism directed toward the U.S. or themselves. Americans, mostly White Americans, had become liars to the world, bullies to the Lesser members, domestic and foreign, and hypocrites to themselves long before Donald Trump threw in his political hat to run for president.

With or without Trump, the U.S. had become a savage nation on all levels of its national institutions and in all aspects of its social relations. (Just for a quick confirmation, go through the airport in Seattle, Washington and go through the airport in Vancouver, British Columbia, only a few miles from Seattle, for comparison and you will see America's pre-Trumpian savagery yourself first hand.) In short, Donald Trump's election and America were a match made in Heaven. The White Majority who voted for him were merely the props, the ring-bearer in this great historical marriage between personality and society.

Indeed, there could be no one more suited to be President of these United States, or better qualified than the quintessential American of today, one Donald J. Trump: A bad president for a bad-society nation. We cannot have one without the other. No matter how nimble the intellectual community is with its compromise and acrobatics, it just cannot wiggle out of this historical dilemma.

To be sure, Donald Trump is frightful; so is America.

Chapter Three

The Day of Revelation

On November 8, 2016, a day that will live in infamy longer and more deeply than Pearl Harbor, everything changed in America: Whatever had been done with certain finesse and stealth, such as racist and nationalist practices, could now be done out in the open. But, unlike the original Pearl Harbor Infamy, this time it is the U.S. that is the perpetrator. More accurately, perhaps, everything about America, a nation built by immigrants, long known for its belief in Liberal Progress toward tolerance and diversity in a Perfect Union since 1776, was *revealed to be false* on that day. This revelation has been so devastating in its consequence that the world is still dazed with the news, as nothing like that happened since the Nazis legally took over the Weimar Republic in Germany in 1933. With a president who has no concept of historical awareness or social consciousness, or even minimal human conscience, the U.S. legitimized all its dark flaws as open and shameless facts on that memorable day.

Donald Trump, the very embodiment of this astounding event, has laid bare the hitherto hidden anatomy of what America truly is, a Superpower armed with hate and brute force: Virtually every hateful word he ever spoke, every violent gesture toward minorities he ever made, every rejection of conventional civilization and humanity in preference of brutality he ever relished and advocated, as a man and as a presidential candidate, is now etched on American historical record and has been witnessed by the world. It is as if a new Holocaust was enacted by the U.S. for the whole world that is astonished beyond belief that the Guardian Angel of world order and peace, a Superpower for the good of humanity, is now the new Nazi who has turned on the world and its humanity that trusted him. Trembling with fear and anxiety, the betrayed world turns to its various Gods and cries: "Lord, to whom shall we turn now?"

By electing Donald J. Trump president, the United States of America transformed itself literally overnight. It ripped off the facade of a Liberal-Progressive-Enlightened leader of the Western democracies to reveal the frightening darkness and savagery of a White-Nationalist-Racist nation, summoning the ghosts of Mussolini and Hitler. What has only been whispered in small circles of social critics, professional and lay, deeply felt but not publicly declared—that the U.S. is actually a police state and a racist nation, cloaked under the veneer of a free-choice consumer society—is now a universally-certified fact. What began as an anecdotal buffoonery in America's political history has now become America's political history itself. The comic relief that gave us indulgent entertainment is now demanding the Pound of Flesh from us for our indulgence.

The emperor indeed has no clothes and he shed his clothes in broad daylight and under the glare of the world, with no shame and no embarrassment, but in full pride and hubris of naked power: The U.S. under Donald Trump is now the recognized Leader of the Un-Free World that openly brags and prides itself over its White Nationalism, racism, jingoism, sexism, and Fascism. Regarding the image of the United States, all bets are off: The pretenses of all past imagery about "America"—that the U.S. represents the Free World of tolerance, multiculturalism, plurality, Liberal Progress in race relations, gender equality and economic justice—are now shattered to pieces. The destruction is so deep and fundamental that neither America's vaunted propaganda machinery nor its habit of trivializing reality can repair or hide it.

It is too vivid as an event and too frightening as an idea to be buried and forgotten even in America's famous short memory. Now that the U.S. is no longer the Leader of the Free World, thinking persons among us may ask, what *is* the United States of America as a nation and as a power? Is it a new America or is it the old America without its façade? Indeed, America's fall from grace is so swift and unexpected, as we all believed in our own self-hypnosis about America as the Good Guy, that historians among us have not had the time to see the Big Picture clearly. We are still struggling with it because nothing like this has been witnessed in our living memory: The Defender of Freedom and Democracy has turned into a Brute Animal overnight. Not since Germany's transformation from a western-style democracy to a Nazi Reich, killing, destroying, and plundering at will, has the world witnessed anything so swift and so terrifying. And not coincidentally, this transformation is led by the new American president who brags about his superior "German" blood. The Jewish inmates at the Auschwitz death camps, under the harsh transformation of their lives overnight, recalled how they had felt "*half* stunned," unable to think or feel clearly about themselves or their new reality: In America, just now, we are *fully* stunned. We are still asking: What does this event, beyond the media publicity and attention, really signify for America?

Our struggle to understand how something like this could happen in the U.S. is compounded by the idea of American Exceptionalism, the idea that the world's turmoil in war and dictatorship can never happen in America because of our unique blessings by Providence and Wisdom. In Europe? Yes, definitely possible, we would say, but not in *our* nation, the citadel of democracy and compromise, so exceptionally protected by circumstances and history, both human and divine.

Some partisan Americans may feel reassured by the fact that Democrat Hillary Clinton won the numerical majority while Donald Trump won on technicality. After all, they might reason, the majority voted to stay with the Good-Guy America. This reasoning is hardly reassuring simply because, had Clinton won the election, the festering "disease" of America, now exposed by the Trump win, would have gone on unexposed for much longer and would have festered much more deeply. Besides, Clinton's America—a coalition of liberal politics, consumer freedom, and Capitalism—would have kept all of us in self-delusion much longer that America was moving ever forward toward a Perfect Union.

It is no wonder that the U.S. is often called an "untried civilization," as we have not experienced the tragic cycles of life—conquest, famine, tyranny, among them—to which most tribes of the Old World have been subjected. Indeed, we tend to think of everything we face in our daily lives as amusing entertainment. Life as anything but a continuing series of joy and pleasure in America, a sign of surely untried civilization, is mistakenly understood as America's "optimism" and its "positive" nature. Although presently caught in the existential contradiction of simple logic and experience, many Americans now may even be prepared to see the presidential unfolding at the White House simply as continuing amusement and entertainment. The impromptu threats and accusations that Donald Trump has been making on his Tweets, before and after the election, for example, are good sources of laughter, never taken seriously, especially by White America. It seems to escape the White Majority that his threats and accusations are always directed to the less powerful of the world, as persons, as groups and as nations, the Lesser Americans. If you are one of the less powerful of the world, Trump is a genuine source of terror. But to most Americans who are not the direct target of his threats and accusations, his words and gestures may just be taken as but another version of "reality TV," nothing more and nothing less. Most Americans, especially those who are active on the computer, make no pretended distinction between the serious and the comical. The mixing of the serious with the comical is already widely accepted and practiced on the digital front and we regularly find the mixing of the serious ("Trump wins") with the comical ("babes in swimsuits") on the same computer screen. "A Bulletin from the (Trump) White House" could now mean anything: A threat, bluff, bluster, joke or nuclear attack announcement on Country X.

II.

Perhaps the most confused, among all those who are struggling to make some sense out of this revelation about America, are the professionals who earn a living teaching what American Society is, namely, the so-called "social study" people: Sociologists, political scientists, social study teachers, those whose job it is to describe the American System.

Now, they find that *all their previously written textbooks are all wrong and useless in describing and analyzing America in light of Trump's win.*

The textbooks, hence the way they teach about America in the past, all assumed that America was a Liberal-Progressive society, with flaws but ever moving forward toward a Perfect Union. In that Perfect Union, as envisioned by the Founding Fathers and blessed by Providence, all Americans, regardless of their social stations, religions, national origins, or races, would enjoy the bounties of Consumer Capitalism in this open and free nation of "Liberty and Justice for All." Well, Donald Trump's electoral win made a living mockery of this assumption about America. Not only did Trump's election completely overturn this Liberal-Progressive-Capitalist image of America, it was *never* like that in America. The professional American-Society teachers are already scrambling to redo their books on America and perhaps are trying to figure out what all this means and how all this has come about. Like the Beatles, they might sing, "Yesterday, all my troubles seemed so far away. Now, it looks as though they are here to stay." Yesterday, everyone, American or foreign, believed in the Myth of a Progressive-Liberal-Capitalist America; today, it is kin to the Nazi and Soviet Nations.

There is nothing more unsettling than to find out that the world in which we lived our daily lives, and the System in which we assumed our daily routines, is no more, and to realize that we are not even sure what it is that we must confront in place of the old, familiar, and falsely comforting. French sociologist Emile Durkheim had coined a suicide type that he called "the Anomic Suicide"--the killing of oneself because things are so confusing and uncertain--for times like ours.

Given what Trump is known to be, most of it negative, it is not unthinkable that America will be divided, at least culturally, between those who supported him, openly or not, and those who detest his electoral-political success. Naturally, then one of the more subtle changes that Trump presidency has brought to American society is the creeping suspicion we have toward other Americans, especially when we see a burly White Man: Is he or is he not one of the Trump supporters, therefore kin to the Neanderthal Nazis and Soviets? Unsaid in this suspicion, especially among the more politically-aware thinking people, is the question: Is he an American Fascist? This is a similar trend that used to be observed in the Third Reich: Is he a Nazi? In the Soviet Union, the similar suspicion and question was: Is he a Communist?

Among the circle of intelligent, educated Americans, the suspicion used to be milder and the question softer about someone whose character they doubted: Is he (or she) a Republican? The Trump supporters tend to be somewhat embarrassed, especially when they are isolated from their fellow mob members and must stand alone, to openly admit that they *are* Trump supporters. Many Nazis and Communists used to be equally embarrassed to openly admit that they were members of the Nazi Party and the Communist Party. In America, Trump support has been equated with support of Fascism and most Trump supporters, especially when caught alone away from their anonymous crowd, went dead-panned if the question arises; many hid their Trump support even from their spouses.

This new social phenomenon has cast a subtle shadow of suspicion, distrust and doubt in America's family, friendship and collegial circles. Indeed, I, for one, cannot now face a fellow American, especially a White one, without raising the question in my mind: Is he or is he not one of the new Trumpian Fascists? It is possible that, especially among the higher circle of education and finances, a certain secret signal, perhaps in the form of the Masons with the putative secret exchanges of their own, those signals only the initiated members can send out and recognize.

Indeed, it might become a fact of shame and curse one must carry for the rest of one's life with the constant fear of discovery that, after all, he will go down in history as part of American-style Fascism that put America's Mussolini and Hitler in power. Future friendship alliances may be determined by the new litmus test, whether they had voted for Trump, thus revealing their true identity as Americans. How intelligent and humane Americans would deal with their friends and associates who are discovered to have voted for Trump is another question. Would they stop everything and holler to the office crowd: "HEY, EVERYBODY, LISTEN TO THIS: SO-AND-SO VOTED FOR TRUMP!"?

Our popular culture also has much adapting to do. One of the first concerns is how Hollywood would portray its heroes, who are almost all White males. Up to now, these White male heroes have almost always been portrayed (even for the anti-hero types) as generous, intelligent, honest, standing for the weak and needy. With Trump in power, now that "white" and "male" in post-election America are almost synonymous with racism, protectionism and chauvinism, all ingredients of Fascism, how would they be portrayed? Even John Wayne, the classic male hero in Hollywood, while sharing some features of Fascism, never kicked a man who was down and always addressed women as "ma'am." The question is quite serious now: How would Hollywood movies portray the post-election Trumpian White male hero, who has proven to be a closet racist, nationalist, white supremacist, male chauvinist and Fascist?

It is not entirely unthinkable that the script writers would feel obliged to insert a line in their dialogue, something like "I DIDN'T VOTE FOR TRUMP!" for the male hero to declare somewhere in the movie. But most ticket buyers happen to be, as in most entertainment events in America, Whites. Now that the great White pretention is over, would Hollywood begin to lionize the "Trumpian" heroes as heroes in real life, without the fear of critical reaction? Time will tell whether having voted for Trump would become a badge of honor or a sign of shame.

In the meantime, there is a small historical reckoning to do. America has been severely divided twice in its past: Once during the Revolutionary War in which the colonial Americans were divided about evenly between those who were for independence and those who wanted to remain British. Again, a century later, America was divided in the Civil War between the North and the South. Now once again, in 2016, Americans are divided, this time between Whites and non-whites, or between those who are for Trump and those who are against Trump, this time with ballots, not bullets. But the implications are just as foreboding: Would the threatened Lesser Americans, like blacks and Hispanics, feel threatened enough to arm themselves for protection from the police?

Social analysts used to be comfortable in referring to "Americans," as in "most Americans" or "we as Americans," and so on. But this can no longer be done, much less comfortably. Americans are divided now along a line as deadly as the Civil War and as unbridgeable as during the Revolutionary War. The intellectual community may go on pretending that there is such a thing as "Americans" once again, but if truthfulness or honesty is any standard, it is no longer possible to do so. As each day passes, and the Trump Administration does this or that, indicating that it is a White Nationalist, or even racist, government in power, we would be reminded again and again how divided we have become with Donald Trump whose very success is defined by how deeply we are divided.

The two great divisions in the past ended only when one side won and the other side was defeated in a deadly armed conflict. Would *this division* follow suit in resolving its own conflict? Again, only time will tell, but at this writing, the prognosis doesn't look very positive.

Chapter Four

The Child with a Loaded Gun

Many in the media community described Donald Trump as "a child who has never grown up." On November 9, 2016, Donald Trump, this overgrown adult with the mentality of a five-year-old child, woke up with a loaded gun in his hand. White America gave him a special mandate to do pretty much whatever he wanted to do with his gun. The world was in shock as much as part of American society that believed that "somebody like Trump" could not possibly win the hallowed title of the Leader of the Free World. The ensuing chorus was heard in one refrain: How did it happen?

In 1860, America elected Abraham Lincoln as its president, a Republican. In 2016, America elected Donald J. Trump as its president, a Republican. Both were elected legitimately so there was no question of force or irregularity in the process; both were the expressions of the Will of the People. Lincoln and Trump, obviously they are a great contrasting pair. When we consider such a contrast, we first notice the difference between Lincoln and Trump as two *characters.* Then these two characters are seen framed by their respective voters who elected them, so we notice the difference between *people* in Lincoln's time and *people* in Trump's time. Then, finally, we notice that the America of Lincoln's time and the America of Trump's time are also two different *Americas.* Our thinking thus moves from the individual characters, to their voters, and eventually to their societies: American society, or its System, creates its people, and these people create their presidents. To understand how the Child with a Loaded Gun became president of the United States, we must understand his parents, the United States as a society and as a nation that bore the voters who bore the president.

Warnings of something like the Trump Phenomenon have been sounded earlier by many observers. Neil Postman wrote about an America where we were killing ourselves with entertainment in a book appropriately called

Amusing Ourselves To Death. More recently, Mark Bauerlein described the current digitally-crazed Americans in his book as "The Dumbest Generation" in history. As early as 1980, Lance Morrow questioned in a *TIME* editorial whether such a generation of Americans, drenched in the most childish and senseless entertainment and amusement, by the most ruthlessly organized self-centered corporate system, could become adequate "Citizens and Soldiers" for their nation. Indeed, what kind of voters and citizens would the victims (or beneficiaries) of such a concentrated assault from their Social System eventually turn out to be? How would a generation of mindlessly entertained and amused human beings, who turn out to be mostly White, think and vote when a candidate is fine-tuned to know how to appeal to their always on, always *amused* and always *self-centered* and always *dumbed* mind?

Have we been amusing ourselves to death? The consensus answer in calm reason is, Yes, we have been amusing ourselves to death. Have we created the Dumbest Generation with our digital development? The consensus answer is also, Yes, we have created the Dumbest Generation in American history. If we recognize that we amuse ourselves to death and have also created the Dumbest Generation, as historical facts, how can we ever think that there would be *no consequences* from amusing ourselves to death or creating the Dumbest Generation in our midst. What kind of parents would be watching their children amusing themselves, day and night, "dumbing" themselves to death, still feeling calm and confident that they would grow up to be upstanding adults and citizens? Could something like the so-called Trump Phenomenon have been anticipated from our death- creating amusement society and its Dumbest Generation?

Donald Trump is a *personality*; his White supporters are a *national character*. Trump's personality makes up his *biography*; the national character of his supporters makes up their *social history*. At the election in 2016, the personal biography of Donald Trump and the historical national character of the White Masses coincided and produced the amazing election result. As personality and biography are written by the larger development of national character and social history, the larger development of national character and social history are written by the nation's and society's System itself. We can never understand the election result unless we find the historical and sociological causes of the national character that produced the voters and the voting result.

In all this, the most insignificant factor is Donald Trump himself, although in the glitz and hype of the moment he tends to get all of our attention. If the White voters weren't looking for someone like him or if America's social System had not produced the White voters as they were, there would be no Donald Trump. Thus, no one really knows what created the personality of Donald Trump in his biographical life. You can play with psychoanalysis or a series of accidents and incidents in Trump's life to explain why he became the Donald Trump we know today, not another kind of Donald Trump. But everything about the origins of Donald Trump is guesswork; we can only guess but can never get to any intelligent conclusion about the making of the personality known as Donald Trump. This is true of all individual personalities, famous or anonymous, and intelligent answers can never be deduced from the individual personality traits or actions. We can say that Event X that occurred in Trump's early life which we think conditioned his personality later. But we immediately find there are contradictions in that the same Event X occurred in other people's lives that did not produce the same personality result. So we can only continue our guesswork to explain Donald Trump or anybody else.

II.

National character is an historical product that can be observed, studied and analyzed. Most national character studies have produced a set of fairly useful and accurate accounts of character types. Let's say the personality traits of Donald Trump are predominantly observed as childishness, selfishness and vengefulness. When we identify such traits among the general characteristics of the White Masses who supported Donald Trump, we do not think of it as a mere *coincidence* among millions of people, including Donald Trump. Since so many persons are afflicted by the same character traits, we say it is a national character that has its origin in a specific social development and historical epoch of the way a large number of people, perhaps the whole generation, think and act. Instead of trying to figure out why Person A, Person B, or Person C has such and such personality traits, we now ask how the society has produced such traits in its generation. Thus, we move from Psychology to Sociology in our quest.

This analytic move from Psychology to Sociology is not as easy as it appears. The psychological studies of someone like Donald Trump tend to be endlessly fascinating. Many cases of criminal personality types, starting with Dr. Jekyll and Mr. Hyde to Gary Gilmore and ending with any mass murderers in recent times, have held us fairly spellbound with their various and intriguing possibilities. But, such personality studies yield nothing tangible or helpful, as one exhausting study does not lead to predicting the similar events not having occurred yet. Even if we discover everything about one Donald Trump, even if it is possible, that would not lead us to discovering the next Donald Trump, not any more than discovering everything about the current mass murderer to the next mass one, waiting around the corner in the next year decade.

But sociological studies of a generation or citizenry, although not as exciting or given to speculation, can look into the larger pictures of society and its Social System as to why such an event—such as the election of Donald Trump—was possible as a historical development. The question ends up as what in America's Society or Social System could have created such a childish, vengeful and Irrational generation. (Studying the "Criminal Mind" is interesting because it is likely to be about somebody else, but studying the "Criminal Society" is not because it is likely to include myself in it.)

As in most societies, American Society has two sides to its existence: One is its open side, the side that is on display for the world to see. It is loud, colorful and visible. As always, this side of America is the Effect of the Other Side's Cause. Most commonly, it is the side of America that is reported on by the media and reacted to by the public. The so-called Trump Phenomenon is one such event that makes up America's known side.

The other is the hidden side, mostly invisible and largely unknown to the public. This is where the Society's System, and its Institutional Sub-Systems, does its work, according to the larger rules of Power and Structure. Capitalism, especially Consumer Capitalism, never sleeps and churns along its historical and structural mandate, that is, enlarging its power to the fullest extent. Consumers eat the food it produces, watch what it puts on the screen, and think the thoughts that are put into their heads. But, few Americans ever think about how such things come to their minds and bodies so that they consume them with certain predictable consequences both on their minds and bodies.

As we see things openly reported and discussed by the media, America's Capitalist System makes its decisions that cause events to happen, slowly, surely and invisibly. Donald Trump is part of such a process. American Society is Dr. Frankenstein and Donald Trump is its Monster, not the other way around. While our focus is on Trump's election or his persona, the event was created by Trump's society itself. Calling attention to this part of social analysis is the aim of our current quest.

III.

To describe the Biggest Picture first: The emergence of Donald Trump as President of the United States coincides with a remarkable social character development in American society that shaped the White Voter and goaded his choice of Trump as his Leader. The social character, now shared by Donald Trump and Whites come in three broad but interrelated traits:

1. We hate work. Both Trump and Whites have grown up particularly disliking work, and would do anything to avoid having to work by finding others to do their labor, thus concentrating their total energy on self-aggrandizement in the pursuit of Power. This trait turns virtually everyone, but mostly Whites, hostile to their jobs and job-related work. Minimalism (but maximal reward) comes with this trait. As they hate their jobs, constantly seeking someone else do the work for them, they minimize the importance of work and seek compensation in intensified pleasurable activities. Hence, entertainment emerges as America's most essential requirement of life. We may simplify this particular trait as "childish."

2. *We live a solitary life*: By historical quirk and Providence, White Americans are selfish, solitary creatures, likely to live and die away from the human community. Unlike the non-whites who live in communion with others, Whites live, work, play and die alone. White people love "connections" with other like-minded Whites, but mostly at the level of social-media and ballgames; in fact, they distrust one another intensely and believe other Whites are liars and hate each other, taking turns as quarrelsome customers and opportunistic trouble-makers. It is doubtful that the Whites who appeared at Trump rallies ever thought of other Whites as brothers or fellow believers. Very likely, they gathered, hollered, and went their solitary ways afterward. We may simplify this particular trait as "selfish."

3. *Trump and his Whites have become savages*: Both Trump and his White supporters, having lived solitary and self-centered lives, have turned into rather vengeful savages, with little or no sense of community or forgiveness. This savage trait is broadly based on the teachings of Capitalism, nurtured and fortified by the incessant consumption of entertainment, amusement and distraction, thus creating a generation that has little or no sense of humanity toward each other, mostly angry and vengeful. In short, they have become very vengeful if alone and very savage if in society. In spite of America's greatness in military and economic dominance, the prevailing historical assessment is that American consumers, meaning mostly Whites who can afford the most consumption, are very dumb and are becoming dumber by the minute. And, as their savagery increases, so does their sense of mutual hate and self-loathing. We may simplify this particular trait variously as "vengeful," "savage," "dumb," or "stupid."

These primary trends have created their secondary behavioral consequences and they are more popularly known the world over as "selfish," "childish" and "stupid" social character traits that are commonly recognized as uniquely "American." Donald Trump and his White supporters are the *bona fide* carriers of such modern American social characteristics. The easiest way to recognize such traits in White Americans is to contrast them with Scandinavians or Canadians whose commonplace social traits consist of "wisdom" (not childishness), "community" (not selfishness) and "intelligence" (not "stupidity").

Although mostly humored and lightly derided in popular culture, most famously in Jay Leno's talk-show, such anti-social traits have their origins in

America's fundamental social structure and its economic system, namely, Consumer Capitalism. In Donald Trump and his White supporters, we find that these traits are shared to a remarkably harmonious degree: They say "great minds" think alike; so do dumb minds. Before Trump, the U.S. was feared only by its sworn enemies. With Trump, everyone, friend and foe alike, fears America's Child with a Loaded Gun.

IV.

Donald Trump's election to the Presidency of the United States has thus given us a chance to observe America's savage nation in a rather dramatic way. But *how* American society has drifted to this state of affairs today is neither so dramatic nor so visible. In a countless, routine way, from corporate boardrooms to average living rooms, from advertising strategies to consumer preferences in America, this slow and mostly unrecognized process of our intellectual and emotional transformation has been taking place.

As you read these lines here just now, the Best and Brightest Americans are plotting to make us dumber and more dispirited tomorrow than we are today. Corporate America never sleeps and that is Capitalism's machineries whose opioids have brought us to this state of transformation (or degeneration). Donald Trump and his Fascist cohorts are merely the actors on stage but the script was written long before their emergence by an agent as all-powerful and all-knowing as God himself: We call it American Society and its Economic System.

Why did virtually all experts fail to predict the depth of so-called "White anger"? The answer is not difficult to get but requires some analytic detachment and independence from the media intellectuals and social analysts. Once our mindset is thus cleared from their influences, we can say thusly: Those intellectuals and professional social analysts, who live and think within their own circles and their methods, believed in their own Liberal and Neo-Liberal propaganda about America's Enlightened Progress toward Racial Equality and Globalism. In this grand vision of things, the U.S. would become the leading light of a world that is harmonized racially and economically, all in great peace and cooperation.

Consumer Capitalism, the center-piece of Neo-Liberalism at the open market, had been quite effective as a theory and as an explanation of how the open market and consumer freedom were guiding the American System and American Culture. Under the Neo-Liberal System and Culture, the U.S. was an open and free society where the Rationality of Neo-Liberal Capitalism was resolving all the kinks of racism and localism toward the ultimate utopia of consumerism where money and pleasure solved everything.

Virtually every politician, every professor, every journalist and every economist underestimated the Power of Consumer Capitalism to corrupt the thinking and feeling abilities of human beings through entertainment opioids, day and night, around the clock, at the open market. Believing their own self-propaganda, the intellectuals and social analysts underestimated how easily the entertainment-drenched society could actually corrode common intelligence and emotion to the level of a child. At the ballot box, the child voted for opioids and everyone was surprised.

In the past three decades or so, with the coming of cable TV and then computers, American society has become an Entertainment Nation, the likes of which were never seen since the fall of the Roman empire. Entertainment everywhere and always and in all varieties gradually made Americans dumb and selfish, like children, making them lose all sense of community and history, and demand only what pleased their senses. This also rendered them vulnerable to easy promises and propaganda. White Americans were affected by the entertainment opioids more than any other group simply because they were more exposed, thanks to their higher incomes, to such mind-killing entertainment. This was one case where being more affluent, not unlike the opium-addicted wealthy Chinese, only brought more woes to them.

Could any citizens, in any nation, or ordinary human beings, of any society or era, survive the American brand of entertainment day and night, researched and developed to the most scientifically and technologically sophisticated degree ever imaginable by their Best and Brightest? No such assault on the intellectual and emotional capacities of humanity has ever been recorded or witnessed, not even in the days of Romans at the Circus and Coliseum at the height of their indulgence. After decades of this, amusing themselves to death and creating the dumbest generation, something had to happen to America's mind. We could not simply pretend that Americans, especially White Americans, the main target of entertainment consumption, could go on unaffected. Donald Trump happened to have been at the right time and in the right place to reap the full benefit of the generations whose minds had thus been corrupted.

When Donald J. Trump was elected U.S. President, it was a stormy event in America and elsewhere. But the Perfect Storm few saw coming on November 8, 2016 was created by the coming together of three elements: Trump the leader, White People who chose him, and most importantly, America's Consumer Capitalism that for decades worked to destroy White People's intelligence and humanity so that they would one day choose somebody like Trump as their leader.

By electing Donald Trump, against virtually every expert prediction, the White Majority proved that America is still a Whiteman's nation, as heir to Rome and the Third Reich, but no more as "America" that once famously declared that "all men are created equal." This Perfect Storm came at the tail-end of a Liberal Society (its extreme form called Neo-Liberalism) based on the premise that Corporate America should supply anything that the consumer desires. While Marie Antoinette may have shouted to the hungry crowd, "Let'em eat cake!" American Consumer Capitalism shouted out to the lonely, solitary crowd, "Let'em enjoy entertainment!"

During the decades of this unregulated anything-goes consumerism, the market changed from the supply of THINGS, like shoes and chickens, to the supply of IDEAS, like entertainment and fulfillment as its main consumer product. White People in America, the main beneficiaries of this economic master trend, now long saturated with opioid addiction, became dumbed down, childish, and self-centered, demanding ever more opioids. Their Pied Piper, Donald Trump, promised to increase their supply of opioids, taking it from non-whites and was elected President.

No one knows, not even Trump himself, how his Trumpian Vision, at once so backward and brutish, recalling the brute powers of Rome and the Third Reich, will eventually play out. Whatever he promised to White People will have to come from the non-whites since it is not coming from the wealthy. That may give Whites enormous psychological satisfaction, but little else. To give them more than this psychological gift, Trump would have to take some from America's super-wealthy One Percent: This One Percent who controls America would never allow to happen. Hence the Fate of Donald Trump is sealed at that point by this limitation: He cannot touch the One Percent.

V.

Trump won the election by creating scapegoats (the Lesser Americans, such as immigrants, Muslims, non-whites) and dropping any pretenses of liberal America that at least paid lip service to liberty and justice for all, effectively contained within the all-encompassing Consumerism. Inevitably, there would be an interesting interaction, even tension, between "President Trump" (official, global, political) and "the Donald" (mean, childish, temperamental, spoiled and vengeful) and the world would be watching him in half horror and half fascination. Obviously, the former role would have a restraining effect on the latter persona. The extent of this restraint determines the fate of America and perhaps the world, not to mention that of Donald Trump himself who might have taken on more than he can handle.

This is the predicament we are in simply because of what had happened to the White People of America who put all of us there. The White People of America put all of us there because of what American Society had done to the White People in the first place that made them selfish, childish and vengeful.

If you have any doubts, notice how our news reporting or news analysis on serious issues--like elections, terrorist attacks, or earthquakes and so on-- are interspersed with commercial breaks and advertisements on one commodity or another. Notice also how the commercial breaks and advertisements have no connection to the reality of news reported or events analyzed. Even after serious election stuff, terror attacks or earthquakes, the commercials that come on immediately are childish fantasies of their consumer-entertainment world where the reality of the news and the fantasies of the commercials are interchangeable. For over three decades of concentrated entertainment and accelerated distraction of the most childish kind, White Americans have been living with these fantasies until that unreality has become their normal habit of mind.

If you wish to understand White Americans and how they could have voted for someone like Donald Trump, just watch the advertisements for a few minutes.

With Donald Trump's ascendancy to President, American society is in no good prospect for a better society: It is caught in the battle between old Capitalism that wishes to extend and enlarge its old power, on the one hand, and new Fascism that wants to muscle in with its White Nationalism, on the other. If the former wins, which is likely, we simply go back to the Neo-Capitalism of market dominance and entertainment-induced popular stupor; if the latter wins, we join the European nationalists with our new brand of Feudalism cloaked in Fascism. It is a Hobson's choice between addiction to our consumption and enslavement to the system.

Chapter Five

Trump's "Moral Immunity"

Donald Trump as President, the child with a loaded gun and a license to do as he wishes with it, has another very powerful, even frightening, weapon on his side: It is his "Moral Immunity," which he shares with God, who is the only other Being that enjoys a Trump-level excuse from moral responsibility. Moral Immunity gives both God and Trump the immunity from blame or criticism no matter what they say or do. God is all-powerful, all-knowing and all-good, therefore the theological immunity is what shields him from moral immunity as well. Who could blame God for being bad no matter what He does? But, how does the mere mortal like Donald Trump get *his* Moral Immunity?

Throughout his pre-presidential life and candidacy for president, Donald Trump, with his massive exposure to public view, built a persona of great immunity from judgment: That Trump "can do no wrong," not because he is always right but because the concept of right and wrong does not apply to him. Donald Trump built around himself a persona that few in history have been able to attain: The freedom from public judgment. Ronald Reagan was called the "Teflon President," mainly for his ability to deflect public criticisms for many of his faults. But Reagan's immunity from criticisms had to do with the public's "forgiveness" of him; Trump's immunity has to do with the public's *indifference*, based on the belief that the man is incapable of anything other than bullying and blustering. He is so free from public judgment, in fact, that, there *is* considerable substance to what he said about shooting someone on Fifth Avenue without hurting his support level. We could actually imagine him strolling naked in the Rose Garden at the White House in full public view, and it would not cause any loud judgment or condemnation. This Moral Immunity—that we in America do not hold him to *any* moral standard at all--is his biggest and perhaps most destructive weapon to be unleashed on the American Nation.

The human equivalent of Moral Immunity is generally granted on a particular social group quite opposite of God--the insane among us. By law and convention, we grant immunity, both legal and moral, *to those who do not know what they are doing,* and the insane (and children and idiots thrown in by community consensus) belong to this category. Except in our case, there is a grown-up, 70 year-old man-child and President of the U.S. with control of 7000 nuclear warheads, who enjoys this Moral Immunity that only God and the insane can enjoy. This man, Donald Trump, has that complete immunity as he could say anything (for example, "grab the pussy") and do anything (for example, he could kill a man in broad daylight and no supporter would desert him). Not since Adolf Hitler received this level of immunity from the Reichstag in 1933, to do virtually anything he deemed necessary to maintain law and order in Germany, has any human being given this God-like moral immunity on such a large scale. With this immunity, Donald Trump as Commander of Chief of the U.S. can start World War III, and the last thought on our mind, as we die in radiation heat, would be: HOW DID THIS HAPPEN?

Under normal circumstances, if he had been an ordinary political candidate, Trump's candidacy would have sunk many times even before it started. Before the Trump Era, other political candidates folded their political tent on matters so minor, it is almost laughable in the Trump Era.

Two examples suffice.

One, in 1964, Nelson Rockefeller, the Republican frontrunner was on the verge of winning the presidential nomination when the news broke that his wife, Happy, gave birth to a baby, reminding everyone of the nasty scandal involving his first wife and his affair with the new lady, Happy. That scuttled his nomination then and also killed any subsequent presidential ambition for Rockefeller.

Two, in 1972, Ed Muskie, the frontrunner for the Democratic Party, had the misfortune during the campaign of crying before the press while defending his wife who had been criticized in the media for her putative drinking problem. His crying and emotional outburst shocked the nation and this episode sank his candidacy for "crying out loud."

Divorce and tears, mild stuff. But, those were different times when the U.S. existed under a moral precept prior to cable TV and Digital Entertainment. Now, fast-forward to the Trumpian World and his Moral Immunity. He is America's first sitting president whose wife, the First Lady, has appeared in the nude for popular magazines in Europe (a far cry from Happy Rockefeller's scandal) with absolutely no impact in the popular perception of the Trumps or the Presidency. If somebody pointed out that the first lady's nude pictures are all over the world media, this might be Trump's typical reaction:

"Yeah, isn't she a beauty? Guess who is sleeping with her every night?" The public response would be big laughter and applause. His "tax evasion" was termed "genius," and his "pussy-grabbing" boast just the boys' "locker-room talk."

During the entire periods of primaries and presidential campaign, it was obvious even to a child that the man had no beliefs of any kind, political or otherwise, no knowledge of any current or historical issues, no intellectual or philosophical reflection, no appreciation of art or nature, no particular feelings for humanity in general, no sophisticated view of the world and the U.S. in it. To him, life was all "violence and retaliation," as one of his British friends described him, all pussy and sex, all power and money, all selfishness and ego, all entertainment and pleasure. He was the quintessential *Enfant Terrible*, with a loaded gun: Yet, none of his defects and flaws caused even the slightest dip in his popularity among his supporters. (At the time, many media outlets reported that his popularity dropped some, which, in retrospect, turned out to be totally inaccurate, as his popularity had remained steady). In essence, Donald Trump enjoys complete Moral Immunity for all his deeds and misdeeds: His famous boasting--his extraordinary God-like weapon--that "I could stand in the middle of 5th Avenue and shoot somebody and I wouldn't lose voters" turned out to be quite prophetic.

Now, to remind us of this most extraordinary phenomenon, we need to re-emphasize that the only *other being* in the universe who enjoys this sort of Moral Immunity is God. (But, even He is repudiated by some of His believers sometimes, such as in the case of the Holocaust, as He was blamed for not preventing it, letting so many innocent human beings suffer). In some ways, Trump's Moral Immunity surpasses God's. It is doubtful that even God would have survived in America after being so savagely eviscerated day after day by every media outlet (except perhaps Fox News). Day after day, the universally recognized Liar and one of the most Corrupt men on earth called his opponent Hillary Clinton "liar" and "corrupt," obviously the case of the pot calling the kettle black, and nobody among his supporters laughed in disbelief. Nobody took even the slightest notice at the comedy and absurdity played out on the order of the Nazis calling the Soviets "Fascists" and "Beasts" during World War II.

II.

This extraordinary endowment of Trump's God-like Moral Immunity—the notion of not being held morally responsible no matter what he says or does—helps us visualize two important facts about Trump:

One, his supporters expected nothing for him to accomplish and achieve as president other than what he had promised them, such as jobs. In other words, they held him responsible for nothing morally taxing or burdensome. They approved of him morally *as he was*, which was close to zero. Here was a man who was devoid of any moral responsibility that is expected of an average human being, not to mention the Leader of the Free World. And his supporters expected nothing of him as a moral being. This is truly extraordinary immunity, that a presidential candidate of the world's sole Superpower was expected to know so little as president, to perform so little as leader, and to be so little as a human being. They never thought of Donald Trump, their nominal Leader and Pied Piper, as anything other than someone who hated what they hated, who would repress and punish those they wanted to repress and punish, and who would resort to brute power as they wanted to resort to brute power. He was *their* source of power and convenience, nothing more. Certainly, his supporters never recognized him even as a normal human being in the sense of being capable of pity, imperfection or forgiveness.

Two, this Moral Immunity confers power on him as President of the U.S. that is great and terrible. This remarkable God-like Moral Immunity may prompt and goad Donald Trump, the President of the United States and the Leader of the Free World, to do horrid things in his executive decisions and actions as Commander in Chief with terrifying consequences. For example, in his bluster and hubris backed by his sense of Moral Immunity, he might provoke North Korea to attack South Korea in devastating warfare on the peninsula; or, in his equal bravado and miscalculation, he might start Armageddon or World War III in the Middle East. His Moral Immunity exempts *him* from responsibility, but not the world from its *consequences*. This dilemma posed by Trump upon America and the world may be best understood as a spoiled child whose indulgent parents tolerated the child's early signs of cruelty and selfishness by considering him as simply entertaining. The child would continue to say and do awful things and his parents would just laugh, thinking it was all for fun and amusement. America's society, especially its media institution, was indulgent with him because he was "good for CBS" as it was good for other media outlets. His antics only caused people to "tune in" and were good for the ratings. His outrageous behavior created a huge demand for more outrageous behavior from him. By the time the entertainer became a presidential nominee, but still wholly stunted in moral growth and intellectual development, the media, his social parents, suddenly realized the mistake they had made on their *enfant terrible.* But it was too late. This sort of parenting mistake—indulgent parents sorrowfully recognizing their errors only too late—has been told and retold many times, including *King Lear.*

Obviously, his speeches in front of a rabid supporting crowd during a presidential campaign may be different from his decisions and actions in the White House. But hanging the balance of the world between war and peace on this slim hope may not be very wise. Dashing this hope, quite promptly, even as he was waiting to be sworn in as the 45th president of the United

States, he seemed to forget he was elected president as he continued his midnight Tweets in anger and with false claims. As Green Party candidate Jill Stein was processing her request for vote recounts in Wisconsin, Michigan and Pennsylvania, Trump lost all his dignity as President-Elect and Twitted that the recount request was a "scam to fill up their coffers," and claimed "I won the popular vote if you deduct the millions of people who voted illegally." As the actual sitting president with all his institutional weapons of power, and with no visible behavioral changes, Donald Trump with his Moral Immunity is a scary prospect, and signs are that his basic character, formed over a life of 70 years, won't change.

Under normal circumstances (and the key word here is "normal") the U.S. Presidency is not a very powerful position, nothing like Russia's Putin or China's Xi Jinping, both of whom could have a man exiled or shot at will. Eric Alterman wrote in his book on the Obama Presidency, *Kabuki Democracy,* how impossible it is for the president to create a "transformative" change in America, especially challenging the One-Percent to create greater equality and justice in society. But under abnormal circumstances, with a Child with the Loaded Gun as President and Chief in Command of the most destructive military power in history, burning with the desire for revenge on his political enemies and punishing the Lesser American minorities and obstinate nations, a chief executive like Trump with his Moral Immunity can do a lot of damage, even fatally, before he is impeached or dies of old age.

If he ordered a military attack on a nation that irritated him, for example, would the Military Establishment, the professional emblem for orderly chain of command and obedience, balk at the orders or obey them? Is America constitutionally sound enough to withstand a president for the next four years who is certifiably childish and vindictive?

Such absurd possibilities are contemplated because Donald Trump is remarkably morality free. *The man has no moral beliefs*. He is a complete *tabula rasa* in his moral compass. He hates nothing and loves nothing. He proposes nothing and opposes nothing. Unlike those Moralists (those who have strong moral beliefs) and Immoralists (those who have strong opposite moral beliefs), he is an Amoralist who has no particular set of moral beliefs or biases in his make up. It is unlikely that he has done anything in his life only because he believes it is the "right thing" to do. Other than the situational notion of doing what's good for Trump, Inc., he is remarkably free of any human moral precepts that afflict virtually all human beings on earth. How such a human being is possible to exist on earth, much less as the Leader of the Free World, is an endlessly speculative question with no answer that is easy or clear. What we cannot avoid is the fact and consequence of an *amoralist* who wields a massive instrument of power of world-destruction as the Commander in Chief of America.

We can reason with Moralists and we can argue with Immoralists, as we know what they want and advocate. But we cannot reason or argue with an *Amoralist* like Donald Trump because the normal discourse of humanity—cause and effect, chain of reasoning, normal everyday logic, such as if you do X, then Y will happen and Z will get hurt—does not apply to those who believe in nothing established. Donald Trump is the most outstanding case of *amoralism* in a world that is, and ought to be, defined by moralism, in fact many conflicting moralisms. Trump's reasoning stops after the X. He will change his mind about anything since he does not believe in cause and effect, and he will deny any of his previous beliefs since he has no chain of reasoning, and our normal everyday logic does not have the slightest effect on him. Since nothing established has any effect on him and his decision-making is swayed by whoever is with him at the moment, nearest him, or most persuasive with him in his childish, selfish and vengeful fancy, the Devil nearest him has his hearing. Hence he is most susceptible to the American-version Svengali or Rasputin that can play with his childish emotion, selfish mind and vindictive reasoning to get his vacuous approval. While he is calculating his business pluses and minuses at the Trump Tower, the calculus determines his decisions. While sitting at the White House, there is no such finite pluses-minuses calculus that can guide him. At the White House, all is political, which is to say, mood-dependent and whimsical, which maximizes the effects of his Moral Immunity.

Indeed, he is so morally free and vacuous that when we hear that he is opposed to abortion or that he wants to "Make America Great Again," purely as moral propositions, we are more inclined to be puzzled than to debate him on his beliefs. Our natural reaction is: *Why* would he believe in one thing or another? For the past 70 years of his life, he was wholly devoted to the morally-vacuous business of adding money to his chest. He has been elected President of the United States in spite of, or perhaps because of, having no moral beliefs, supported by White America that is equally vacuous with their moral belief. Both found what they wanted in the other, Trump in pursuit of power for power's sake and his supporters in search of their psychological satisfaction.

III.

Eric Alternam writes (*The Nation*, January 30, 2017): "Mainstream journalists are used to collaborating with politicians to tell the truth a little bit at a time. Lies are accepted when they fit the master narrative, but they need to hover within an acceptable range of plausibility. At the very least, they require the pretense of evidence, however specious it might be. (But) they have no experience of covering an American president who *doesn't even pretend to care about truth.*" It is interesting that Trump's lying is unconscious in that he does not deliberately concoct something that is contrary to truth, for example, having done X and saying that he did not do X while *knowing* that he *did* X. For Trump this business of lying is slightly different because, unlike common liars, when he says he has not done X, when everybody else has remembered that he did X, he doesn't remember or think that he did X. Technically he is a liar, but morally he is not, just like a child or an insane person who does not really remember that he indeed committed X. The whole world that witnessed Trump's doing X calls him a liar, or a "serial liar" as he continually does this, but Trump has absolutely no concept of having done X and lying about it: Why? By the time he makes a statement about X, he has forgotten about it altogether (I cannot officially diagnose this particular syndrome, but there is something about him being a "sociopath" or something like that which includes the symptom of such forgetfulness about his actions that have social and moral consequences.) The trouble with having a president who is a technical, if not conscious, liar is that his lying has enormous consequences on people whether the liar consciously knows it or not. Lying may have no negative consequences for the liar but it may hurt those who must live with the president's lies in all his policies and powers. Such is the explanation as to why Trump doesn't even pretend that he is aware of the difference between truth and lie. Hence, the real significance of Trump's presidency is not that we have an unconscious liar for a president, but that we have a president who has no concept of the difference between lies and truths.

During the campaign, those who supported Trump tended to see his inability to distinguish between lies and truths as a sign of his "honesty" and "truthfulness." Indeed, Trump has been remarkably restraint free in saying what he wants to say (sometimes *doing* what he wants to do) quite consistently whether in public or in private. When a person is so free from guile or consciousness that shape the person's recognized public persona apart from his normally reserved private self, the world is left to deal with him as he is, the way he has been shaped by his upbringing and social circumstances. Apart from our private personality, what we as average human beings present ourselves to the world in public is made up of many things that are publicly formed, such as education, moral values, history, religious doctrines, and other factors that make us what we are. But when the person has no such "public" factors in his personality formation and no hidden "private" agenda deeply suspected, as in the case of both Jesus and Donald Trump, we are only left with what each person is as he appears to be: For Jesus, it is in all he said and did in the scriptures, which is not much. What we have in Donald Trump the president, as recorded, observed and concluded from the mountainous quantity of information about him, is a moral immunity that consists of intellectual emptiness, philosophical vacuity, and childish impulsiveness. If we add the enormous institutional powers of the presidency that he now controls, the implications are staggering beyond imagination. No wonder, as when Eve ate the fruit at the Garden of Eden, the earth groaned when Donald J. Trump was inaugurated as President of the U.S. on January 21, 2017.

Why are we in a situation currently with our society in the hands of a president with no moral beliefs whatsoever? Because American *society* itself, after decades of Consumer Capitalism, an economic amoral system of its own, has become a vacuous society. For, of all human enterprises, consumption takes place in a wholly vacuous moral emptiness, as a two-year-old child can consume and consume with immunity as long as he has the money. Consumption is largely living in a vacuum, which is a cousin to lying. Americans, especially White Americans, have been living with sweet lies for decades (consuming fiction, make-believe, fantasy, advertisement, propaganda) created by Hollywood, Disney, Madison Avenue, Wall Street, and other institutions of Corporate America and facilitated by the timely computer technologies. Unlike what we might be inclined to believe, Donald Trump's moral beliefs, or his lack of moral beliefs, are more "American" than those of his opponent would have been: Consumer America and morally-vacuous Trump are such a match made in Heaven, and the match materialized only because both are selfish, childish and vapid.

Chapter Six

Who Created the Monster?

Depending on the calculus of what prospect is in store for each individual, group and nation in relation to the man in the White House, the world is now recovering from the shock of seeing Donald Trump elected President of the U.S., each speculating what would happen to them. Trump, the reality TV host, businessman and now the president, is easily the most talked-about, discussed and written-about person in our modern era since Charles Lindberg, the hero of trans-Atlantic solo flight. It's been Trump everywhere, on the TV screen, on the Internet, and on the minds and lips of anyone who is awake.

TIME magazine, predictably, made him 2016 Person of the Year with this comment: "It's hard to measure the scale of his disruption. . . For reminding America that demagoguery feeds on despair and truth is only as powerful as the trust in those who speak it, for empowering a hidden electorate by mainstreaming its furies and live-streaming its fears, and for framing tomorrow's political culture by demolishing yesterday's, Donald Trump is Time's 2016 person of the year." All very proper for a popular magazine--intellectually vigorous, but vaguely undecipherable and polite, emotionally neutral--and still recognizing that it's all Trump who did it. He is indeed Person of the Year: *Trump is the man.*

Really?

What most people do not remember or think about, while they are intensely concentrating on the person of Donald Trump, is that it is American Society that creates its heroes and villains. It is America's cultural and political hunger that created the persona of Donald Trump, the Entertainer and the Snake Oil Salesman. In spite of all his entertaining tricks and all the outrageous and often savage character traits that make up his persona, it is

American Society itself that decides who is to be famous and who is to be forgotten or discarded. Donald Trump is no exception.

As quirky and infamous as he is, all of Trumpian persona would amount to nothing but a small comic relief or annoyance among those who must work with him. As famous as he is, and now as powerful as he is as a political figure, his rise to fame and certain-to-be fortune *has little or nothing to do with himself or his personal skills.* More specifically, it is America's voters, reputedly White Americans, whose yearnings and aspirations—mostly nationalist and racist--found him suitable for their quest. All credible media researches and investigations have concluded that the Trump Phenomenon is uniquely a "white" phenomenon, mostly white men and some white women. If it were not the deep-seated yearnings and aspirations of these Whites who were seeking someone like him, to return to the world where Whites were White and non-whites were non-white in their proper respective places, there would be no Trump.

In order to understand Trump, we must first understand these White People, men and women, educated and uneducated, affluent and not so affluent, who found a savior in him. In order to understand these Whites, by the same token, we must understand American Society itself, its most dominant features and institutions and their history, that have created these White people in its image and molded their thinking and feeling in its design. If the electoral result with Trump is the Monster, and the White Voters its creator (Dr. Frankenstein) who created Dr. Frankenstein? Without question, it is American Society itself that created Dr. Frankenstein who created his Monster. While the Monster gets all the attention, we must not forget what is above all social actors and actions, to make them all possible to be staged and seen.

In short, to understand these White people, their thoughts and feelings, that drove them to someone like Trump, we must understand how America's dominant social system, namely, Consumer Capitalism, with its dominant products, created its most dominant consumer group, namely White Americans. Even famous men do not create their own fame, as it is always the society and its larger history that create and produce them in their respective roles. If Trump had been born in another era where social norms were different, and certainly without its Media Circus, he would have merely been a buffoon, fool or egomaniac with little or no attention, much less love, from us. Before America made him what he is, we are certain, he was just another young American in search of his place in his society.

Donald Trump, among all the presidents and presidential candidates to date, is perhaps the easiest person to understand. His whole persona is made up of three most common character traits among most White Americans: *Self-centered, vengeful and childish.* (You can throw in *Anger* as a side-effect of the above traits combined*)*. Trump's daily behavior has been childish as he is wholly unaware of anyone but himself, his goal in life has been selfish, and he has always been violently vengeful as he never forgives the slight done him. No celebrity has bared all the inner and outer ingredients of his make up in more glaring detail than Donald Trump himself. There is nothing interesting in Trump's persona and character because of their clarity and simplicity, except that these ingredients of Donald Trump (selfish, childish and vengeful) are also the basic ingredients of the White Majority in America who eventually chose him for their leader. In short, Donald Trump and the typical White Americans are the same kind of people; they are two peas in a pod.

The surprising part of the election results is that, while the media knew Donald Trump well enough, they did not know White Americans as well. The media professionals did not quite understand how stupid the White People had become, after decades of assault, day and night, with trash after trash supplied to entertain them. Obviously they underestimated the power of America's Consumer Capitalism--giving people what they want—that had destroyed the intellectual and human capacity of White people to the extent of total mental stupor. They misjudged Trump-supporting Whites: The media professionals believed that they were smarter than they actually were. They believed that if they condemned Trump, White people would also condemn him. If they found Trump's behavior stupid, the White Majority would find it stupid. There was so much in Donald Trump to condemn that the media thought the whole world was with them in their condemnation of Donald Trump. They were quite mistaken in that there was a large gulf between the intellectual-media community and the White Americans. While the media professionals were made up of America's best and brightest, the audience for whom these smart people created the media products had stayed quite dumb. As a rule, the media professionals worked day and night to keep Americans (largely White audiences) stupid, and when they needed to asses the success of their works correctly, they vastly underestimated their success.

It has always been the media hubris in America that they can mess with their audience's mind at will—alternately serious and frivolous, smart and dumb, human and inhuman, morally righteous and morally stupid—as their business required. The end-result is that, subjected to such confusing and contradictory messages day and night, the audience naturally *becomes nothing in particular with themselves*: They become neither particularly serious nor particularly frivolous, neither particularly smart nor particularly dumb, neither particularly human nor particularly inhuman, neither particularly morally righteous nor particularly morally stupid. What indeed is this thing, *becoming* nothing in particular? Like a child who has had no particular upbringing—with contradictory messages showered upon him all the time— the White Majority has become aware of nothing but themselves as agents of self-centered consumption, demanding whatever their desire for consumption demands and being fulfilled with whatever pleases their consumer desires. It is for this reason of what the Great American Media, and its Greater American Society, has done to the White Majority that very little, virtually none, of what Trump declared in public or in private was a topic suitable for policy debate or public discussion. Like a petulant child, he simply declared whatever he wanted to declare and that was the end of debate or discussion.

Under the circumstances, the shock of hearing that White Americans just elected Trump president of the U.S. is like hearing, as we should recall it here, that a 6-year-old child just shot and killed the president of the U.S. with his father's six-shooter. Naturally, the child would become an instant object of our attention. But this attention on the child, although natural and logical, is mistaken. In order to understand the child, we must focus our attention on his upbringing, his parents, his community, and ultimately his society. Likewise, to understand the White People who just elected Trump president of the U.S., as shocking as it is and as tempting as it is to focus on Trump and all his electoral strategies and vicissitudes, we must shift our focus to the social factors that created those who created Trump: Of the three factors involved in the 2016 election—Trump, Whites, and America—Trump is the least significant of the three factors. He is the child who finds a smoking gun in his hand and is just as surprised at what he has done as the next person. To understand how it happened, we need to understand the largest of the three factors, that is, American society which created White Americans who created Donald Trump.

II.

But, first, the most immediate question we need to raise and resolve is the one about our Democracy. In America, a nation with no feudal experience, not even a dictatorial past, has nothing but the "democratic" process in its political arsenal. For America, it is democracy or nothing. Because there have been no cultural forces to balance out our democratic process that other societies have—such as the Crown, their tribal history, their religion, their trials and tribulations as a nation, their folklore, their legends, their treasured Collective Wisdom—the democratic risk is peculiarly American. Alexis De Tocqueville noted this as American democracy's "tyranny of the majority."

Given this historical past, American democracy lives and dies on citizen intelligence, as expressed in their voting power. But by its nature, the freedom to vote as one wishes is identical to the freedom to spend one's own money as one wishes. Both can and do lead to childishness, selfishness and vengefulness. It has been understood among theorists and scholars, variously from Locke to Jefferson, from Rousseau to Lippmann, that the voter's personal wishes, often called "local interest," eventually coincide with the larger nation's wishes, called "General Will" or "national interest." It is in this process of coincidence between the private citizen and the larger collective community that the personal and the national come together to form a coherent whole.

But, what if the two factors do not coincide? Two possibilities emerge: The first one is that the private interest (childish, selfish and vengeful) wins out because the "private interests" of the majority drown out the national interest. Here you have the realization of De Tocqueville's Tyranny of the Majority. The second one is, if the national interest (in whatever guise and ideology) out-powers the private interest of the citizens, we have plain Totalitarianism. The role of leadership is to make sure, through the process of persuasion and influence, that private interests and collective interests coincide so that neither consequence comes about.

When totalitarianism is the alternative to the majority's tyranny, most would prefer the latter as the expression of history and progress. After all, isn't the democratic formula, the majority vote, asking for this possibility or eventuality? The question this possibility or eventuality raises is answered by Lysander Spooner in his classic book, *Trial by Jury*. In it, Spooner, a libertarian of the Jeffersonian mold, argues that the power of the citizens, as represented in the Jury, is absolute, above the Court and above the Law: In essence, he argues, the Jury (and the citizenry by extension) *is* the law above all things, absolute and final. The Power of the Nation, in the Jeffersonian and Spoonerian sense, is vested in the People of the United States. But, the nagging question is: What if the majority has become Selfish, Childish and Vengeful to the extent that their majority would merely be the majority decision to commit collective suicide that will destroy the nation?

The workings of democracy assume as its cornerstone that citizens are well educated and are relatively free of self-destructive impulses. The idea of democracy is defended only when there is enough free flow of individual freedom to change our minds according to the process of persuasion. That one can be persuaded by someone as one can persuade someone else, by the exchanges of ideas, is what makes democracy possible and preferable. Such democratic ideals collapse instantly if citizens, or the majority, are so rigidly brainwashed that they are beyond persuasion or argument. Hitler came to power all democratically and what he did in the next 12 years of Nazism was all legitimate and democratic. But few people in the modern world would be persuaded that the Third Reich under Hitler was *really* a democratic nation. However, it is relatively easier to see if the *procedure* was legitimately democratic than to see if the *voters* were legitimately democratic.

After the Trump election to the presidency of the U.S., we can raise the same question: Is America *really* a democratic nation that elected Donald Trump president of the U.S.? When the process is proven to be legitimate and there is no question about Trump's win being legitimately democratic, the next inevitable question is, *Were the voters, who voted for Trump, in their right minds?* When the question shifts from procedures to voters, we shift our analysis from Quantity to Quality, from who got the most votes to what happened to the voters? We raise these questions because of the simple fact that these voters who voted for Trump, the White American Voters, happened to have lived for several decades through the most mind-killing system called Consumer Capitalism, which is not a neutral system of life. Consumer Capitalism is different from its predecessor, Industrial Capitalism, which supplied Americans their material needs arising from their life's demands, which require chickens in the pot and shoes on their feet. Unlike Industrial Capitalism, Consumer Capitalism supplies entertainment and fulfillment, vaguely associated with happiness and pleasure of the moment while supply lasts. Addicted to entertainment and enslaved to fulfillment, consumers slowly lose their minds to Consumer Capitalism's relentless supply of trash. Now, after three decades or so of this process of trashing the American Mind, the White Mind in particular, these mind-trashed Americans go to the voting booth and cast their ballot for one Donald Trump. If we could understand the inner workings of how Consumer Capitalism actually succeeded at destroying the White American Mind, we could at least comprehend the frame of mind in which the White supporters did what they did: We could find the sociological explanations for their collective madness.

The Founding Fathers, ever suspicious of the untried "majority-led" democracy in America, instituted a saving mechanism in the form of the Electoral College, which, in theory, could override the majority vote. Under the circumstances in which we live today, the Electoral College vote being cast *independent* of the General Will, cast as the national vote, is unthinkable. (For one thing, no Electoral College member who changes his vote would survive politically upon returning to his hometown.) According to the formula we have in America, the presidential election is like a round-robin playoff system: First, the candidate wins one round, the mass vote, and then, he goes on and wins the Electoral College round. In theory, although Hillary Clinton lost the first round to Donald Trump, she could still win the second round, the Electoral College vote. Given the circumstances, this possibility exists only in theory. If the Electoral College, when the body convenes in Washington and casts its vote and, God forbid, cast its votes for Hillary Clinton to save the nation from the Tyranny of the Majority, they would certainly be massacred by the White Majority.

III.

Given who Donald Trump is and what he portends to become and do as the president of the U.S., this normal political process is no longer deemed normal in America. Although he won the process fair and square, we recall

Adolf Hitler's own fair-and-square assumption of Germany's Chancellorship in 1933, and question why this "normal" and tried-and-true democratic system has not worked in America in 2016, in substance if not in form. Again, the question is the same: How could the majority, the White Majority in America, still stand by their man in the face of the nation's all-out attack and criticism from virtually every intellectual, professional, scholarly and journalistic community? What made their mind or brain absolutely immutable to human emotion or intellectual reason, almost suicidal historically and culturally?

The answer might be in this supreme irony: Virtually all the members of the intellectual community were engaged for decades in making the voting American White Majority what they were. They worked for Consumer Capitalism to make White consumers as childish and as self-centered as possible. The editorial board for the *New York Times* and *USA TODAY*, for example, condemned Donald Trump as unfit for president and endorsed Hillary Clinton as fit for president. But, ironically, it is these intellectuals at the *New York Times* and *USA TODAY,* as well as at college campuses and on TV and computer screens, who invented everything for Consumer Culture. Their entertainment and brainwashing eventually produced the monumental White Majority's childish-selfish-vengeful decision to support Donald Trump, who is almost universally described as an unfit president, even an unfit Human Being. But, it is these great intellectuals who made White Americans to be unfit voters in a democratic but unfit society by supplying entertainment opioids that killed their minds.

In the meantime, we should remember two things about America: One, the present generation, fittingly the dumbest generation ever, is quite different from the previous generations that were equally childish, selfish and stupid at times, but not at their fundamental makeup. Previously, the generations before our digital generation had some sliver of wisdom from their elders, America's political leaders, or simply their collective community. Today's digital generation has none of these helpers: They are completely and wholly the product of digital messages at their fingertips. No human mind has ever existed in such a precarious and perilous state.

Two, given the conditions of our present technology and psychology assaulting our senses and intellectual in a way never before, the so-called Trump Phenomenon will continue into the future. The whole Trump Experience is by no means an overnight phenomenon but has developed over a slow and meticulous process from Consumer Capitalism, which is unlikely to be modified or fade. It would behoove American society as a whole to wisely brace for many more future Donald Trumps. The White Majority will not suddenly become un-selfish or community-conscious overnight. It has taken decades to make them what they are, and it would certainly take decades to un-make them. But, first, we have to understand the former process thoroughly (how White Americans were made) in order to understand the latter possibility (how to reverse the process).

Our prognosis is not very promising: Reversing the process of idiotizing White Americans that took decades of Consumer Capitalism, which produced the Dumbest Generation, requires that we reverse Consumer Capitalism itself. Given the addiction and enslavement created by our Social System, this would certainly require more than what we human beings can do. Just imagine asking an average American, whether White or non-white, to give up his smart-phone, for the sake of humanity and posterity, and you can guess the nature of our difficulty.

Chapter Seven

The Nature of "White Anger"

It is now universally recognized that it is "White Anger" that elected Donald Trump. What is this thing called "White Anger"? Why are (or were) White Americans angry? The conventional wisdom is that White Americans were angry at the *status quo* and voted for an alternative to the *status quo*. To get at the root source of this anger, media professionals have interviewed White people who told them what had made them "angry." The causes of their anger varied, from jobs to government, from the economy to trade relations, from welfare to Obamacare, whatever. After sifting through all their unhappy issues, all that remains, we conclude, is that they were angry.

Should they have been angry to begin with? Was their "anger" justified?

The one unquestioned principle in a democratic system is that *voters are never wrong*. (The existence of our Electoral College system indicates that they could be wrong.) Of course, questioning whether voters in any election could be wrong, morally, by electing a candidate of their choice for the reasons that they elect him, would destroy the very system in which the democratic faith, with its secret balloting, resides.

Rooted in this tradition, the general post-election analysis is always focused on why the voters elected Candidate X. They ask the voters for their reasons behind their electoral decision, and when they are told that Reason Y is what prompted them to cast their votes on Candidate X, then Reason Y is reported to be the reason. Thus, the analysts conclude that voters elected X for reason(s) of Y. However, the *legitimacy* of Reason Y is never questioned any more than the election of X. If they say the reason for their going for Candidate X was that his opponent had a very elitist speaking habit that annoyed them (typically by Adlai Stevens against Eisenhower), then the question never arises whether their dislike of his speaking pattern *should* have been the reason. But, the focus would be now on why the defeated candidate had not fixed his speech habit to fit the voters' preference. The principle is that the voter has *carte blanche* with his vote: *He can vote for any candidate and for any reason,* period, which is the reason why elections in America degenerate to absolute childishness and the advertising cost sky-rockets with each election as voters become more and more like children at a candy store and the candidates more and more like merchandise to sell.

This brings us to the sociological, not technical, question of why the White Voters chose their candidate, Donald Trump. Technically no one can question why voters choose to vote for a particular candidate. The voting system *ipso facto* contains the right and justification to choose any candidate of one's choice. In the case of Donald Trump, somehow the question arises as to why, strictly sociologically, White voters in America voted in a way many believe they should not have voted. We do not question whether Hitler came to power in Germany legitimately, as he was appointed to Chancellor of Germany according to its constitutional process. But we raise the question of how Hitler came to power over and over again, historically and sociologi-cally, because somehow it seems unthinkable that Hitler had come to power at all, and legitimately. Similar reasoning applies to Donald Trump's ascen-dancy to presidency. This certainly goes against the principle of the Unques-tioned Vote. But, again, our interest is sociological and historical in drawing the Bigger Picture about generations and their society in America, not the technical one of learning how to win the next go-around for one party or the other).

As noted above, the puzzle of White support for Donald Trump has been discussed and answered in a social phenomenon loosely identified as "White Anger." Virtually all media interviews of White people in America who were supporting Trump described their motive in general terms of anger, mostly that their national government was paying more attention to the hitherto-neglected minorities than Whites and they felt ignored and unloved.

Our analysis here deviates from the traditional post-election pattern in that the so-called White Anger is not taken as the beginning and ending of how Trump won. But our focus is on White Anger itself, not as the reason and explanation for the electoral result that put Trump in the White House, but as a legitimate sociological topic as part of the Big Picture. (To the traditional-professional journalist in the media, White Anger itself *is* the Big Picture.)

Two questions arise: Should Whites in America *feel* ignored and unloved by their society and government? If they should not, yet they still feel that way, what is the *cause* of this widespread anger among Whites that has no sociological basis? The answer to the first question is easy enough to identify as it involves a few factual reminders, which we shall discuss below.

But the answer to the second question is a bit more complicated as it involves the larger picture of the American Economic System, more specifically, its Consumer Capitalism that has systematically destroyed the White-man's Mind in the last three decades. The consequence of this destructive social phenomenon has only now resulted in the election of Donald Trump, which is dramatic enough to be noticed worldwide.

Now, the answer to the first question. Whites in America, as a whole, have been enjoying all the benefits of the 16-trillion-dollar consumer economy that is available to them. We say "available to them" because 90 percent of America's economic wealth goes to the top One Percent. Of whatever is available to the working people in America, high and low, the lion's share goes to Whites. The common reference to the Trump supporters as mostly "poor whites" or "working whites" is a myth. The *Nation* magazine identifies the Trump-supporting Whites' income as "20,000 dollars higher." *Newsweek* says, "As exit polls showed, Trump didn't win among poor Americans, as was expected; the majority of voters (52 percent) with a total family income of less than $50,000 in 2015 actually voted for the Democratic nominee, Hillary Clinton." In general, the average personal White income is almost twice as much as the Black average personal income, and this has been so since the Brown vs. the Board of Education decision by the Supreme Court that formally ended Jim Crowism in 1954. Jamelle Bouie writes in a *Slate* article the day after the election that "Trump didn't just win working-class whites—he won the college-educated and the affluent." All the top positions of any consequence in America, say the CEOs of the *Fortune 500*, the generals in the military, the lawyers and professors, doctors and scientists, the presidents of the U.S. (except the current one) are and have been Whites. Non-Whites get arrested more often, get shot unarmed by police more often, are twice as much more likely to be on death row, and own only 10 percent of what Whites own in assets. Culturally, also, Whites' supremacy in America is unassailable: Almost all cultural icons of "good guys," "heroes," "role models" are occupied by Whites; when kids learn about the Great Americans, they are likely to learn about Great White Americans. A month is allocated to Blacks Americans, another to Asian-Pacific Islanders, another to Hispanics, and so on, but there is no White Month simply because every month *is* a White Month. Whites spend more money on entertainment, on leisure activities, and on arts and hobbies. Major spectator sports are predominantly White businesses: They are owned and patronized by Whites, while non-white players are owned and controlled by the owners and coaches who are White. (NFL quarterbacks, considered "leadership positions," are normally reserved for White players and non-white players are discouraged from trying out as quarterbacks.) Digitally, Whites enjoy greater access to computers than non-whites, prompting the talk of the "Digital Divide" that keeps non-whites from enjoying the digital benefits and thus falling further behind.

II.

No wonder, being "white" in America is still a vastly privileged position. When a black man is pulled over by a cop on a lonely county highway in Texas in the middle of the night, he is not just worried about the cost of the ticket; he is worried about his life. This sort of extra stress of life is not suffered by Whites who would only calculate the ticket cost. To be sure, nothing special, by way of privilege, just lands on the Whiteman's lap for him to enjoy over his colored counterpart. But, the average Whiteman expects, and generally gets, the reward of life according to what he puts into it. Life for American Whites is fair enough, in expectation as well as in result. Not unlike black Americans who expect life in American society to be inherently unfair and are urged on by their parents that they must put in a 150-percent effort to get a 100-percent reward. An average White does not have to suffer this sort of injustice as a matter of daily routine expectations. American society is so stacked to favor Whites in so many visible and invisible ways (from hailing a cab to applying for a job) that it is *incalculable* as to how privileged White life is in American society.

What *is* a privilege and where does it come from? Two points are pertinent to our discussion of social privilege: One is that in order for a privilege to exist—a special advantage of life not available to all—it must *deprive* someone or some group or some nation of the privilege that is now afforded another person, group or nation. For White Americans to enjoy any kind of privilege, say, not worrying about getting killed by a white cop, a black man must suffer *extra* worry about getting killed by a white cop. For a general or a colonel to enjoy the privilege of exclusive parking spaces for them at any American military base, forbidden to the lower-rank drivers, the latter must forego the enjoyment of the comfort that the generals and colonels enjoy with their privileged parking spaces. For someone like Bill Gates to enjoy the privilege of his extraordinary amount of wealth, others must be deprived of *their* privilege by that amount. (Germans in the Third Reich enjoyed their 2500-calories-a-day ration until the very end of WWII, but for their privilege of good nutrition, all occupied countries had to give up every morsel of food to the Nazi occupiers who shipped everything to their Motherland.)

The second point about social privilege is that those who enjoy the privileges not available to others, slave masters and aristocrats, high-ranking officials and wealthy persons, for example, *as a rule do not recognize that they are enjoying a privilege.* I have been teaching college sociology courses for three decades and have found virtually no White students in my classes who ever recognized or acknowledged that they *are* privileged persons in American society. (Could there be "racism" without its creating privilege? Could there be privilege without its going to those who maintain the racist system?) The simple enjoyment of parking comfort for the generals and colonels are likely to go unrecognized or acknowledged at American military bases, even at theaters, PXes, restaurants where there is no apparent military urgency for this privilege; what's worse, most of the time, these privileged parking spaces go unused, thus demonstrating their extraordinary nature of privileged-ness. Likewise, I doubt that the super-rich in America believe they are living a privileged lifestyle, as they probably think it's completely normal and routine for them and they *deserve it.*

On all levels and in all aspects, from Wall Street to Hollywood, in sports and computers, in courts and in classrooms, physically and psychologically, America *is* a White Society. Whites own it, control it and benefit from it. When *TIME* magazine predicted that America would be a "nation of color" by 2050, as the new immigrants would not be European descendants, one commentator said, "So? Whites would still own all the money and power in America." How could there be "White Anger" at the loss of privilege in American Paradise that is built and exists for Whites?

In spite of the benefits that they enjoy overwhelmingly, Whites are *unhappy and angry,* unhappy because they are not satisfied with the *status quo* and angry because they are not getting more. They feel more is going to the non-whites than coming to them, for example, through the Affirmative Action Program, as this federal policy has been one of the most grievous bones of contention among Whites. But, look at it within a family context and we get a very different picture: Let's say the black Americans are late comers to the family with certain physical handicaps; the Affirmative Action Program was instituted to help out the slow-moving and slow-learning handicapped new child in the family to bring him up to speed; the older child, spoiled and selfish and used to getting the family's whole attention, sees this special attention from his parents paid to the new slow brother and feels neglected and angry. In the meantime, the slow brother is thrilled with the help and attention he is getting and feels sunny and positive about life.

The *Nation* magazine reports that despite the fact that they bear the brunt of racism and poverty and late start, non-whites in America remain optimistic about themselves and America. "Black Americans are consistently and significantly more optimistic about the direction of the country than their White peers. . . Like black Americans, immigrants report consistently more optimistic views of the nation's future than do Whites."

Understanding the anger that Whites have felt in America may be better explained by the source of the optimism felt by non-whites: Non-whites look to a future in the nation and in their lives, while Whites concentrate only on their lives *here and now*; and perhaps more importantly, non-whites live together as a community, while Whites live, play and die alone, in great solitary loneliness and misery. While non-whites sing the tune of optimism and happiness, Whites seethe in lonely anger. While their feelings of neglect and anger might have been somewhat alleviated while Trump was promising all sorts of special privileges for them, now that the election is over, they are back to their solitary lonely life, vaguely awaiting Deliverance.

Now on to the second question: What caused this *inability* for White People in America to think intelligently and feel optimistic, seeing nothing but doom in paradise, being unhappy in the land of abundant pleasure, and living solitary and lonely lives in the networking heaven of social media? In short, what destroyed the White Mind, reducing it to the level of a spoiled child amid all the toys he is playing with?

Chapter Eight

Trump between Capitalism and Fascism

The election of Donald Trump proves that a world-spanning superpower cannot pretend that it is a just, fair and humanitarian good guy very long. Now that Trump is the sitting president as our daily wakeup call, the pretended reality, even with its prodigious propaganda machinery, cannot go on. No previous superpower, not the Romans, not the Nazis, the most famous superpowers in history prior to the present superpower, could do it forever. Whichever form it takes—imperial Rome, world-conquering Nazism, now the present Superpower U.S.—they all fall to the fate of all superpowers: They eventually show their true color, their power, as in super-power, and their eventual *hubris* and fall. In present U.S., our dominant system, which is Capitalism, is encountering its cousin, Fascism, as a political challenge to its dominance. Every day, the world hears what Trump says and watches what his Cabinet does, and everything that the world hears or watches is the inevitable conflict (or at least discomfort) between old power Capitalism and new power Fascism.

This "struggle" is shown, in a reverse psychological way, in the "peace-making" comments that Warren Buffet made about how the economy (capital) would do under Trump: "I think it'll work fine under Donald Trump. Trump won't ruin the economy or the stock market." On the other hand, economist Richard Wolff foresees a different outcome in the economics-politics relationship: "Trump is declaring war on America's large corporations," says Wolff, "who have invested hundreds of billions of dollars for the last twenty-five years in China, India, Brazil and in countless other places on the promise that they could pay low wages and bring the product to the U.S., to the working classes, that can afford it. If that's going to be blocked (by Trump) they will be out of great deal of money. Then they are going to be *the enemies of Mr. Trump* (who) cannot afford it." Obviously the capitalist class is watching how the Trumpian power will affect Corporate America. To sum up what goes on between Trumpism and Capitalism, writes Tim Mullaney for *MarketWatch:* "The honeymoon is over: Wall Street is finally taking Trump literally. . . A struggle between the essential stability of the U.S. economy and the 11-day old instability of its political institutions is being joined before our eyes."

How, indeed, do Capitalism and Fascism, as ideological systems, stand in relation to each other?

Both Capitalism and Fascism are systems of control: Capitalism controls the Majority who work and consume in the mainstream of society and derives its power from the wealth it collects and possesses; Fascism has the majority controlling the minority, deriving its power from the pleased majority. Capitalism tends to avoid uses of direct violence, as it prefers the neutral appearance of the "marketplace" or "free enterprise" or "consumer choice," or "courts" and so on; only rarely does it rely on something physical and violent, such as "Debtor's Prison." Fascism, on the other hand, is less shy about using violence, especially legal violence, from the street-level skirmishes to the military-level war-making, as its operational mode is the direct demonstration of strength and manliness.

Both systems believe in control by power, the simple equation of all social relations among individuals, groups and nations: *THE STRONG RULE THE WEAK*. Capitalism's focus is on *economic* power as its main attention, while Fascism's is more on the political movement of gaining and keeping *political* power.

To be sure, although both systems may conflict with each other, as will happen in Trump's America, they share in them their dependence on the naked, and cruel, use of power—brute, military, legal, educational, spiritual, cultural, media—to dominate and control the masses and the weak, respectively. In America today, Capitalism accomplishes its goal primarily with the market's work on consumption and entertainment; Fascism in the Trump Administration is expected to see free and open reliance on the military and legal means of punishing the Minority. Although both are mean and cruel systems of power, Capitalism uses the gentler approach of propaganda and self-addiction while Fascism is more likely to adopt the more brutal and direct approach of force and action.

Fascism, being an ideology of power, is a simple, clear-cut, uncomplicated system (although its local expressions vary a great deal) that says the powerful rule the powerless. This fits the character of Donald Trump perfectly: He is like a precocious child who is cunning, clever, and unsophisticated but single-minded to a cause, strong but without blood-deep commitment and remarkably free of self-reflection or doubt. In biographical detail, Trump comes from a very different world of life, quiet alien to most ordinary

Americans, where it is full of paranoia and fear that he might lose the next Darwinian contest for power. Trump as a Fascist displays many contradictory traits, some of which are also observed among White Americans: He mostly swaggers but shrivels into fear like a child when he is scolded; he has no sense of generosity or forgiveness and even the slightest of slight sends him into sleepless nights and lonely Tweets; his bravado and bragging are always expressed in power and wealth, and without them, he is afraid that he fades into nothing in America; and like a typical Fascist, he cannot stand being wrong and as President who cannot be wrong or wronged, he is quite cable of starting WWIII just so that he, Donald Trump, can be proven right.

Donald Trump, as the new American-style Fascist leader, is an ardent practitioner of Capitalism, if not a dedicated believer of Capitalism. He has made the transition from cruel Capitalism to cruel Fascism as he entered the political field. He is the same man merely changing his scenery, from a successful Capitalist to a successful Fascist. How successful was he as a Capitalist businessman? Here is how I described him in a book entitled *American Paradise*, published in 2010 when he was a practicing Capitalist and a popular TV showman:

"(Trump) loves the game of business power, and managed to parlay that into a popular TV show. 'There is something very succinct and very beautiful about the words 'You're fired,'' says Trump about the joy associated with those words used in the 'reality' show. 'It's so definite and final.' Yes, so definite and final that they can be delivered only by an absolute tyrant to a wholly powerless victim who cannot fight back. 'I love the way [the program] shows the city,' speaking of New York City where his show takes place. 'The beauty, the viciousness, how it eats these [apprentice] kids alive. I really like that.' But, as power-hungry and boastful as he is, he is so distrusting of people that he is a terrified child of a human being. He is so fearful of people that, reminiscent of another tyrant who distrusted people, Howard Hughes, he refuses to shakes hands. 'It's barbaric,' explains Trump in a magazine interview. 'Studies have shown that if you shake hands, you catch colds.' (He conveniently ignores another long-term study that shows if you live, you die). Another report describes him as so paranoid that dinner guests at his mansion noticed the Uzi guns sticking out of the bodyguards' coats while they were guarding the guests around the table. This is at a dinner in his own home entertaining his friends. He admits his personal misery to the interviewer when he says, 'My life is much less glamorous than people think.'"

Still, the lure of power—the ability to make someone else's life miserable--is much greater than the pain of loneliness and paranoia the process demands of the player. All players in corporate America are one step away from hearing the words—"You're fired!"--pronounced on themselves. If they survive this random terror of the night and fear of the day, then their day comes, when they can inflict the terror and fear on others. In the meantime, they 'play hard, make as much as you can and work all the angles....and dream the American Dream,' as the report describes Trump's life."

This is the kind of human being, showman and businessman that Trump was and, most amazing of all, American Whites liked him and his show, and eventually his candidacy for the President of the United States. It makes us shiver to ask the question: *What kind of people would have liked this kind of human being and this kind of "reality" TV show, where the strong simply devoured the weak?* Of course, the answer is: The White people who eventually voted for him as their Leader. Those who enjoyed his show are the same kind of crowd that enjoyed the gladiators and Christians fed to animals at the Roman Coliseum. Could the White People who voted for Trump *not* distinguish between a TV showman and the President of the United States (not to mention the Leader of the Free World)? Obviously not.

Trump did not create cruel Capitalism, he merely personified it better than anyone before him or since. If school children wanted to learn about what a typical Capitalist is like, the teacher could do no better than just pointing to the persona of Donald Trump. Now, how does he fit into the new power system in America as a Fascist? From Capitalist cruelty to Fascist cruelty is but a small step and Trump has crossed the gap nimbly. In an article in *the Washington Po*st (May 18, 2016), entitled *"This Is How Fascism Comes to America"* Robert Kegan writes about Donald Trump and his Fascist supporters:

"We're supposed to believe that Trump's support stems from economic stagnation or dislocation. Maybe some of it does. But what Trump offers his followers are not economic remedies — his proposals change daily. What he offers is an attitude, an aura of crude strength and machismo, a boasting disrespect for the niceties of the democratic culture that he claims, and his followers believe, has produced national weakness and incompetence. His incoherent and contradictory utterances have one thing in common: They provoke and play on feelings of resentment and disdain, intermingled with bits of fear, hatred and anger. His public discourse consists of attacking or ridiculing a wide range of 'others' — Muslims, Hispanics, women, Chinese, Mexicans, Europeans, Arabs, immigrants, refugees — whom he depicts either as threats or as objects of derision. His program, such as it is, consists chiefly of promises to get tough with foreigners and people of non-white complexion. He will deport them, bar them, get them to knuckle under, make them pay up or make them shut up.

"That this tough-guy, get-mad-and-get-even approach has gained him an increasingly large and enthusiastic following has probably surprised Trump as much as anyone else. Trump himself is simply and quite literally an egomaniac. But the phenomenon he has created and now leads has become something larger than him, and something far more dangerous."

Notice the striking similarities between Capitalist Trump and Fascist Trump in the above two descriptions, one from me and the other from Kegan: The threat and actual use of power by the strong ("You're Fired!") on the weak (all others, not White America, are meaningless, irrelevant, marginal, and even sub-human). Now, he is, at least nominally, no longer a practicing Capitalist; he has to become a full-time practicing Fascist in his new job as President of the United States.

II.

How much of a "Republican" (containing both Capitalist and Fascist traits) is Donald Trump, many have asked. On the political level of analysis, in elections and platform articulations and as such, not much. On the sociological level, such as in capitalism, racism, nationalism, militarism, individualism, social Darwinism, male supremacy, and Fascism to tie them all together, however, he is very much in line with traditional Republican values. Trumpian Fascism that requires a massive and effective intellectual paralysis and manufactured emotional state, is after all a child of Consumer Capitalism and its relentless supply of Opioids, all part of the Republican strategy of Neo-Liberalism.

In the end, Trump is neither a dedicated Capitalist nor a card-carrying Fascist; he just finds the basic philosophy of both Capitalism and Fascism to his liking largely because the way Power simplifies all human equations. Trump is a classic "amateur" who ran for president on a lark and is as surprised as anyone, by beating a thoroughly "professional" Hillary Clinton. It's ironic that a normally tree-hugging amateurish humanitarian Democrat has been thrashed by a true amateur whose selling ticket was Fascism, American style.

It is truly ironic that no man before him has come to the White House as the American President with virtually no ideological bag. No man before him has ever been able to escape all public issues of ideological beliefs and free himself of all thinking clutters and concentrate his whole energy and being on himself. What does wealth mean to him? Just a tool of his power, no other philosophical or philanthropic meaning attached to it. What does sex mean to him? His penis penetrates the vagina, and after some repeated minimal moves, he ejaculates. What does "America" mean to him? The citizenship paper says he is an "American," but it is wholly accidental and the nation means no more than an address for his business empire. What does Humanity mean to him? Just a source of labor and wealth for him to exploit and own. All no more, all no less. During the campaign, the American Psychiatric Association forbade its member from "psycho-analyzing" Trump. Think how much fun he would have generated if this had been allowed?

How would this meeting of Capitalism, the fierce *economic* machine, and Fascism, the angry *political* machine, fare for him?

In the U.S. we are about to witness a rather rare historical event unfolding in front of our eyes: The contest between two powerful ideologies, Capitalism and Fascism. Depending on which power wins, White Americans could become the Dumbest Generation ever (if Capitalism wins) or non-white Americans could become the most repressed since the Jews in Nazi Germany (if Fascism wins).

Donald Trump as president is caught between an irresistible force and immovable object, almost: The *new political power* of his supporters that demands rewards and the *old economic power* that wants to keep its rewards. No society or era had an even split or unified compromise between these forces: It is always one or the other power that rules. Up to now, to cite some examples, Russia and China have had *the political* ruling the economic; the U.S., on the other hand, has had *the economic* ruling the political. This new political development in the U.S., with its strong-ego President in Donald Trump, is like the Russian or Chinese corporations suddenly challenging its political leaders. The world would notice with curiosity and interest in the outcome. The curiosity and interest multiplies for the U.S. for its dominant Superpower status and its ego-driven chief executive.

III.

Among all existing societies and nations, the U.S. is alone in being an "economic society," in which the Economic Power of Capitalism rules its society and nation. Its control of America is complete and absolute, both physical and mental, in that we eat, think, watch, wear, and play whatever they supply us. Politics, education, the military, and religion, among the big institutions, merely function as back-up agencies of the economic. With this backdrop in mind, now we have president Trump who must please his supporters with his political machineries, which might not please the Economic-Powers-that-be. Established Capitalism might not like the Fascists that Trump represents and tries to please. Our new president might very quickly find himself between a rock and a hard place.

Ever since the "Classic Liberalism" of Jeffersonian America was replaced by Corporate Capitalism, the Capitalist System has ruled America, first by the Industrial Capitalism that sold things and then in the last few decades by Consumer Capitalism that sold ideas. Throughout its power and fame as America's unchallenged ideology, it taught us to accept one cardinal fact of life: *Economic Power rules*. By creating the world's largest wealth gap between the One Percent and the Masses, and, more importantly, training

Americans to accept the inequality of power as natural, it also trained White America to accept another, similar fact of life: *Political Power rules.*

It is but a small leap from money ruling America's masses to political power ruling the marginal groups in America—the non-white Lesser Americans. If the money-haves could rule over the money-have-nots, why could the political-power-haves *not* rule over the political-power-have-nots? The dollar is mighty over those who don't have it; so is the vote over those who could be ruled by its power. For over a century, White Americans learned, in the format of social Darwinism, that greater wealth rules the Lesser by their natural right; now, through the persona of Donald Trump, White America has learned to rule the Lesser politically. So, rather suddenly, American society has two branches of power elite: The Economic Elite and the Political Elite. So far, they have not clashed over any major issues simply because the Trumpian politics has carefully skirted the money-and-wealth issue and Trump's White supporters, somewhat busy with the non-white minorities, have not made a strenuous issue of economic power in America. But, sooner or later, the two branches of power will clash.

It is indeed mind-boggling to speculate: What if the White supporters of Donald Trump, so deeply committed and unswerving, *voted against the wealthy elite in America*? The economic elite in America, the One Percent, has often been warned by its best and brightest, as in the famous Citi Group's letter to the wealthy, that its greatest fear should be the votes of the 99 Percent that can start a revolution. Something resembling a revolution did occur when Trump was elected by White Americans. But this "revolution," which did happen, was not against the wealthy elite as such revolts should be, but against the poor minorities. Perhaps the fact that they had been trained over a century with the idea that money's rule is absolute, or perhaps because their chosen leader happens to be one of the wealthy elite, the idea of revolting *against the wealthy* in America had never occurred to the Trump supporters.

It is supremely ironic that what will save America from this rising Fascist movement is *not* the liberalism of Thomas Jefferson or Abraham Lincoln, but Capitalism, not for America's sake, of course, *but for its own sake.* In this meeting of two power systems in America, one established and the other challenging, the Established System is the savior and the force to restrain, even destroy, the new kid on the block, the muscle-flexing Fascist White America.

Capitalism, dramatically represented in the One Percent, owns most of America's capital and controls most of the American Way of Life, that is, the way most Americans, especially White Americans, think, feel, eat and defecate, the whole ideological arsenal. As Corey Robin said, "(Capitalism) governs labor, telling workers what to say, how to vote and when to pee." In a "capitalist" society, where all things depend on capital, naturally capital controls everything and those who own capital rule everyone else.

It is this power (that capitalists have) and its natural fear (that they might lose what they have), in the face of the sudden political movement that put Donald Trump in the White House, that will save America from Fascism in the process of saving itself. The Capitalist System, since the ascendancy of Corporate Capitalism, has never been seriously challenged before in American history. In a way, this new kid-on-the-block Fascist rise is a wake-up call for the comfortably slumbering One Percent who had all ideological and physical machineries in America—political, legal, cultural, religious, educational, media—humming its way nicely, up to now. Its ascendancy and domination have never seen this kind of threat and challenge to take the center stage in American life and society.

Neither the native movement of Edward Bellamy's American Nationalism of the *Looking Backward* fame, nor the catastrophic downturn created by the stock-market crash and the ensuing Great Depression, nor the wave of protests by the Flower Children inspired by the anti-Vietnam-War, nor the Bernie Sanders Socialist fervor, to name the memorable few, has ever challenged the American Capitalist System, both as a faith and as a lifestyle. In a somewhat strange way, Democrat Hillary Clinton, nominally critical of un-bridled Capitalism, is as much a "Capitalist" as billionaire businessman-tycoon Donald Trump, which shows how dominant and all-powerful Capitalism has been in America. It is so dominant and all-powerful, and so well integrated into America's body and soul, that its famous critic and its famous practitioner, good friends in real life, live well with one another and harmoniously, while equally benefiting off the same capitalist trough.

IV.

During the campaign, Trump never clearly articulated what he was going to do with Capitalism, if he got elected, other than the vague promise that Wall Street would be heavily taxed. As in most other things mentioned in the Party platform or policy talk, Trump left only a very vague idea and a general set of promises to his followers. Very likely, he had no idea about government and, more likely, he didn't think he would win the election. Nor did his followers, White America, know what they wanted to do with Capitalism in specific terms.

Strangely enough, the intellectual sector of America in the media and academia, have rarely worried about the *evils* of Capitalism, only its "failures." Traditionally and conventionally in the Liberal-Capitalist rubric of a market-based, consensus-driven Enlightened Society in America expected to resolve all social-political-economic issues in the ever-expanding market freedom. Deeply and naturally immersed in the public acceptance of Consumer America, where free choice and free marketplace captured the popular imagination and intellectual complicity, no one really seriously thought of anything challenging this Capitalist order.

Along with the new tide of globalism and digital revolution in universally common lifestyle, both the U.S. and its market alliances the world over took the Liberal-Capitalist mantra as the gospel of the 21st century. Good or evil, it was going to be the now and the future way of life for the world. One middling scholar even gained his fame by declaring the "End of History" in that the Liberal open market within the Capitalist system would dominate the future world. Then came Donald Trump's Fascism to America in a dramatic fanfare, sudden and strong enough to shake up this Liberal-Capitalism complicity and its consumer haven to their very foundation.

The conventional wisdom does not oppose Capitalism and Fascism as two contradictory philosophies. On a larger scale, as noted, they are closer than they appear in America's political landscape today. In a way, they are two branches of the same tree, like Protestantism and Catholicism on the same tree of Christianity. Certainly, Capitalists and Fascists have more in common with each other than with the workers or the minorities, respectively. In the same way Donald Trump and Hillary Clinton have more in common with each other, perhaps two branches of the same tree, than with their respective constituents (Trump with White Americans and Clinton with non-white Americans). But the entrenched One Percent in America does not like, and feels uncomfortable with the populist engine that moves Trump's locomotive to its pinnacle of power in U.S. Presidency. By this very significant difference in their respective power structures—One Percent against Ninety-Nine—America's Capitalism and Trump's Fascism face each other as competing forces.

Trump is not a man in favor of delicate give-and-take negotiation. He is more of the proverbial bull in a china shop, given to bluster and threat of bare-knuckle power play (which obviously appealed to his White supporters). Except now, he actually has the physical ability in the military, government and law-enforcement to carry out his bluster and threats. He has neither the deep wisdom nor the necessary patience to bring a difficult issue to a win-win conclusion (after only three days in office, the media already called him a "lazy" president). That shortcoming puts him in a very peculiar position as president, a position he has never been in before. Neither his business experience of win-or-lose, nor his campaign experience of rousing the crowd to cheap passion, would help him in this new peculiar position. As Don Regan, Secretary of the Treasure and Chief of Staff under Ronald Reagan, painfully learned when he moved from business to politics, Donald Trump cannot simply holler, "You're fired!" every time he doesn't get his way.

During the campaign, he only faced Hillary Clinton, not the whole forces of Liberal-Capitalism that lined up against him. As much as he wailed against the "media bias," the media was extraordinarily good to him simply because he was good business. As Les Moonves, Chairman of CBS, said during the early days of Trump: "(Trumpism) may not be good for America, but it's damn good for CBS." A critical question naturally arises: *What if Trump is not good for Capitalist business?* What if the media, and its Liberal-Capitalist System, are no longer amused and indulgent because he is bad for business and his bad-boy presidency goes beyond amusement and begins to worry the Capitalist Establishment? The media wing of the Capitalist Establishment, which often deliberately boosted his ratings value before, will not be so amused or indulgent when President Trump cannot use his usual crowd-rousing low-blows and Fascist disturbances for a good orderly market. As President, Trump will be isolated from his Fascist crowd who had earlier given him his daily energy and power. But no more. The Liberal-Capitalist Establishment of America, once aroused by its deep fear and threat from Trump's Fascist policies and actions, will go all out to tame or destroy Trump's Fascism and return America to its Liberal-Capitalist tradition of comfort and money-making.

V.

Even before his inauguration, the wheels of Capitalism were already turning on "how to stop Trump from destroying the (financial) world," as Steve LeVine wrote for *Quartz*. He describes an organization called "Syneidesis," mobilized by a quintessential American billionaire, William Doll, who believes in the righteousness of the Capitalist System, with the "reward of wealth going to the equity owners of enterprise." Doll and other billionaire members of Syneidesis, meaning in ancient Greek "conscience," see Donald Trump as a threat to the Liberal-Capitalist World Order. By enlisting the 2,000 billionaires the world over, they intend to stop Trump's disruptive political Fascism, which threatens many capital investments and projects, such as in trade and climate technology, from which a profitable return is expected by the capital investors. Combining profit with "conscience," the billionaires declare, "We need to show the fallacy that the (capitalist) elites are only in it for themselves. You need to stand up and show the good you can do." To accomplish this and prevent Trump from making destructive inroads into their hitherto-predictable and orderly Corporate Capitalism, Doll and his billionaire colleagues want "an international coalition of prominent families—a UN of (finance) families that *control the world*." (Parentheses and Italics added.) Levine views the activities of Syneidesis as a microcosm of the Capitalist Order mobilizing itself against the looming political challenge from Trump.

There are three ways that the Capitalist System will put pressure on the seemingly-freewheeling President Trump: First, the Capitalist infrastructure in America, controlling all the institutions of any meaning (government, education, religion, the military, among the main ones), is just too much for one man, even the wayward president, to bear. Second, Trump himself is a businessman and owns billions in business assets, all of which are quite sensitive to economic speculation and consumer mood, none of which he would want to jeopardize by upsetting the System. And third, he owes billions of dollars to banks, the System's storm-troopers, and can be under enormous pressure, direct and indirect, to behave himself, or else, the vice of debt might squeeze him to death.

Since he has no political agenda, ideological substance, nor national plans transcending Twitter messages and crowd-pleasing, President Trump would be quite vulnerable to the concentrated assault from the Established Capitalist Power. In this sense, as in many other ways, he resembles one Adolf Hitler at the time of assuming his power as Chancellor of Germany as he remained vulnerable to the Established Power, in this case the military, for the rest of his life. Capitalism, especially Consumer Capitalism, has been slowly destroying American society, its White consumers who elected Trump being the most dramatic casualty to date. Yet, it might end up saving America from Fascism. We, the chickens in the coop, feel ambivalent: Should we be grateful to the fox for saving us from the wolf?

Chapter Nine

The Nation Divided, Once Again

What did White Americans want from Trump? The answer would come in several "political" items, such as jobs, better trade agreements, secure borders, and so on. But if we cut to the chase, the answer is: Punishing the Lesser Americans so that their (Whites') jobs would be securer and their place in America would be stronger in the rising tide of multiculturalism and liberalism championed by the federal government. In their calculus, the evil of America was manifest in the Minorities—the non-whites and immigrants and Muslims—and Donald Trump was the man to "Make America Great Again (for Whites)." In this single-minded quest to punish the Lesser Americans—to get Trump elected and to get back to White America--the White Majority had to endure some extraordinary obstacles. One half of America was determined to win its battle against the other half.

Indeed, the support White People showed Donald Trump in spite of all that the intellectuals and the media professionals had thrown out to defeat Trump is nothing short of greatness, shown in history only few times. It is in human nature to be swayed by what one hears all the time by way of persuasion, and what the White Masses heard during the entire presidential campaign was enough to turn even Satan away from Trump's cause. Day and night they heard how terrible Donald Trump was as a human being, as a businessman, and as would-be president. Yet, Whites stuck by him.

As the campaign drew near November 8, some major media outlets, like the *New York Times, USA TODAY*, and the *Huffington Post*, and others, made their most dramatic move: Putting all their institutional prestige and authority in one basket, they endorsed against Donald Trump; for good measure, many individual editors and journalists also made scathing remarks about Donald Trump. There seemed hardly anyone of education or sense who would not have negative opinions about the Republican candidate.

To get our bearings straight and recognize the almost epic endurance that White Americans demonstrated for their Leader, we need to look at some of the things the media people said about Donald Trump. (The actual quotes are in Italics for easier reading).

Joe Klein, *TIME* Magazine, October 24, 2016: *"Our harvest of Trump grotesqueries."*

Editorial Board, *New York Times,* Sept 24, 2016: *"we believe Mr. Trump to be the worst nominee put forward by a major party in modern American history."*

The Huffington Post. For months (prior to November 8), every story on the *Huffington Post* about Trump came with the following note at the bottom of the article. *"Editor's note: Donald Trump regularly incites political violence and is a serial liar, rampant xenophobe, racist, misogynist and birther who has repeatedly pledged to ban all Muslims—1.6 billion member of an entire religion—from entering the U.S."*

USA TODAY, Sept 30, 2016: *"Donald Trump is, by unanimous consensus of the Editorial Board, unfit for the presidency. He is erratic. He is ill-equipped to be commander in chief. He traffics in prejudice. His business career is checkered. He isn't leveling with the American people. He has coarsened the national dialogue. He is a serial liar."*

Nation Magazine, Oct 24, 2016, in its cover montage of Donald Trump with the following words to make up the face: *"Racist. Misogynist. Buffoon. Totalitarian. Clown. Liar. Bile Fraud. Fear Monger. Thin-skinned. Nasty. Asshole. Male Violent Sexist. Vicious. Bankrupt Loser. Bluster. Deplorable. Unqualified. Abusive. Hubris. Scam Artist. Prevaricator. Simpleton. Calumniator. Egomaniac. Fascist. Cheat. Dictator. Misanthrope. Swindler. Authoritarian. Sociopath. Malevolent. Jingoist (there is more). . ."*

British Journalist, name unavailable: *"How violence and retaliation are constant themes in Trump's rhetoric."*

THE DATA TEAM, November 4: *Only 4 percent of Danes would vote for Trump,* as opposed to 50 percent of the U.S..

Joe Scarborough, *MSNBC* Host: *"Is Donald Trump a sociopath?"*

A Northwestern University professor *publishes a 9000-word psychological evaluation of "Trump and Narcissism"*

Mark Singer, *New Yorker* writer: *"Trump aspired to and achieved the ultimate luxury, an existence unmolested by the rumbling of a soul—exempted from introspection."*

David Brooks, *NY Times.* Feb 26, 2016: *"Trump represents the path the founders rejected. There is a hint of violence undergirding his campaign. There is always a whiff, and sometimes more than a whiff, of 'I'd like to punch him in the face."*

Matthew McWilliams, political scientist, *"found the one trait that best predicts whether you're a Trump supporter is how high you score on tests that measure authoritarianism."*

The Guardian. *"Trump hints at assassination of Hillary Clinton by gun rights supporters."*

Patrick Kennedy, former Rep from Rhode Island: *"Calling Trump 'crazy' demeans people with mental illness."*

The New York Post, August 10, 2016: *"Trump barely reads anything---watches television all day long—he lacks the attention span to focus."*

What people and organizations have said against Donald Trump is monumental in volume, in kind and in intensity. But this much is enough to demonstrate what the White Masses in America had to overcome, whose heroic resistance belongs to the citadel of courage exhibited in Mao's epic Long March in China, Hannibal's crossing of the Alps, and Joan of Arc's victory over the fear of Death by Fire. What the White Half endured for one Donald Trump will remain in the annals of political history simply because of who Donald Trump is as a human being.

It is indeed remarkable that there is a human being, even as an American entrepreneur, who so absolutely lacks any redeeming value, who not only exists, but has become elected to U.S. Presidency. Donald Trump is a singularly ego-driven man. There is only Donald Trump and no one else in his calculus. The Presidency to him is merely an extension of his ego, just another building that bears his name. Never since John Milton described Satan in *Paradise Regained* has there been a living, breathing being without a single ongoing human virtue or an anecdotal incident to show that he was once a human being, surely a sweet baby when he was born, as the member of a social community.

He is contemptuous toward everyone who is not Donald Trump, even toward his own White supporters as he is superior to them all. On his Superior Self, he said that he believes in eugenics, the science of selectively breeding human beings, a favorite topic of one Dr. Josef Mengele, the infamous Nazi doctor at Auschwitz who experimented with inmates. Trump says human intelligence is inborn and he was born superior. He said, "I am very proud to have that German blood, no doubt about it. Great stuff." Under normal circumstances, such a comment would raise the specter of anti-Semitism: A man who talks like this is obviously a Nazi. But anti-Semitism is a belief that requires some hardy intellectual-emotional commitment to maintain and control. It is unlikely that a person like Trump would be capable of believing in anything—a concept, a theory, a system, a philosophy—outside Donald J. Trump himself.

What the media had said about Donald Trump, as highlighted above, was enough to have destroyed even God Almighty and all His theological fortress on earth he had built. No mortal before Trump could have withstood the barrage of firepower concentrated on one man to destroy his image and reputation. But he withstood it all with aplomb and got the last laugh. How did American Society create such citizens and voters, namely, the White Half? What kind of a mindset, now single-mindedly dedicated to destroying the Lesser Americans would ignore such universal outcries against their chosen candidate and still vote for him? To find answers to these questions, we must backtrack to the very concept of "political majority" through its various historical changes in America.

II.

In the 19th century, a scholar named Alexis De Tocqueville visited the U.S. from France to observe the world's first pure democracy in action. The result is his classic two-volume tome, *Democracy in America,* in which the most significant central theme is known as the "Tyranny of the Majority." The Tyranny of the Majority refers to the greatest nightmarish possibility in a purely democratic society: In a society where the majority rules absolutely, as in 19th-century America, *what if the political majority is wrong,* politically and morally? This concern for the Tyranny of the "Majority" was later replaced by the Corporate Elite, whose small minority (roughly "one percent") could spawn a new kind of nightmare, the Tyranny of the Minority.

Does the presidential win for Trump mean a return of the Majority once again to center stage of American power? No, because Trump's political majority came to power by destroying the other "majority," the non-white minorities (in reality a demographic majority) that have now become political minorities. In America today we have "two majorities," White Americans and non-white Americans, one of which happens to have been outmaneuvered electorally. To see how confusing America's ideological and philosophical landscape has become with the election of Donald Trump, just witness two events: One is the remark made by Melania Trump, then the candidate's wife, who spoke of American culture having gotten *"too mean and too rough."* Too mean and too rough? Described by the wife of a candidate who *personified* these cultural trends, mean and rough, for American culture? In response, an incredulous reporter asked: "Has she seen her husband lately?" The other is a pro-Trump website criticizing the collusion between Monsanto and the government by giving Hillary Clinton's old law firm (who listed Monsanto as one of its clients) as an example of this collusion. Trump's wife criticizing America for being too mean and too rough and Trump supporters criticizing Monsanto and Clinton together as responsible for producing unhealthy food for America?

This ideological confusion in Trump's America is also revealed by his supporters as well, from the mainstream supporters to conspiracy theorists on one side and to the militia types on the other: Among themselves, they complain a great deal about government corruption and its threat to individual liberty and freedom, the urgent need to protect the Constitution, and so on. This is a confusing combination of "libertarian" and "classic-liberal" political philosophies, which are bitterly expressed by Trump supporting Whites. While reading their commentaries, one can only wonder if all these comments could possibly come from Donald Trump supporting Whites. But, while being harsh on the political sector of America, they are mostly, and strangely, *silen*t about Corporate Capitalism in America as a factor even remotely connected to government corruption, the threats to individual liberty and the American Constitution, and so on. If you just read their comments about the political aspects of American society, you would think that there is no role that Capitalism plays in American life: Does Capitalism even exist? This sidestepping of Capitalism, by way of sidestepping their real target in the Lesser Half, is quite revealing in itself.

"(According to the militiamen) the federal government has become tyrannical and the country's customs and culture are being destroyed," reports Shane Bauer for the *Nation* magazine relating his stint as an undercover militiaman during the presidential campaign. "We lose more and more rights (Bauer quotes a militia commander), more and more freedom, everyday." The militiamen in particular and Trump's mainstream supporters in general are concerned about losing the (White) American Way of Life, but they almost never think about how Capitalism may be at the center of all this. They voice worries that the "Founding Fathers' republic" is being replaced by "government tyranny," but they never go into mentioning the Wall Street bankers, corporate CEOs, or the mighty mind-controlling power of the media and entertainment.

The four main sectors in this American political landscape—Whites, non-whites, the government, and Corporate America—are so tangled with one another that sorting the System out in their minds is not easy. Just see how tangled their interrelations are: Corporate America controls Whites, non-whites and the government but stays neutral to the White-non-White conflict as both are valuable cannon-fodders and consumers; Whites hate the government for protecting non-whites but never say so openly and have no idea what Corporate America does to them; the government, beholden to corporate interest, treats Whites and non-Whites according to the political winds. White Trump supporters, the most self-centered generation ever, must contend with their two equally-strong impulses: The desire for job security and the hatred for non-white Americans; and still trying to use the conventional idioms of American tradition and politics to hide their racism, Trump supporting Whites speak of "liberty," "freedom," or "the American Way of Life." *The Los Angeles Times* interviews typical Trump supporting Whites and they insist that they "are not racists."

It is not odd that there is a strong feeling against the federal government among Trump followers as the Protector of the Non-Whites, nor is it odd that they conspicuously leave out the economic sector culprits, Corporate America, from the responsibility of corrupting America. Somehow Americans in general, long before Trump, always felt freer to criticize the politicians as agents of corruption, than the economic movers and shakers as the culprits of American corruption. True even in popular Hollywood movies. This example is from the conversation between Superman and Lois Lane in *Superman I*:

> Lois Lane: "Superman, why did you come here?"
> Superman: "For Truth, Justice and the American Way."
> Lois Lane: "You will have to lock up every politician in America!"

It is interesting that Lois Lane did not say, "You will have to lock up every *businessman* in America!" Perhaps we assume that all businessmen *are* crooked, beyond criticism, and that, by criticizing the economic sector, we are by implication criticizing ourselves as its main consumers and customer. The famous "Lock her up!" chant among Trump supporters was, of course, not about any crooked businessman or –woman, but Clinton who was a full-time politician. Donald Trump's election to presidency is confusing the political-social-intellectual landscape as well, throwing the whole neat Neo-Liberal-Capitalist-Progressive matrix of American history into great chaos and disarray. Until Trump appeared over the horizon, virtually all intellectual elements of America—anyone who had any interest in what was going in American society—assumed that things had been *moving forward*. Here the concept of "moving forward" meant the historical concept of progress and enlightenment, that American society, like all other modern nations, were moving ever forward toward the "light" of history: From Feudalism to Democracy, from Closed Society to Open Society, from Serfdom to Freedom, from Superstition to Science, from Caste to Mobility, from Tyranny to Liberty, and from Oppression to Brotherhood. In this movement of progress, the U.S. took its leadership as the first free nation to declare that all men are created equal and are entitled to life, liberty and pursuit of happiness. Even De Tocqueville's worry seemed to have become insignificant in this great assumption of the inevitability of progress that benefited all.

III.

Corporate Capitalism, first in the form Industrial Capitalism, made the claim of America's leadership in historical progress somewhat awkward simply because a certain amount of freedom and equality had to be sacrificed for many to justify progress. Some social critics, like Thorstein Veblen and C. Wright Mills, saw the contradiction between America's basic promise of political and economic liberty and the capitalist reality of corporate ascendancy in American life. In short, American society was rapidly becoming the victim of rising Corporate Capitalism in which the rich were getting richer and their workers, the vast majority of Americans, were being reduced to anonymous masses of nameless and faceless employees. (These nameless and faceless employees had to fight it out among themselves—conveniently between Whites and non-whites—in the era of diminishing economic opportunities, setting up the stage for Trump's White Half. Unlike the European nationalists and racists, however, Trump's nationalist and racist supporters still had to speak their minds using the language of Jeffersonian America, among them, that we are a nation where "all men are created equal." Hence the confusion.)

But. in the meantime, this intellectual perception and tension of America's Mass Society began to fade away in the rising tide of Consumer Capitalism, laying the foundations for later version called Neo-Liberalism, in which, literally, Americans were offered anything they wanted by way of entertainment pleasure. First with cable TV that multiplied their television-viewing distraction, then with the rise of Digital Revolution that opened entertainment everywhere and all the time, this rising tide of Consumer Capitalism made any critical assessment of America, in the fashion of Veblen or Mills, impossible. When people get everything they want, everyone asked, isn't the ultimate reality of Life, Liberty and the Pursuit of Happiness, the new Garden of Eden, the Nirvana, the Kingdom of God on Earth? Any political, cultural or intellectual misgivings that might be felt in America's souls and consciousness, quickly vanished in the great caldron of pleasure and distraction, the greatest in variety and intensity the world had ever seen. The new wave of freedom and pleasure, the great combination of Neo-Liberalism and Capitalism, found its flowering in the Marketplace. It was through the Marketplace that America found its Peace, Harmony, Happiness and Progress. There was no greater defense of America's Progress than simply pointing to the great masses of people enjoying their daily entertainment and distraction: Day and night, around the clock, at such small costs so that virtually anyone with a wage-earning capacity could participate and enjoy.

What little critical element that was left, not overwhelmed by the great Consumer Capitalism and its material boon, was alarmed by the rising dominance of Corporate America that monopolized America's consumption and its vast wealth. While people were having fun with the Consumer Capitalism, its Capitalists were getting ever richer, controlling more and more of America's wealth. The difference between the rich and the not-rich was getting so great that the popular division between the One-Percent haves and the Ninety-Nine Percent have-nots became a handy reference to America's inequality. Critics lamented that the Ninety-Nine Percent was dead and silent like the serfs during Feudalism, fatalistic and powerless, and becoming alarmingly stupid—and anxious once they realized that this mirage of life's fun and sweetness could disappear anytime their money ran out and their money came from their employment. It is indeed difficult to say how much of their nationalist-racist impulse toward non-whites originates from their entertainment-caused stupidity and how much from their genuine economic anxiety.

Then came Donald Trump and his supporters, raising havoc in the very neat concept of America into One Percent and Ninety-Nine Percent. What are the Trump-supporting White Voters in the large scheme of American history? Are they part of the hitherto slumbering American Masses, the 99-percent of the "Dumbest Generation" suddenly awakened in the tidal wave of political consciousness? Or, now that they have the non-whites to kick around, are they joining the traditional elite of kings and lords?

What is so confusing to the great American conventional wisdom is that the Trump supporters, although numerically a majority (after a fashion, since they won the Electoral College, not the numerical majority vote), are *not part of America's forward-moving progress. THEY ARE A MOVEMENT BACK-WARD*, to Feudalism and all that is pre-modern and pre-enlightened. Instead of America's traditional assumption of moving forward toward greater Life, Liberty and the Pursuit of Happiness in the Perfect Union, the Trump supporters represent Nationalism, Racism, Xenophobia, Jingoism, Sexism, all of which are summed up in modern Fascism. Fascism, Trump's brand of politics, is a cousin of Capitalism, which is a cousin of Feudalism. Together, Fascism and Capitalism are atavisms that take humanity back toward the Cave. Capitalism has been surviving, even thriving, in America, supported by both Republicans and Democrats, because of its coupling with the Neo-Liberal consumer freedom ("give-'em-what-they-want"). When the vast majority of Americans, White and non-white, feel free and fulfilled with their great consumer binge, who could complain about Capitalism?

As an ultimate irony in American life, this paradise capitalism--which gives you everything you want—also takes away everything it gives you, thus creating a level of anxiety (for fear of losing everything you have) and confusion (not knowing whom to blame for your anxiety and fear) the Humanity as a whole ever experienced. So, the more enjoyable Life became, resembling the paradise at Eden, the deeper their Anxiety became; the deeper their Anxiety became, the more urgent their desire to find their Scapegoat to blame, to hate, and to punish. Hence the division between Whites and non-whites, and the endurance of the White Trump Supporters to endure hell and high water to get their job security and continue their life enjoyment in paradise. And the White Half's willingness to obey the famous dictum of Jay Gould: *"I can hire one half of the working class to kill other half."*

As their manager to carry out this task, Whites elected a man who is neither for Consumer Capitalism nor against Consumer Capitalism. Nor are the electors of Donald Trump clear about Consumer Capitalism, the real cause of the division. They have created a revolution for Donald Trump's career but what they created is not in the framework of American Progress toward greater happiness and for all. But wholly against this American assumption of progress, they made a gigantic leap backward to an era, like the Cavemen, where the strong simply ruled the weak in brute power. This is neither historical nor American. We have seen many European-style nationalist atavisms, but never thought it was going to be witnessed in America. Intellectuals are quite confused as to how to read the Trump Revolution because they cannot quite tell how they can fit these Fascist rebels into any known patterns of history, both American and world.

In the end, the so-called Trump Revolution fulfills the prophecy of Jay Gould who prophesied the ease with which workers could be commanded to defend their economic security by destroying, not their master, but other workers. The one half of the Ninety-Nine Percent has been ordered by the Liberal-Capitalist system to kill the other half. Donald Trump has won his election with the White half, sworn to kill the other half, the Lesser American Masses. Strangely enough, the American Masses are turning on each other, White half against non-white half, instead of the One Percent who is the common enemy of both halves of the Masses. The White Half of America does not know that their real enemy is *not* the non-whites, but the One Percent that owns and controls them, both the White Half *and* the non-white half. But they know not that they are barking up the wrong tree.

The field of social analysis, part journalism and part social science, has never faced a challenge this momentous and this baffling. Like much of the crowd who watched the Crucifixion of one carpenter from Nazareth two thousand years ago, we are not sure what it is that we are witnessing and hearing about day and night from the media. Questions are many but answers are few, as the events unfold as we live through them ourselves. We do not enjoy the luxury of historical chronology or emotional distance. It is all here and now, all urgent and all remote, but we must press on with our quest.

Chapter Ten

The End of a Demagogue

Then, Trump as the latest in the line of populist demagogues, in America and elsewhere, there is the small matter of the *end of all demagogues* that inevitably follows their easy rise to power. For all pursuers of power at any time and in any place, the temptation is always incredibly strong to use the crasser and baser way to reach their goal. Lying comes easier than truth, ignorance easier than intelligence, selfishness easier than community. But, then, there is the reckoning in the end.

As congratulations pour in from all the leaders the world over, and he takes his victory lap over and over again, the man of the hour, Donald J. Trump, may be wishing he could run away from all this. His moments of fun and games are over and nothing but drudgery is ahead for him. With his win over Hillary Clinton, all the fun world for Donald Trump ended: After the win, it is now nothing but endless work of running a country he never once thought about running. He is a born dramatist, not a negotiator; a star, not a stage director. He never once worked for or thought about the wellbeing of others. The sociological and philosophical concept of "others" has never occurred to him in the sense that these "others" are human beings just like himself. (Dr. Gustave Gilbert who worked at the Nuremberg Trials later wrote that the most striking characteristics of the Nazi leaders was their lack of "empathy" for others. This is also one of the striking things about Trump, who has no concept about "other" human beings.) The entity called "America" never meant anything to him other than as a financial trough from which he would draw his profit and benefit. Trump's indifference to America is so not necessarily because he is pathologically selfish who is unaware of anything else, although to some extent this is true, but because he is just a quintessential American businessman. The grueling day-to-day, detail-to-detail is nothing short of Death for Donald Trump who has never spent a minute of his time not devoted to the fullest exploits of his fun and games. His aim in the political foray was, like all his business deals, the pleasure of the hunt and the thrill of the chase, not what he actually gained.

It is in the very nature of what a businessman is *supposed* to be. If every student in Business 101, Business 102, Business 103, and so on, were to follow what they are taught in their classrooms and by the textbooks, *they would be exactly like Donald Trump.* He is as much a quintessential American of 21st century America as John D. Rockefeller or Henry Ford was of 20th century America, as Davy Crockett of 19th century America, and Thomas Jefferson of 18th century America. Just simply think of Donald Trump as the most *popular* man in America of his time. After all he was elected by the majority of the Electoral College vote, fair and square.

He has never been an administrator type who paid attention to daily details of organization and personnel for the sake of orderly management. Details always bored this hyperactive thrill-seeker to death. He is so hyperactive he could not concentrate his mind even for a few minutes to read a book. If it is not about himself, he has no interest. He is "lazy" in the classic aristocratic mold, doing only what he wants to do and avoiding what he doesn't want to do, making others do it. Most people most of the time do things they do not wish to do mostly for reasons that they are not powerful enough to decide. Donald Trump, by virtue of his wealth, has been able to live the life he wanted—in full pursuit of what he desires and nothing else.

It is said that Donald Trump denies that climate change is for real. He denies climate change as a major issue not because he has a philosophy or knowledge that denies the climate change, but because he is too lazy to recognize it. It is not because of anything he believes or disbelieves in the climate issue, but it is not "fun" enough to recognize and follow up on. For him, climate is the least-exciting thing in which he wishes to be involved. (It would certainly kill him if he were condemned to watch the clouds for an hour as punishment). The same reasoning goes with art, economic justice, racism, poverty, feminism, and even abortion. He is not interested in any of them simply because none of them is an interesting issue enough for him to plunge fully and continually into. Many people recognize that Donald Trump is a "shallow" person. But, it is wrong to call him shallow because shallowness indicates a certain level of depth—however shallow—about Life in general. Donald Trump has no depth whatsoever, not even shallow, either in his knowledge or in his feelings. In such aspects of life and society and humanity, larger than Trump himself, he never grew beyond a five-year old and embodies the culture and spirit of most White Americans and their social development who have a similar arrested growth.

The best of Donald Trump is already behind. The days of fun and games are over for him. The only thing he can do is to maintain his popularity among his supporters by drifting to the extreme right (fashionably called "alt-right") and oppressing the Lesser Americans all he can. The thrill of the chase is over and he is now subject to the withering scrutiny and criticism heaped on him by the media each day. Once enthralled by the freshness of Donald Trump, the media will undoubtedly be after his blood, now that he is President. He *was* the darling of the media, but as the Chief Executive, he is no longer solely for entertainment. He can rely on new shocks and new Twitter messages to keep White America entertained only so long. He will soon find out that being President is a nasty business where he cannot lash out at everyone as he used to, especially when the One Percent gets pissed off at him. His White Praetorian Guards cannot rally around him as easily as in the days of Candidate Trump. He will seethe and fume, and wish he could just go back to one of the Trump Towers and hide. Now that the election is over, so is the game. Donald Trump's hair is rapidly turning gray with the frustration and exasperation of a caged animal, and a caged animal he is, in the prison called the White House. What else could he do that would satisfy his moment-by-moment quest for excitement and thrill?

Donald Trump has no ideology—neither political, philosophical, economic, religious, intellectual or even personal—but is a man of intensive self-absorption on the level of an autistic child. Without any belief either about life or society in general, he has had to spend all his energy and wits in winning the battle at hand, exclusively at making money and at self-aggrandizement. Nothing else has ever mattered. Presiding over a cabinet meeting to discuss the issue of tariff on Chinese-imported steel, or something as mundane, bore him to premature death. The U.S.. government under Trump may have to open a new chapter in the style of governance that we might call the "Regency Government," where the actual administrator runs the country and President Trump spends all his time doing play things that keep him occupied with pleasure and amusement.

Winning the battle, whether in business or in political contests, was all-important to him. Trump never realized, much less thought about, what kind of man-killing boredom would follow as a reward for his electoral win. Dealing with the daily routines of government, not the continuous drama of public limelight and popularity, is tantamount to the Death Sentence to this man. By winning the biggest lottery of his life, he now wishes he could run away from it all. Sooner or later he must be reminded of what Don Regan, the secretary of the Treasure and chief of staff for Ronald Reagan, said about the difference of running a business and running a government: In business, everybody jumped when he gave orders; in government, everything had to be negotiated. Donald Trump, given to a lifetime of giving orders, would find that the Presidency is his coffin for his early death. Indeed, to Donald Trump, the Presidency is a losing proposition all around. He cannot increase his private wealth using his position (not blatantly at least). He cannot fire people arbitrarily and at his whim (as civil servants are protected by law). He cannot grab female pussies whenever he sees pretty women and gets the urge. What does he gain from the Presidency? He can certainly start a war when he wants to, but there are no nations that he particularly hates and wishes to destroy (if anything, Trump is an internationalist where the relations are determined primarily by business consideration). Besides, he owns property in just about every country and would not want bombs dropped on any of them.

(It is possible, on the order of heavenly miracles, that somehow the spirit of the Republic, or the ghosts of the past leaders that still reside in the White House, can awaken the sleeping or stunted human development in Donald Trump and he suddenly grow into his new job as President. But I doubt any betting man in Las Vegas would wager on this sort of conversion happening to Donald Trump.)

II.

Political Power is the only reward that can be granted by the masses in a political society to the select few whose service to the nation is recognized or is promised. John F. Kennedy's war heroism, John McCain's honorable endurance as a POW in Viet Nam, or John Glen's space exploits are examples. Or, their previous experiences in government as governors, like Bill Clinton and Jimmy Carter, are given credit for their next job. Donald Trump is the only person who has become president without any useful services or experiences that are publicly recognized. He came to power by way of demagoguery, the easiest but most dangerous path to power. It is the easiest way to power because appealing to the darkest, and most persistent, natural call is what humanity most often responds to at its lowest and most unthinking moments. It is most dangerous because the price is always there to be paid in multiples as humanity as a whole wakes up one day and is sorry for what it has done or has not done in its collective insanity. Demagoguery is a backward move toward the cave and always looks bad when the passion cools and reason returns. The proof of this inevitability is easy to obtain: Names like Mussolini, Hitler, Joseph McCarthy, just to name the famous few who came to fame and power using demagoguery as their chief weapon, only evoke shudder and shame. Trump's free ride to power, almost in catastrophic contrast to Hillary Clinton's 30-plus years of service to the nation in various capacities, entails a great price. Mussolini was killed by those who put him in power, his body dismembered and put on display. Hitler rose to power in a similar fashion and died in suicide, his body disappearing forever, his name being mentioned only in infamy. Joseph McCarthy's name is synonymous to a national shame and nightmare in America that we would rather not mention. At this moment, Donald Trump is on schedule to replace McCarthy at the Pantheon of American Shame.

What would be Donald Trump's price for his rise to fame and power with the easiest, perhaps lower than first-graders', appeal to White Americans' reason and intellect? Without a conventionally recognizable power base (although nominally "Republican"), he came to power on the votes of a very angry and mindless group of Americans, the entertainment-crazed and distraction-corrupted White Masses, full of childish discontent and selfish demand, with an emotional hate toward minorities and foreigners of all kinds. How would these Masses turn on Trump, their one time savior, as such crowds inevitably did time and time again in our historical past? And why should we think of this tragic end as inevitable for Donald Trump as inevitably as the proverbial Wheel of Justice and History?

As of now, this is the situation that Whites and non-whites face in America. For White Americans, their extreme right-wing days are ahead. Most top government officials appointed by Trump will be tough on non-whites and foreigners in America, thus giving vicarious Fascist pleasure to the Trump supporting Whites. But these Whites are, even after the Trump win, still the same cannon-fodders and slaves working under the Capitalist Masters. In spite of their alt-right pomp and circumstance, nothing in their working enslavement has changed and will change. While kicking the minorities and foreigners while they are down, their working and playing life will remain powerless, stupid and mentally dead.

Non-whites, in the meantime, are facing the consequences of Trump's rigorous exercises of White Nationalism and Racism, under the rubric of American Fascism, and of an unfriendly federal government run by Trump's unsympathetic men and women. A form of Police State, under the thin veneer of legalism to cover up a new kind of domestic terrorism against blacks and Hispanics, may start a new era in American law and order of repression. But the non-whites command one great advantage in enduring Trump's Fascism over Whites enduring Corporate Capitalism: They have one another, they have a community, and they have a future.

Whites have none of these essential social characteristics that can keep human beings human against obstacles: Whites live alone, play alone and die alone. Humanity is kept alive and meaningful by each other; non-whites have each other, but Whites have only their solitary selves, alone, surrounded by cut-throat competition, dogs eating dogs, the White Majority distrusting themselves. Concepts like "community," "society" or "humanity" have no meaning to them, just living for the here and now, nothing in the future that promises greater happiness together or deeper satisfaction with one another. They can cheer at the Super Bowl all they want; they can decorate their Christmas trees all they want. But, at the end of the day, loneliness, misery and meaninglessness overwhelm them, more than their vaunted entertainment and drugs, legal or otherwise, can overcome.

III.

This is all beyond what Donald Trump can solve. He is, after all, a carbon copy of the White Masses--selfish, childish and vengeful—their groveling Follower, not Leader, whose end will follow all the ends of history's past demagogues. This point highlights the question of his delicate relations with his supporters. Remembering that the once-ardent supporters of Mussolini and of Hitler both turned against their Leaders, what can be predicted of Trump's relations with his own supporters (who share much in common with Mussolini's and Hitler's followers) is a delicate matter. Unlike Hillary Clinton whose "best" effort would be understood and acceptable to her supporters, Donald Trump's best effort is virtually meaningless to *his* supporters who demand something specific, tangible and pleasing: Their wish is not to share America with the non-whites, but to *monopolize* it. Like Hitler, Trump must give his White supporters *all or nothing*. Given the trade between him and his supporters, nothing short of the Pound of Flesh will do.

We should now turn to that part of our speculation. Right off, it is not easy to see Donald Trump, president-elect at this writing, as a tragic figure, just as, after vanquishing the entrenched establishment rival, he is riding the crest of power and fame. But an honest analysis into a foreseeable future in American society in which his presidency is to be established and tested, we see no other fate that awaits Donald Trump other than the inevitable fall.

His ascent to power has been on the back of two very dangerous forces in political ascendancy: An angry, and not very intelligent, crowd and its high expectations. Trump cannot satisfy the crowd without threatening, or at least greatly discomforting the stability of the Capitalist Order (normally known as the One Percent) who needs continuing stability and peace for its own prosperity. At the same time, he cannot disappoint the angry crowd who put him up to power. He is riding on the proverbial back of a tiger: He cannot get off safely and he cannot keep on riding safely. Either way, there is a great risk and danger.

The moneyed elite will be watching him carefully and critically for any sign of threat to their power and prosperity. It is possible that Trump and his ilk will be able to walk the tightrope with political savvy and good luck and effective propaganda, but not for four years. Inevitably, his circus act is severely tested in reality and the reality that awaits him is the "established America," the One Percent that controls Corporate America. This America, using all its institutional tools (such as government, the media, academia, legal agents like laws, judges and lawyers, churches), will fight every step of the way against the disturbances that the new political kid and his supporters may create. The established America indulged the new political movement as an amusing public spectacle while Donald Trump was wading through the political process to fame and power. But, now that he is actually in power as a threat to its peace and wealth-making, it changes its view of him and will oppose him all the way. Could Donald Trump, now that his popular base is merely a backgrounder, win the new battle against America's economic elite?

Trump's crowd was never his dedicated army, not Napoleon's Grand Army who would die for their emperor; the Trump supporters were expectant, but angry, children whose Pied Piper had promised Great Things for them: Now, he has to deliver them. ("Deliver!" a white woman who had voted for Trump declared to the *Los Angeles Times* reporter [January 1, 2017] who asked her what she now expected from President Trump; she promised that White Americans would "rock the boat again" if he failed to deliver.) To deliver them what he had promised them, he has to fight the Established America, the One Percent who owns everything that is to be owned and controls all aspects of American life, body and soul that are to be controlled.

IV.

In Donald Trump, we have a president in the U.S. the likes of whom we have never seen before. He is such a character, perfectly made for America's media-dominant society that we forget to recognize the larger structure of the American Nation that has created Trump as it creates all personalities and events. As a person he is such a comic entertainer that we can ignore him when we are tired of him, but as President he is powerful and dangerous and we cannot turn him off when we are tired of him. As a person he belongs to himself; as President he belongs to all of us and all of America. If we have never seen a president like Trump before, we have likewise never seen an America like the present one before, which took decades in the making. As American society has become such a peculiar social system, it has also created a president who is such a peculiar personality. As America goes, so does its individual personality type. As America's System goes, so does its president.

It is an understatement to say that America today is nothing like anything America has ever been. The society in which we live, work, play and die has no resemblance to the various models of America that the U.S. as a nation has passed through. It is nothing like the Jeffersonian agrarian model of freedom and equality; it is nothing like the Industrial Capitalist model in which factories produced things to be used in daily life; it is nothing like the post-war Affluent Society in which the U.S. balanced the economy with practicality and comfort.

The U.S. we witness today is at the most advanced stage of Capitalism where the market has been selling *ideas* (like entertainment and fulfillment) as its main commodity for decades, accelerated by the Digital Revolution. When the object of our consumption is no longer material and concrete, like shoes and chickens, but something as undefined as "happiness" or "satisfaction," the consumer character changes radically. It is more like the crowd at the Roman Circus where the consumers search for something vaguely fulfilling in the form of entertainment to please themselves. This search is quite different from the physical comfort or convenience that was the object of quest among the 19th-century Americans as Alexis De Tocqueville decried as America's preoccupation. Nor is it like the consumer desire for convenience that accelerated in the post-WWII period where refrigerators, indoor plumbing, and automobiles were their popular preoccupations.

What today's Americans, mostly White, have been subjected to for several decades now, first with expanded cable TV, and then with the always-on digital media, is hardly for comfort or convenience. It is wholly non-material and non-physical so that it is impossible for consumers to think more rationally about spending their money on them. Nor are the effects of consumption the same on the mind as they are on the body. Things we consume we can be smart about; ideas are the play of *minds*, and, while it is possible to think about how to find the best pair of shoes for oneself, it is impossible to think intelligently about ideas and feelings in the avalanche of mind-managing advertisement and propaganda. Donald Trump is a product of this mind-era and one of the most successful.

Today's Americans, again, mostly White, have been subjected to the most scientifically-researched and technologically sophisticated Pleasure Machine the world has ever witnessed, whose intensity and variety even the crowd at the Roman Circus could have never imagined. This new kind of pleasure pursuit (for which the world lags way behind the U.S.) creates a whole new society in America because the Consumer Mind is now in the driver's seat in his decision-making, not the rational-physical needs-calculus of supply and demand for comfort and convenience of earlier generations.

The Mind has been demanding, and getting from its corporate supplier, something akin to what the Chinese opium addicts craved and demanded and enjoyed. The more this new supply of consumer goods becomes available, the more its new style of pleasure and enjoyment affects the American Mind, as a consumer, as a neighbor, as a voter, and as a pleasure-addict.

Because all forms of the new opioids cost money, the group that has become most affected by the new consumption is naturally made up of those who can most afford it. This group, logically White Americans, as the beneficiaries of this new mind-consumption, have become extremely childish, self-centered, and dumbed down as a result. The Whites, under the incessant effect of entertainment as life's fulfillment itself, naturally become the most seriously-affected victims of Consumer Capitalism. When we imagine these White addicts of opioids, a smart-phone in their hands and a TV set in front of them, all very self-centered, childish and stupid as a result, it is not hard to imagine a Donald Trump as their President around the corner.

These new Americans, in that they are unlike any previous generations in their entertainment addiction, resemble the aristocrats of a previous era where only the privileged few, mostly aristocrats, could afford to be so Narcissistic and pleasure-driven. Most importantly for our analysis, the new consumption of pleasure has created a crowd, now identified as Trump's nationalist-racist Whites, with a political turn of mind that appeals to a simplified solution to everything, namely, Majority Power.

For decades, the White consumers under sedation from entertainment and pleasure did not act or stir. When they finally did, under the cumulative effects of Opioids and propaganda, drugged and stupefied, they did something quite different from the last time they united for the Civil Rights Movement: They called on Donald Trump to lead them to the promised land of Fascism. The old saying that we can judge a person by the company he keeps may apply here: We can judge a president by the supporters who elected him. Those who voted for Hillary Clinton believed in her and this faith in her was based on Clinton's proven records of public life, good and bad. Those who voted for Donald Trump, however, knew nothing about him, other than the media images of him as a billionaire entrepreneur who had nothing to do with the White Majority, neither in ideology nor in lifestyle: Their meeting of the minds was purely coincidental, subject to a breakup if the supporters would not get what they expected. Their one-night stand would be severely tested in the coming days.

As noted earlier, Trump's greatest asset is his Moral Immunity, his ability to withstand any kind of criticisms from society. But this immunity applies only to *Moral* issues (such as good and evil in the purely moral-theoretical-philosophical sense), even including war and repression, but not to economic issues that would affect Wealth and Power. The top One Percent would tolerate anything and all things, including mistreating the Lesser Americans, *except what would affect their own money.* That's where Trump's greatest risk lies.

Chapter Eleven

The American Character

Here we are about to move up a level in our analysis of how it happened that the nation's White Majority supported a blatant charlatan with neither a political belief nor personal integrity as the Leader of the Free World. (Obviously, he is neither the Leader that we assume he is, nor is the Free World really free.) To understand this puzzling development, we must open up a topic that deals with the Trumpian Whites as a *national character,* a social unit of behavior traits formed by the society itself.

We often speak of the "German character" as industrious and disciplined, with cruelty and inhumanity thrown in from the memory of the Holocaust. We speak of the "British character" as resilient and traditional, shaped by their conduct against the Nazis in WWII. We speak of the "Japanese" character, the Samurai ethos leading to WWII, then Kamikaze spirit in WWII, and the honest-stoic post-WWII character. Often mixed with stereotyped cultural characterizations, the national character studies have invited popular jokes as much as serious scholarship.

Among the latter, the "American character," as the first child and symbolism of the Enlightenment, has also been subject to much analysis, from the classic writings of James Bryce, Harriet Martineu and Alexis De Tocqueville on American national character to more modern studies by Thorstein Veblen, David Riesman and David M. Potter whose book in the sixties described American national character as a "People of Plenty." More recently, Paul Roberts spoke of American character connected to impulsive consumption in his book, *The Impulse Society: America in the Age of Instant Gratification.*

All of the character studies, whether classic or contemporary, portray the behavior of people, the way they think and act, as determined by the historical stage of their social circumstances. In De Tocqueville's time, America's national character was shaped primarily by the factors of frontier-democratic

individualism in America; in the sixties, Potter described America's character in terms of the economic plenty that came with the post-war affluence; in
Roberts' time, today, American behavior can be described largely by its
consumer impulse and instant gratification.

Roughly in the last three decades or so, coinciding with the radical expansion of entertainment culture in America with the advances in cable TV and
later digital ascendancy, America's national character, mostly affecting its
White Majority, has been shaped and formed by Consumer Capitalism. This
particular brand of Capitalism is different from Industrial Capitalism which
produced and sold *things* that people needed, such as shoes and cars. In the
past few decades, Capitalism has been exclusively concentrating on entertainment, with the *idea* that happiness is in the feeling of being fulfilled.
Entertainment has no material reality to it as it is not something we eat, wear
or use. It is all in our heads and minds, and in the fact of consuming. The
utilitarian functions of shoes and cars are quite different from the effect of
entertainment, happiness or fulfillment on the human mind. This peculiar
economic system in America, Consumer Capitalism, has had its full political
and government support in the theory of Neo-Liberal Market Society, where
the American People (mostly White) must be able to consume *whatever they
demand.* Likewise, the Neo-Liberal-Capitalist response has been *"Give them
what they want."* Obviously, when people get whatever their hearts desire,
that affects their personality and, considered together as a group, their *national character*. Here we see the formation of the White Majority's childish,
selfish and mean traits through the Consumer Capitalist stage of America's
historical development.

We now conclude that there is no understanding of the Donald Trump
Phenomenon without understanding those Whites who voted for him. By the
same token, there is no understanding of those who chose Trump without
understanding the Society that created those voters. Eventually, all things
Trumpian are all things American, and that explains why we, as Americans
whether White or non-White, are incredulously *closer* to Donald Trump, in
our outer aspirations and inner character, than we like to imagine ourselves.
Donald Trump is what America is, and what America is is what we are, all of
us, deep in our selfish and childish Capitalism-corrupted character traits.

As noted, for the past three decades or so, the American economy
changed from selling *things* to selling *ideas*. With the rise of cable TV and
Digitalized Society, America's Consumer Capitalism has steadily corroded
White intelligence and emotional capacity: When we say Americans have
been "dumbing down" or that we have the "dumbest generation" in history,
we are referring to the toxic effect of Consumer Capitalism upon its victims.

Who are these "victims" of Consumer Capitalism's dumbing down effect?
None other than White Americans. Why? Because they are the main Beneficiaries of Consumer Capitalism. It is the Whites in America that are the targets of

virtually all advertisements; when Hollywood makes movies, generally they are for White audiences; when ballgames are staged, the audience is predominantly White, quite beyond their population proportion; with few exceptions, TV programs are produced for Whites and White Children; billboards and bumper stickers are all for Whites; all the writings on T-shirts and sweatshirts are for Whites. Just about anything that is designed, marketed and sold for the pleasure of consumers in America is for White Consumers. Consumption goes with the dollars and dollars are (mostly) with Whites.

Naturally, every member of the Best and Brightest cadre in America, from Harvard to MIT, from Stanford to UCLA, who is hired to dumb down Americans, thinks about Whites as their target audience. Every image conjured, every slogan created, every word written down, every event staged, virtually anything and everything that materializes in American society for the market and market profit is for Whites. The magnitude, intensity and variety of ways that Consumer Capitalism assaults White Americans are so great that its total effect is impossible to calculate or fathom. It is a foregone conclusion that the Greatest Selling Machine for America's Consumer Capitalism has eventually produced the Dumbest (White) Generation ever, who has in turn produced Donald Trump as their Leader.

Does Consumer Capitalism consciously think of White People as their target? No. It is just the nature of marketing and demographics. It is Whites that have the money and it is Whites that are most numerous in America. In politics, culture, economy, education, military, religion and all other things social and ideological, the "American Nation" has always been a "White Nation." In the great flow of history and power, the non-whites, like Blacks, American Indians, Asians, and Hispanics, darker immigrants and Muslims, and others, always waited in the margins to be included in things "American." Their number has grown with the rise of immigration by non-white groups that has altered the image, if not the reality, of America's social development.

Whites, their minds corroded with incessant consumption and entertainment for decades, felt cornered and threatened by the rising tide of colored immigration and decided to act in the most direct and symbolic way in the election: Vote for the one most appealing to their inner calling. With Trump's election, the assumption has become an assertion, declared, demonstrated and dominant.

As loud as his election is, however, what the President of the U.S. can do is limited, especially in the way money is distributed in America: He cannot alter the way of who gets what in America's wealth any more than he can alter the flow of the Mississippi. He cannot take the money away from the rich and give it to his White supporters. But, such is not the declared purpose of Trump's Presidency. His presidency is more for the show, given his own personality and the political reality, than substance. But this show may be enough to alter the fundamental cultural and historical nature of American society.

What he *can* do, with the blessings of indifference and even cheering from the White Majority, can be quite formidable: He *can* build a wall between the U.S. and Mexico and make the latter pay for it; he *can* keep all the Muslims from entering the U.S.; he *can* bully the weaker trade partners into making concessions to the new-version agreements; he *can* stop new immigrants from coming to America; he *can* make the lives of American minorities hell on earth, including a new stop-and-frisk style and trend; and many other such things he *can* do for no other purpose than he *can.*

Because he is so unpredictably self-centered, so insecure yet so boisterous, unanchored in any conventional ideology or philosophy, he can start WWIII without any second thoughts, only because he *can.* And that is what makes him and his presidency as a Child with a Loaded Gun so destructive and dangerous.

To cap it all, he tweeted one of his messages soon after he was elected (November 29, 2016): "Nobody should be allowed (he said) to burn the American flag – if they do, there must be consequences – perhaps loss of citizenship or year in jail!" The technicality of this proposal is irrelevant, as the Supreme Court had upheld it in 1989 as free speech. What is so instructive for us in this Twitter message is this: Donald Trump sent out such an outrageously stupid and un-American message to his White Supporters (who else?) because he *knew* it was *safe* for him to say such a thing. What is so revealing for us is not that Donald Trump is stupid and un-American (maybe he is, maybe he is not), *but that his supporting Whites were stupid and un-American,* according to their own Leader's assessment of their intelligence. This assessment is on the order of not knowing the location at which the "Gettysburg Address" was delivered or the place where the "Battle of Waterloo" was fought. Was Donald Trump's assessment of the intelligence level of his followers correct? Obviously. He won the election.

Perhaps Donald Trump and his followers are a match made in Heaven. As Trump himself thought nothing of his supporters' intelligence, and his supporters thought nothing of their Leader's intelligence. How else could we explain the fact that these White Masses would choose as their Leader a man who has absolutely no redeeming human value? No matter what Trump said during the campaign that could not be repeated in good company, they accepted it by ignoring it; no matter what Trump did during the campaign that was ugly and unbecoming of a nation's leader, they accepted by making no value judgment on it. It was as if Donald Trump was never taken seriously as a human being with any decent intelligence. It was as if they were saying to Trump: *"Donald Trump, no matter what you say or do or have done, we don't care, because we already know to expect nothing from you, as a human being and much less as our Leader. Just make us feel good!"*

It is sad, indeed, that the greatest citizen revolt since 1776 is not to strengthen the American ideal that declared that "all men are created equal," but to create a Fascist State in America that declares that the strong rule the weak. Most grievous of all, the Capitalist System, with its powerful Consumerism, succeeded in dividing up the Ninety-Nine Percent into two halves of workers and ordering one half to kill the other.

II.

Who are the so-called "Trump Supporters"?

We recognize that they are overwhelmingly *White*. How overwhelming? The *Atlantic Monthly* magazine puts it at 90 percent. The name generally given to this Trump Bloc is the blue-collar type "White Working Class." But since there are reports that educated high-income Whites are also among the Trump Supporters, we need a new name that is handy and all-inclusive for this group that elected Trump: Let's call them the WATS, for *White American Trump Supporters*. (On the other hand, we should create another handy reference for those Whites who did not support Trump and we will call them the WANTS, *White American Not Trump Supporters*.)

It has been widely established beyond doubt that people at the ballot cast their votes according to their *self-interest*. The absolute secrecy that shrouds the vote sanctifies the principle that the vote is cast purely according to the voter's intention and the intention is his own self-interest. While reporting on who the Trump Supporters might be, the *Atlantic Monthly* article applied the word "shocking" to the fact that 90 percent of the Trump Bloc is made up of White people in America, which is virtually a Soviet-level bloc voting.

But, it would be more shocking if the Whites *did not* vote for Trump who represented the White-Interest. What Trump advocated, so clearly and repeatedly, was obviously good for Whites and this is what Whites voted for. Everything Trump ever said made Whites feel good about themselves. Only a demagogue plays this sort of populist game, the strong against the weak, and a good politician normally avoids this route. But Trump obviously chose a demagogue's model as being closer to White America's national character, not a good leader's route (both sides were numerically pretty even in size). Voters don't vote for good leaders (it would be contrary to the very nature of the "vote"), they vote for the one who best represents their self-interest. When Trump called Mexicans "murderers and rapists," he obviously implied that only Mexicans murder and rape, not Whites. This made Whites feel good and it would have been shocking, actually, that Whites would not have voted for a candidate who made them feel good and promised to make them feel even better in the future if they voted for him.

All so-called campaign strategies are geared to make their constituents feel good, appealing to their self-interest, at least their "local" interest, while keeping the candidate's dignity intact. But the temptation to play demagoguery is so strong for every candidate that it is a constant struggle within each electoral round. Building a wall between Mexico and the U.S. to keep the murdering and raping Mexicans out is much more appealing than building strong bridges and good schools. Unlike most other candidates in the past, Trump was the first to acknowledge that he *is* indeed the emperor without clothes and he didn't care if he was naked to the world. Instead of doing something shocking, the WATS did what they were expected to do: Vote for their self-interest. Only four percent of the Norwegians, who had no self-interest in the U.S. election, preferred Trump as their candidate. (Too bad that people who have no self-interest do not vote in the American elections. Perhaps given the enormous impact that the American leadership has on the rest of the world, people outside the U.S. should be allowed to vote, maybe to make up a certain portion of the Electoral College vote?)

III.

Now, there is this small inconvenient fact that some Whites did *not* vote for Trump, the WANTS. It is quite understandable that Whites voted for their own self-interest. It is equally understandable that non-whites voted for *their* own self-interest, as the WATS did theirs. But the WANTS voted in a way that was against their own self-interest, at least not personal, immediate, and psychologically-satisfying self-interest. In fact, the WANTS voted for something their tug of heart told them *not* to do. This makes the WANTS, White Americans Not Trump Supporters, the most interesting group among all voting blocs in America that demands our serious sociological attention.

What, then, did the WANTS vote for when they cast their ballot not for Trump but for a candidate who would not give them everything that would appeal to their self-interest? The "Stronger Together," as noble as it may be, is not as appealing as calling Mexicans murderers and rapists or threatening to build a wall between the two countries. Obviously, instead of voting for their own personal, immediate, and psychologically-satisfying self-interest, they voted for something not personal, not immediate, and not psychologically satisfying. It is clear that they thought of themselves as "American" before they thought of themselves as "White." As Americans, the WANTS voted for what they considered to be Americanism, what America stands for. As Americans, the WANTS voted for what is good for all Americans, including Whites themselves, whereas the WATS voted for what is good for themselves, personally, immediately, and psychologically-satisfying. What is really shocking here is not the way WATS voted, but actually the way the WANTS voted, seemingly against their own natural self-interest. The WANTS obviously judged that what's good for all Americans is also good for Whites too. But the WATS judged that what's good for all Americans didn't leave much for themselves, as, in their view, Whites were the only legitimate "Americans" entitled to the bounties of America. Although they once came and took it from the Indians, they were now determined to protect it from the later invaders, the non-whites, who came as the new immigrants to the New World to share the bounties.

What separates the WATS, the Whites who supported Trump and the WANTS, the Whites who did not support him, and explains the separation, is this matter called Human Nature. Nothing is more important in the emergence and development of "Americans" as the concept of "Nature," as the U.S. is recognized as history's first and only "Natural Society." In the total conception of America, the shortest way to understand American society (its character, government, economy, education, culture, everything) is through this concept of Nature: Americans are natural people and like to do what their nature calls for. What nature calls for is that we do what we naturally desire within us: Being childish and selfish in search of amusement and power over others. But, keenly aware of this, the Founding Fathers, notably Thomas Jefferson, placed a strong condition (sometimes called the "Lockean Proviso" among philosophers and political economists referring to what John Locke wrote on the subject) which says this pursuit of natural desires *must be done to the benefit of all Americans*. In a more simplified way, this condition is expressed in the declaration that All Men are Created Equal. Do whatever your heart desires, the condition says, but make sure that we do it all equally in America. Traditionally, the Democrats have supported the condition more strongly, and the Republicans have been more insistent on being "natural" for each American to get whatever he can, regardless of the savage consequences as a result of the struggle. (When Melania Trump complained about America being "too mean and too rough," she was referring, ironically, to the savage "Republican" consequences of this natural struggle, which, incidentally, her husband ardently personifies.)

As the U.S. has historically developed into a Capitalist System, especially its Consumer Capitalism variety, it is more and more difficult for any American to believe in the Jeffersonian idea of equality for all, much less practice it in his daily life. So, the Whites in America dramatically have split between the Jeffersonians and the Trumpians. While the Trumpians follow the call of their nature, the Jeffersonians respond to their "society," where individuals subsume their individual passion to promote welfare for all. This frame of mind is often called "social consciousness" and the resulting product "community." Trumpian America believes that we can live without social consciousness and without community, and the election plainly demonstrated a brave absence of social consciousness and a strong disregard for community in White America. What is social consciousness?

Social consciousness is an awareness of "others." It is a uniquely human attribute as only human beings have formed an artificial entity called "society," to live with each other in peace and harmony. In nature, we live as our animal nature would dictate for survival and protection. In society, we live as human beings in the company of other human beings. In this sense, in an ideal society (say, in Scandinavia or among the Amish) our individual self is made up of, in equal parts, ourselves and others. In it, others are as important as ourselves, if not more. Some extraordinary members of humanity, we call them martyrs, even live and die for others in complete disregard for themselves. Social consciousness is thus a testimony to our constant struggle, and balance, between what our nature calls for in utter selfishness and what our society calls for in our existence in the midst of our neighbors.

Even in our more callous and selfish development in Capitalist lifestyle of consumption in America, we had always tried to balance out nature and society, if just for the sake of appearance. America was known, or wished to be known, as a nation that balanced freedom and pleasures of natural life with the idealism of justice, humanity and morality. To be an American, as the image was established, one was balancing self and others, nature and society, and freedom and obligation. In the last several decades of Consumer Capitalism, and especially with the advent of Digital Life, however, the balance tilted toward self. This tilt has been most dramatically demonstrated in the White American Trump Supporters who completely abandoned even the facade of balance between nature and society. From now on, the WATS declared, it's natural power that rules, for me, me and me. Politics without social consciousness is an extension of nature's naked cruelty, savagery and selfishness. Jeffersonian political equality was possible because of the economic freedom Americans enjoyed in their abundant land that ensured their *equality and freedom,* normally an impossible combination for humanity. Our historical development and existential experience tell us, especially jolted into awareness with the WATS, this Jeffersonian America will never happen again in this land called the United States. The WATS and Trump declared that we will be more cruel, more savage, and more selfish, among ourselves and with the world in the coming years, and we had better brace for it.

Just how many socially-conscious WANTS, the White Americans Not Trump Supporters, are there among us? Very few. We arrive at this pessimistic conclusion by doing simple math: The WANTS are all American voters minus the Trump Supporters and those non-whites who supported Clinton. The latter non-whites cannot be counted among the socially-conscious simply because the rule of self-interest among voters must apply equally to non-whites too: We must assume that the non-whites also voted for their self-interest. (Those non-whites who voted for Trump, on the other hand, could not be counted among the socially conscious simply because of the existential reasons: We just don't understand why the victims of Trumpian policies would actually vote for their tormentor.) Among all Americans, White and non-white, the socially-conscious citizens are thus pitifully small. This leaves the WANTS as the only certifiably socially-conscious Americans that still believe in the Jeffersonian ideals of America, that our pursuit of freedom and pleasures of nature must be available to *all* Americans.

Conventionally, America's open indulgence in hedonism and epicurean-ism was a forgivable sin, in America's self-explanation as well as in the perspective of the world, only because it was done in the rubric of *egalitar-ianism:* That America's famous self-indulgence was being carried out, at least, by *all* Americans, something that had never been seen anywhere before in any other society on that scale. Now, Trump and the WATS have openly declared an end to the Jeffersonian façade. At the same time, there are few of these Jeffersonian Americans left, those who truly believe that all men, white and non-white, men and women, are equal Americans and thus side with the Lesser Americans with their lives and fortunes. And the trend does not prom-ise that such Americans would rise to greater numbers or somehow American society would, even in pretending, claim the Jeffersonian ideals again. If we remember that ours is the "dumbest generation" ever and we are "amusing ourselves to death" daily, confidence or hope that there is a future in America is an intellectual luxury we cannot afford, not for us, not for our posterity.

IV.

How did this happen? To answer the question, we must now do some back-tracking and witness what America's Consumer Capitalism has done to de-stroy the brains and minds of White Americans who, in their stupor, elected Donald J. Trump. What did America's Consumer Capitalism feed the White Masses for the past several decades that turned them into the children and idiots? Never in the history of humanity, stretching to the Romans, has there been a people, White Americans, so relentlessly assaulted by a determined class of money-mongers, the Capitalists in America, with the sole purpose of destroying the White minds with around-the-clock trash. Never in the history of arts and sciences of human persuasion, has there been such a system of manipulation as effective in killing the spirit and soul of a whole nation as Consumer Capitalism in America. This is uniquely "American," different from anything known before in history or elsewhere in the current experi-ences of other nations.

Analysts and scholars tend to see the Trump Phenomenon in light of what's going on elsewhere in the world, two most notable events being Brexit and the French election in which Le Pen's nationalism is seen as the French equivalent of Trumpism. These writers think what's going in the U.S. and what's going on in the rest of the world are quite similar and tend to conclude that what goes on in the U.S. is part of what goes on world-wide. They think politics in the world in general runs along the liberal-conservative cycles in which voters get tired of one government and look to replace it with its opposition, almost regularly. The

Trump Phenomenon, like Brexit and French nationalism, comes at the end of the "liberal-capitalist" era in the U.S. which will revert back to the traditional-type after Trump's term. While comforting and reasonable, what they fail recognize is that politics in the U.S. is not like all the traditional patterns of national politics in Europe and elsewhere: While in Europe and elsewhere, the *people* are organized as *political groups*, the U.S. has no such thing, especially among the White voters, who live, play and die as solitary individuals without any political or even human connections among them as a group. Social media or ballgame gatherings do not lead to political bonding. Unless you *protest together*, there is no *political together*. (There is more "political" interest among non-whites in America simply because of their minority status that requires the strength of unity among them).

In other nations, politics is normally the most serious business there is, and their economic interest is subsumed under their political activities. Especially in Europe, with a long history of Feudalism, they believe political power cannot come from anything but political activities and political activities are ineffective unless they are organized. In the U.S., under great propaganda effects from Capitalism, politics and economics are completely separated. White Americans rarely think economic gains are achieved through collective political activities, such as union organization or collective pressure. In their view. it's all individual struggles and personal career choices that determine their economic fortunes. Add to that frame of mind the relentless preoccupation with entertainment that numbs their minds into idiotization and childishness, and you have a very different chain of cause and effect that has led to the Trump Presidency. The process may be political (election cycles, party conventions), but the substance is highly cultural (solitary entertainment, consumer society). Naturally, it is those institutions that control cultural consumption—the Capitalist System and its Consumer Society—that controls all parts of American life, including its "political" process. One might say that the U.S. is the first and perhaps only *democratic* society that has taken politics out of its national governance. Thus, unlike any other nationals, Americans are governed daily not by their national government or their municipal communities, but by Hollywood, NBC or the National Football League. In this era of post-industrial, virtual existence, politics has been replaced by cultural psychology, and one of the end-results is the emergence of Donald Trump.

We move onto the next stage of progression to explain why this historical atavism has occurred in America. But, before that, we need one last summary rearview look at how Donald Trump came, saw and conquered America.

Chapter Twelve

Trump's Conquest of America

It is the year 2016 and the U.S. is gearing up for the business of choosing its 45th President. Consumer Capitalism, thanks to America's best and brightest talent, had done its work: For decades now, American Consumers, mostly White, had been effectively reduced to five-year-old children, deeply selfish and vengeful. It is relatively easy picking for someone as clever and shameless as Donald Trump to come to the scene and conquer America.

The ultimate irony in the Trump win of 2016 is that White Americans did not do exactly what Corporate America had trained them to do: They voted for Donald Trump, not Hillary Clinton, as the script called for. Consumer Capitalism that had fed America its trashy distractions for years forgot the widely-accepted wisdom of its own: *Garbage in, garbage out.* You feed Americans garbage, and you get garbage Americans. White Americans, numbed for years with sewer-level entertainment, had become immune to reason, and the established power did not recognize the change.

For decades, Consumer Capitalism (politically called "Neo-Liberalism") showered the consumers with whatever they demanded, often even what they did not demand, reducing them eventually to a point where normal intelligent human thinking had become quite alien. Thus dumbed down, White Americans had become disciplined workers (although they longed to quit their jobs) and obedient consumers (Mental Trash being their daily supply), exactly as designed by Corporate America and its best and brightest minds. The established power of Corporate America did not know just *how idiotized* Americans, especially White Americans, had become under its system.

While Corporate America maintained a firm grip on Consumer America, the "political game" went on as scheduled. "Your vote is important!" the voters were told over and over again. Predictably half of the voters did not bother to vote. The vote exists only on the premises that America is a democratic society run by its citizen-voters; the vote thus represents this citizen power for self-governance; the representative government, voted on by its citizens, is the legitimate voice of the American People. Why, given this premise of American Democracy, then, traditionally, do half of American voters refuse to believe this Great American Civic Premise?

The vote represents one of the two things that make the Commoner the king of the day—the other being the dollar--when he has them in his possession. We cannot imagine an average American throwing away the dollar when it is given to him as a democratic gift from his nation *half the time it is given to him.* But why does he throw away the gift of the vote half the time it is given to him? This voluntary abdication of his civic power can mean only one conclusion: He does not *believe* his vote means anything real or true or powerful. In his commonsense understanding of the American political process, he intuitively senses that his vote means nothing because the "political game," whereby elections are held and his vote solicited, is just that, a *game,* that is played according to the rules of the game that are already predetermined. We never have to tell people, "Your dollar is important!" but we have to tell them over and over again that their vote is important because it decidedly is not. (It's like hearing on a recorded message from a corporate business office, "your calls are important to us…," et cetera, and the first feeling we get is that our calls are *not* important to them. If our calls *were* indeed important, why would they try to convince you that they *are*? On this level of our existence, "being important," like "being loved," is felt, not demonstrated.) This emptiness of the Political Game was amply shown when it was widely reported that the Russian government intervened with the election in America by releasing certain information to the American voters: The very fact that whatever is released by a foreign government can affect the election shows how flimsy the electoral process is in America. The vote is so insignificant that it can be thrown away at the slightest rumor or innuendo.

But, the usual pomp and circumstance of the Political Game went on with great attention paid from the media on each presidential election as if they are covering the Super Bowls and Olympics,. The commonly-accepted political idea is that in our Liberalism-Capitalism balance in America, the Republican Party puts its weight on the "Capitalism" side and the Democratic Party on the "Liberalism" side. Although this scoring of the American political game is widely understood, neither party ever tried to make an issue of "class warfare," meaning the "money issue," which was almost always a taboo in American politics. (In America we generally separate the "economy issue" from the "wealth issue," the former being the day-to-day nickel-and-dime pocketbook variety whereas the latter involves millionaires and billionaires and their Capital. The former is freely argued and discussed, but the latter is rarely mentioned). Thus alternating between the two political parties, like the National Football League circulating the Super Bowl Champions among the teams, the political system would keep America in political balance and economic imbalance. This system worked to perfection until Donald Trump came on the scene in 2016, making a wholly unexpected jump from gutter-level TV and sewage-level populism to the White House. Of all the politicians, we can now see it clearly in sociological retrospect, only Trump knew that White Americans had become gutter-level citizens and sewage-level voters under Consumer Capitalism's relentless Mental Trash. The conventional wisdom, smug in its driver's-seat comfort and security, did not know of this change that it had created for White Americans itself: The intelligence and humanity of the White voters had been destroyed worse than anyone, except Trump, had realized.

Still, through the last few elections, wholly unaware of the great seismic shift in the intelligence and humanity of the White Majority in America under the relentless working of Consumer Capitalism, the political Super Bowl was staged every four years. John McCain and Mitt Romney had represented Capitalism in the "Liberalism-Capitalism" equation and were defeated by Barack Obama who represented Liberalism. America's Consumer Capitalism would have prospered just as well under either choice, perhaps with but a slight change in emphasis, depending on whether the government would be Republican (Capitalism side) or Democratic (Liberalism side). That Wall Street was known to support Hillary Clinton, a Democrat, rather than its standard-official friend from the Republican Party, makes this point clear to everyone.

II.

In 2016, Donald Trump changed the rules of the game radically by offering a "third" choice, instead of the traditional two, Liberalism and Capitalism, or more commonly, Liberal-Capitalism, in the "consumer-capitalist" society. What Trump offered was an entirely different altar at the Temple of America with entirely different sacrifices. Prior to Donald Trump, the choices that White Masses had been offered were those *without sacrifices*. Whether Republican or Democratic in the election result, the unifying idea was that *all Americans,* both White *and* non-white, were going to prosper in their temple of government and administration. The candidates were merely competing to do this *better* than the other. What Donald Trump offered was something quite new: He told the White American voters that they, the Whites, were going to get something more than just the standard share of the Great American Dream. They were going to get what Trump would take away from the Lesser Americans. He promised them that they, the White supporters, would not have to get disappointed with the all-for-everybody kind of promise of the traditional opponent, whose slogan was "Together, Stronger." The slogan was typically Clintonian, positive, inclusive, traditional and virtuous, but quite meaningless to a White voter who had lost his sense of normal intelligence and humanity in the decades of mindless entertainment and consumption.

Here, the whole concept of "America" itself was altered by Donald Trump. Prior to Trump, the "United States of America" was deemed different from the Old World in one particularly crucial point: In the New World of America, revolution was not necessary to achieve social-political-economic justice; it might be required in the Old World, but not in America; the New World was blessed with so much of everything, material and immaterial, for everybody that this sort of revolution was *unnecessary* in America. The reason socialist rhetoric and unionism generally held little appeal to most Americans is simply that this kind of radical political transformation did not fit the conditions of the New World where everything was abundant. Even though the top One Percent in America became wealthier and wealthier, their wealth was always considered secure from mob attacks and socialist assault. In fact, wealth in America, whether in the bank or in one's private possession, was considered *most secure* in the free world, rivaling that in Switzerland.

But Donald Trump was offering White Americans something very "European." He was saying to them that White Americans (although he never mentioned the word "White" in public) were not getting their just share and it was about time that they took it, by force if necessary, from the non-whites and non-Americans. Given the selfishness, childishness and vengefulness that had become the hallmark of (White) American character, all shaped by Consumer Capitalism, White Americans loved what he promised them: A radical departure from all that was "American," to be sure, but White Americans by then had become politically more Fascist (in the mold of Mussolini and Hitler) than Jeffersonian or Clintonian.

Through McCain and Romney's candidacy, the promise of sharing America's wealth was skeptically viewed but reluctantly accepted, seeing no better alternative, by the White voters. (The Republican had gone as far as benign neglect of the non-whites but never articulated such "un-American" policies specifically or boldly.) What Donald Trump offered on the new alter was concrete and tangible, bracing and brazen, savage and Fascist: He would fatten up the Whites by shrinking the non-whites' portions. Under normal electoral circumstances, the Republican candidate would hint at such things (for example, Romney's infamous 47-percent speech), but Trump made it his central campaign theme: Non-whites are dangerous and un-American and we will take away their bounties and give them to Whites. Voters are naturally skeptical of such promises of largesse, especially when they are spoken as a political promise. But Donald Trump was no normal politician and his promises were nothing like the normal promises offered by politicians. He was very specific with his language and unambiguous with its meanings ("Mexicans are rapists and murderers") such as no other politicians would have been reckless enough to make public. Not even Barry Goldwater or George McGovern, the two "radicals" from both parties, talked like that or promised like that.

Like McCain, Romney and Obama, Hillary Clinton was of the old school, where manners and tradition of the Political Game had been instilled in her as her second nature. There was something very "old school" about Clinton, her manners and her promises, so polite, so proper and so rational. This sort of old-school mannerism had become passe in Trump's America and for most American Whites. Trump had come from the cutting-edge frontier of the cable-TV-and-digital culture where most of the American White voters had settled. The intellectual community was shocked by Trump's boldness and recklessness, it turned out, much more so than were the White Masses who eventually voted for Trump's promise. For Hillary it was a Political Game which was familiar to her and her predecessor candidates. For Trump, it was a War, a Total War, as in his previous Business War, of survival or destruction.

In retrospect, the old established order had become complacent about what it had achieved with the White Masses. After all, for decades, it had trained and brainwashed the White Masses with the wonderful world of Mental Trash and Freedom of Choice and Democracy, and whatever else it deemed necessary in its arsenal of propaganda. Underlying all the training that it had subjected the Whites Masses under Consumer Capitalism and all its wonderful joy was the central theme of *selfishness.* It was selfishness that drove the White consumers to the malls, to the ballgames , and to the computers. This focus on Self was enough to create a Mental-Trash culture in America, to sustain the Neo-Liberal-Capitalist system that kept the rich rich and the consumers consuming.

Then came Donald Trump who offered a new brand of selfishness that the old-school Liberal-Capitalist America had never seen or anticipated before: It was a selfishness not seen since Mussolini and Hitler roamed their respective countries. It was savage and naked, the likes of which might be considered acceptably normal if they were manifest in Russia or China, but not from the "United States of America." After all, the U.S. of A. was known for its Exceptionalism, as "the City on the Hill" as much as the land of Abraham Lincoln and Henry David Thoreau. The old-school established order in Corporate America was amused at first with Trump's new brand of low-brow comedy disguised as politics. For the media Trump was good business all around and everything he said and gestured was front page stuff. The media's tone changed once Trump became set as the Republican candidate. The amusement continued, as Trump continued to provide good copy, but this amusement was now combined with serious journalism that saw the dark consequences if Trump would get elected president. While anxiety and un-certainty tinged the many reports and stories on Trump, the media itself had become addicted to Donald Trump by then (because Hillary Clinton was just too much of an old-school ma'rm to write anything interesting about). The White Masses had also gotten addicted to Donald Trump by then who prom-ised them Heaven and Earth.

Could he get elected president, the media wondered but its own answer was: *No way.* To make sure that it would not happen, because it was "un-thinkable" that somebody like him would actually become president of the United States, the media started attacking him in earnest. The established media still believed in the conventional wisdom of manners, tradition and reason: Surely, Americans could not possibly elect somebody like Trump. Dividing Americans between "White Americans" and "non-white Americans" had been vaguely assumed as reality but still not openly dis-cussed among intellectuals and commentators in polite society. "Stronger Together" was trite but still more acceptable than calling Mexicans rapists and murderers. Trump was still too "unthinkable" and what was intellectual-ly and emotionally unthinkable could not possibly happen in America. The faith in this old America was bolstered by the simple fact that the sitting president was a Black man, twice elected. How could a nation that had elected a Black president turn around and elect a racist Fascist? (What they forgot was the fact that "America" did not elect Obama; just half-plus-one of America did and eight years of a Black President was too much for most White Americans although nobody would say this aloud or in good compa-ny.)

III.

The electoral system in America at first glance is an odd thing, as it was assumed that, aside from the times of wars and disasters, the president is a figurehead. America was and is controlled by money. The real power in America was vested in Wall Street bankers. The "political" process was merely a window-dressing, both in substance and in image. The very circus-like procession that characterized the political process clearly demonstrated that the Political Game was just that, a game that was played out periodically to satisfy the Founding Fathers and the "99 percent," and a nod to the world that still believed in democracy.

If the reality of America conformed to the image of America, the "politi-cal process" should have long disappeared from America: Government should have been run simply by corporations. Even the most "radical" of all recent presidents, a Black president, could not make much of a difference in

America's real system of rule, which is to say, by Corporate America. This political game had been played for decades just fine.

Presidents of both parties came and went, and all without leaving any visible trace of their having been there. The rich kept getting richer and richer and no president could do anything about it. In all honesty, none of the last four contenders—McCain, Romney, Obama, Clinton—would have made any difference if we just selected one of them randomly. No wonder, the old establishment of Corporate America was smug enough not to worry about any possible "political revolution" from the masses that were certifiably stupid and selfish and childish, addicted to Mental Trash and enslaved to their employment by their economic necessity. The Law and law-enforce-ment worked for the money class. The military was keeping the trade routes and coffers secure. Colleges were training and indoctrinating the future em-ployees of Corporate America. Congress was passing laws to favor corpora-tions and their interests, thanks to lobbying power. And the best of all, the government was all under the proper control of the Wall Street CEOs and their cohorts. All seemed just fine for Corporate America and its Consumer Capitalism and its Mental Trash power. So, why worry about the little "polit-ical game" where the Masses do their noisy but insignificant voting in their funny little ballot booths? The only clear indication of the extent to which the White Masses in America had become dangerously vengeful, vapid and sav-age was the "blogging culture" among the computer users, but even that was dismissed as a small blemish in an otherwise well-disciplined society and people under control.

Then came Donald Trump's election. And a shocker it was: Is his election shocking because it violated the assumed predictive omniscience among the intellectuals as well as America's tarnished image overseas, or is it shocking because of what his election might actually do to alter the Established Order of money and power? If the answer is the first, after some shame-facedness of the media leaders, things would calm down. If the answer is the second, we have more to discuss. In the meantime, the one thing that Trump's win told us that is of great significance is that the White Masses had become much dumber and more selfish under decades of Mental Trash and Consumer Capitalism than Corporate America had ever imagined possible. In fact, it is very likely that the whole Capitalist Machine that had turned White Americans into dummies and selfish children had never realized what kind of "White Americans" they had created with their relentless assault on their minds and souls.

By the time Donald Trump had come to the White Masses, they had already been destroyed: They had become so stupid, so selfish, and so child-ish that when someone like Donald Trump promised them bounties to be gained by crucifying the other half of America, they acted as if they had found their Messiah, their Fuhrer, their Savior. This was a pyrrhic victory at its worst,. Destroying half of America to bolster the other half was destroying all of America. Equally pyrrhic, Trump promised to repress one half of America to free the other half, which would eventually make all of America unfree. Corporate Capitalism that had destroyed White Americans didn't even know how successfully it had done its job. It should not surprise us at all that people so corrupted by the stupidest kind of entertainment day and night and dumbed down by the worst kind of self-deluding propaganda for decades would grab anything, Trump or no. In this, Donald Trump was as clever as Machiavelli and as shameless as the Devil in the Garden of Eden. Or, simply and more sociologically, he was just at the right place at the right time.

This is our parting picture of Trump's Americans: If you are a "typical" White American Consumer, you are *expected* to be of low intelligence and lower social awareness. The sad part is that you cannot protest against these quite degrading and dehumanizing expectations. What the one-percent supplier of America's daily essentials feeds you and entertains you with is enough to convince anyone that such expectations of the majority held by the minority are all true. All the things the masses eat, watch on TV, browse on their cell-phone, whatever, would convince anyone in the world that it is indeed true that the White Masses in America are of low intelligence and lower social awareness. If you disagree with these descriptions of average White Americans as portrayed and expected by the one-percent, simply watch TV and advertisements produced exclusively for you, the Average White American. One or two segments, if watched analytically, should quickly convince you of your low level of existence basically as a dumb self-centered child. In this sense, you fit the character of the man you voted into the White House.

IV.

The White American worker, perhaps contrary to the images of large boisterous gatherings we have gotten used to during the Trump campaign, is quite obedient and docile. The idea is that workers will do whatever they are commanded to do. To elaborate on a famous quote, loosely attributed to 19th-century financier Jay Gould, who was asked if he was afraid of worker revolt, he said no, he was not. To explain why he was not, he said, "I can hire one half of the working class to kill the other half." When this saying is repeated, it is always mentioned as a joke intended to get a laugh or two from the audience. (Indeed, the saying gets a laugh or two whenever I mention it to my students, sometimes followed by a silent musing on the meaning of the quote as it sinks in. As revealed by their classroom writings later, the meaning of the quote has a terrifying effect on some.) The laugh as well as the silence affirms the truth in the saying: Yes, the working class can be controlled by their own foolishness and powerlessness; yes, you tell them what to do and they will do it obediently. At the same time, this can be said only in jest, intended to get a laugh. Any serious use of the quote--or the existential meaning of the quote--is harmful to the health of the speaker. It is just too painfully true to say it in earnest in America.

White workers in America have just decided to kill the other half, non-whites, by voting for Donald Trump. Whatever else Trump's election may have accomplished, one thing is undeniably clear: It split the working masses into two groups, Upper-working class Whites and Lower-working class non-whites. The ruling class simply has a buffer zone--better than the vague and easily-disgruntled Middle-Class--that stands between One Percent and Working Masses. Jay Gould's working class has become Trump's storm-troopers. As Trump's voters, the White Masses swore that they would take whatever they can from the Lesser Americans, to make themselves more powerful and pleased. In this they have learned well from Hitler's Germany, but little or nothing from Jefferson's America.

Now, the only Great Unknown that remains to be seen is not what Trump would do; he has already said what he would do: The truly Great Unknown is what Corporate America would do against the upstart Fascists who may disrupt the nice established way of making and keeping money in America, namely, Consumer Capitalism.

So, what continues for all Americans as the American Way of Life is to consume. The life of a White American begins and ends as a consumer. What is a consumer? A consumer, especially the solitary-living and unconnected Whiteman, is a free human being when he spends his money in consumption. The strange truth is that whenever you make a "free choice" as a consumer you make an *idiot's choice*. The most prominent among his free choices is what we call Mental Trash, which is what most White consumers choose most of the time. That is the very law and nature of consumption that have shaped America's thoughts, feelings and passions in the last three decades. Thus, Mental Trash, as the key ingredient in Consumer Capitalism, connects White Americans to Donald Trump's election and explains their catastrophic mental and moral deterioration.

It is this Mental Trash to which we now turn our attention next.

Chapter Thirteen

Mental Trash

Of all facets in American Life, the single greatest "improvement" in the last few decades has been in *entertainment* and its ability to affect our mind. What is normally celebrated as the beginning of the Great Society, with its Affluent Generation in America, has turned out to be nothing but the flood of the crowd gathering at the Circus to enjoy the day's amusement. As the number of TV channels multiplied, as our computer dependency exploded, and our mind slowly adjusted to the great variety and speed of entertainment, our ability to think and feel as human beings and citizens also vanished: When we gather, we do not form a public; when we connect, we do not form a community; when we collect information, it does not lead us to enlightenment; when we are pleased with our daily spectacles, we do not feel the pleasure as our happiness. The "improvement" in entertainment has been so great and terrible in America in the last three decades that we might foresee the future History of America simply as the History of Mass Entertainment— or Mental Trash—in its all-encompassing presence in American Life.

White Americans brought Donald Trump to power, the man universally recognized as "unfit" to be president. This shocking turn of events caused the world to wonder what had happened to the *White Voters* who did such an unthinkable thing. It turns out, for decades they had been fed mind garbage— Mental Trash--in the form of mass entertainment day and night that eroded any remnant of humanity and intelligence from these Trump supporting Whites. For the last few decades for all consuming Whites, virtually all things *conceived*, *produced* and *consumed* in the entertainment and digital sectors of society have been mind-killing products of one kind or another. Thus, the single most important factor that destroyed the intellectual and human capacity of American Whites who supported Donald Trump, we can say with confidence, is this Mental Trash: Never in the history of humanity and its wildest imagination, has a generation of real human beings been so completely controlled by what society's economic system (Consumer Capitalism) has fed them. The Donald Trump presidency happens to be the most dramatic manifestation of what a trashed mind can and will do.

Mental Trash represents the concept of life and society that is identified with perpetual amusement. Society exists, according to this conception, to provide perpetual amusement, and life to experience this perpetual amusement. In our Digital Era, where the very concept of Mental Trash finds its true meaning, all of society and all of life come through the Digital Channels: In essence, it creates a "mental-trash society " as the totality of life itself. Thus, to live in American society is to be amused at all times; to be amused at all times means so much Mental Trash must be handled through our mind; to handle so much Mental Trash means our mind must function as a Mental Trash Receptacle, or a trash can that processes what is mentally useless.

In this conception of society and life, the mind must remain empty at all times in order to accommodate the flow of mental trash. In the U.S., the Mecca of the world's best mental trash production and consumption, and the proto-type of "mental-trash society," the average American mind either (1) stays empty , or (2) is presently in the process of being emptied , as a Human Mental Garbage Can.

With the advent of personal computers and smart-phones, the Mental Trash Processing has been rising dramatically, almost geometrically, so that we might now foresee that such trash-processing activities will occupy virtually all of our non-working hours.

In America's social reality, Mental Trash performs functions for the masses quite similar to what drugs do to drug addicts:

Both Mental Trash and drugs create the feel-good effects for their consumers, which pacify them into a state of inaction and keep them from an active confrontation with reality : Both Mental Trash Receptacles and Drug Addicts can be kept in a permanent haze of mind and infancy of intellect with a continuing supply of both substances.

Both Mental Trash and drugs are cheaply available on a massive scale of production and supply, with a minimum cost and financial burden to their respective consumers. All Mental Trash and Drugs, both legal and illegal, can be obtained daily with a minimum hardship to the masses. Most important to the System, both Mental Trash and Drugs are addictive : Once formed as a daily expectation, it is nearly impossible to stop the habit of continuing consumption.

Unlike the Drugs, which are known to have quitters via various methods and therapies, mental trash's addictiveness is impossible to quit. Mental Trash is universally encouraged, praised, and defended by all propaganda machines of society, such as political-economic leaders, religious teachers, school curriculums, and the best and brightest of American creativity. Various outlets on the Internet, like Facebook , make it so respectable that not enjoying mental waste is considered something of an oddity in American society.

In America, this mental waste is like the air we breathe: It is everywhere and so much a part of our daily lives that we don't even realize that we are processing Mental Trash every moment of our existence. Like air, we recognize its presence only when its supply stops for the reason of mechanical malfunction or non-payment. The addictive state is so routine that such a wasted repetition has settled in as the Life, the Truth, and the Way for the American Masses who have no idea of what has become of their mental state: Few, if any, are known to have successfully quit this Mental Trash addiction. American society has even coined an innocuous-sounding name, the Millennials, to designate these new digital addicts.

There is nothing we throw out faster than something presented to us as amusement that is not amusing. Once we deem it no longer amusing, we instantly define it as *trash*. Nicholas Carr describes in his book on the Internet, *The Shallows,* what happens when we are constantly exposed to the Internet, the biggest Mental Trash Maker in our digital era: "Our brains turn into simple *signal-processing units*, quickly shepherding information into consciousness and then back out again." (Italics added). What he is describing here is the technical process of how Mental Trash enters our mind and is thrown out. As a "signal processing unit," our mind does this trashing virtually all day.

This "trashing" occurs when our mind determines that there is no need to retain it in our permanent storage of memory because it performs no vital cumulative function in our lives. A typical example would be an item on the evening news which you cannot recall the moment the news moves on to the next item: When something enters our minds and very quickly leaves our minds, sometimes as quickly as the click of the mouse, it has run one full cycle of collect-and-discard mental-trash processing at the speed of our clicks. Not surprisingly, this Mental-Trash Recycling Process is the sole activity of most American minds. In America's Consumer Capitalism today, virtually all things conceived , produced and consumed in the entertainment and digital sectors of society are mental-trash products. We can visualize the process in the way (1) something is collected and discarded and then (2) we ourselves turn into a very efficient Trash Can.

In the process, Americans have become *Living Trash Cans*. All Americans, as TV-audience or computer users, and as various entertainment-product consumers, exist as the Living Mental-Trash Receptacles, just so that they continually receive and throw away all their living experiences as they occur. Naturally, the time between collecting and discarding is becoming shorter and shorter, all moving toward the point of instant trashing. What we normally call "instant gratification" is nothing but instant collection and instant trashing, *happening at the shortest interval.* (After all, what do we do when we are satisfied with something? We throw it out the instant we are satisfied.) The shorter the processing time becomes, the more mental waste one can process, and therefore the greater the satisfaction or pleasure. At the end of a daily cycle, perhaps thousands upon thousands have been collected and discarded by a typical Mental Trash Receptacle, the Typical American Consumer. Not surprisingly, the newest rage on the digital market, Snapchat, *guarantees that everything that appears on it would disappear soon after it appears.* Never in the history of Humanity, has a society developed a mass culture whose *very purpose* is to produce and consume something that has no existence.

Thus, newer models in electronic gadgetry and service, like *Snapchat*, compete to boast greater power for Mental-Trash processing, claiming they can out-perform other models in the collect-discard cycle. All entrepreneurial and human aspirations and enterprises in digital U.S. consist of inventing ways (technologically and psychologically) to design, market and consume at the level of 100-percent Mental-Trash processing. At this level of collect-and-discard cycles, the human mind would have *no room* for retaining any of the ideas, images or events that entered their mind even for a few moments as the trashing has to be instant. In fact, *Snapcha*t's very fame rests on the fact of its fast-disappearing act that is guaranteed by its program. At this level of speed, the human mind's sole function (aside from working) would be as an instant Mental-Trash Can and little else. Likewise, a considerable part of social esteem in American society (economic, political, social, cultural) is now defined by the amount of the Mental-Trash discarding ability in one's possession. It generally goes by the name of "consumer activity:" The faster we tend to, or desire to, process our Mental (sometimes material) Trash into non-existence, the more "successful" we are deemed in society.

Why is *Snapchat* the rage of the Millennials, especially those between 18 and 24, that attracts so much capital interest, a sure thing? It is the Internet's first *nothing* invention, in which the images you send or receive are pro-grammed to "disappear" as soon as you see them, and it is deemed to be the future of life in America in general and on the Internet in particular. Its premise, and promise, is that everything in American life is going to become a temporary, ephemeral and meaningless daily repetition. The blank faces that stare at the TV screens and the voter who cries at a Trump rally, as if she were at a revival meeting, are the consumers of *Snapchat* which is made up of *nothing*, as what you glance at once is unlikely to be retained in your memory after it vanishes into thin air. Billions of dollars would be invested in *Snapchat* because smart money is betting on America spinning surely into generations of intellectual dummies and emotional children in the coming years. Not surprisingly, *Snapchat* is not shaping America; it is merely con-firming it, in the same way Trump's election confirms this Garbage-In, Garbage-Out America, but has not created it. In essence, *Snapchat*'s America is Trump's America, as much as it is the America of those blank faces and minds gone dead.

What then happens to our minds and thinking habits when we are into the daily routines of Mental Trash processing day after day? The following *symptoms* tend to change our perceptions and behaviors, completely disrupting the unique distinction of Thinking Humans--*the Homo Sapiens*--itself, when the Mental-Trash processing becomes our daily pattern:

Reality-Fiction distinction disappears. All become "interesting" momentary events. While "connected" to a "larger" "community" of "networking," Americans in Mental Trash spend their time increasingly alone, physically and psychologically, in their solitary, separate, artificially-created virtual worlds. (Perhaps in a near future, all computer-dependent Millennials would become ADHD-types or autistic as their normal behavioral features.)

Private-Pubic distinction disappears. All become matters of "personal" approval or choice in curiosity or interest. In all social matters, the private-to-public transition requires time and thought. But, in the Mental Trash era, it is instant: What is private becomes instantly public, to be instantly forgotten: What is instantly created is instantly trashed.

Past-Future (Historical) distinction disappears. All become here-and-now experiences. No historical perspective remains and the "past" and "future" lose their continuity as everything pivots around the "here" and "now."

Time-Space (Here-There) distinction disappears. As the grid that fixes our own existence's location and psyche, all local, geographic, and seasonal distinctions vanish. The location of the "*self*," wherever it happens to be at the consumer moment, becomes the center of all things, constantly moving and constantly evaporating. In the process of time-space fusion, everything is like everything else. This also invites the next symptom, relativism.

Relativized Reality: Perhaps most serious for our analysis on America's hunger for Donald Trump, all political-social ideas become relativized into comedy, indifferent tolerance, and meaninglessness, thus leaving us the slender thread of self-interest to connect and evaluate all public ideas. (Even the Pope adapts to this and says religious faith cannot be "absolute" even among the faithful.) All ideas (isms) become non-descript and indistinct. If I like it, it's good; if I don't, it's not good. One religion is like another, one ideology is like another, one perspective is like another: None having any distinct concepts or connections to our real society and life. Scholars play with "postmodernism," "deconstruction," or "political correctness," and so on, strengthening our relativist tendency in Mental Trash. This "relativism" leaves all things equally insignificant (such as race, religion, national origin, gender), except the existing system of power, economics, and Mental-Trash consumption, and the *hierarchy* it creates and maintains. Everything is like everything else, except Consumer Capitalism and Mental-Trash which are held as absolute for their dominant functions in the U.S. (In some ways, the Trump Phenomenon may be thought of as a White Revolt against this relativizing correctness in America. But, Whites by and large are victims of Consumer Capitalism and its relativism more than they are Rebels against the System.) In the absence of distinctions and definitions that set ideas apart from one another and clear as ideas, the only factor that matters is the *self* at the moment: All things center on "me" "right here" "right now" and "what I feel" Language becomes corrupted and thoughts become unclear in *relativist* perspective, and therefore the masses remain inevitably captives of the Present System and its Power Relations. Mental Trash naturally tends to encourage relativistic thinking in the absence of any stable ideas and systems in the person's thinking patterns where everything has merit and nothing stands out. That leaves, in a very dangerous way, the *status quo,* the System (unconsciously) and Myself (consciously), as the legitimate authority. Nothing else is significant enough.

II.

The effect of Mental Trash can be more personally recognized when we see what has happened to the place called the "living room." The living room in an average American household used to be a place where the family actually gathered and *lived* as a small community. It is now a place where we go to die, as our "dying room." With all the media equipment ready to entertain us, with all sorts of digital machines and programs, that's where we *are entertained to death.* We stagger into our formerly Living Room now *to die*: We turn on our daily Mental Trash with clicks of the mouse and remote control, and wade through the maze of amusement moments, interesting nothings, dead to the world. In utter irony, the *dying room* is where we "come alive" as zombies and consumers as if nothing else exists except our moments of comatose self-absorption, busily processing Mental Trash, trash in and trash out, trash in and trash out, click, click, click, flicker, flicker, flicker. . . . It is *oblivion* that passes for *living* in America.

Our current digital industry represents humanity's first non-material society and its first non-material era, where everything created is everything to be destroyed at the same time it is created. The Digital Industry may be described as a Dr. Frankenstein constantly creating new life which he must destroy as soon as he has created it. For the ordinary consuming citizen, this is experienced as his daily "Mental-Trash Processing." It is a peculiar situation that faces us in the Digital Era: On the one hand, we live as biological creatures, eating, mating, defecating in our physical routines; on the other, we play with mental waste which does not exist in any material reality; in the latter, we don't eat, we play only with images and senses, and we don't defecate anything as we don't eat anything. In the latter world, we just process one image after another, creating and destroying at a dizzying speed.

The time span between creation and destruction is becoming ever shorter in the industry and, especially, in each individual consumer. In fact, a few seconds may be all the attention the consumer is willing to give any digital creation that happens to cross the consumer's consciousness. For the propaganda machines of society, this is the precious few moments of consciousness in the consumer's mind that are open to their manipulation. The propaganda machine must go all out to capture the attention of the consumer as the moment is likely to flicker away at the next click of the consumer.

Knowing this, the opinion-leaders, "spin doctors," advertisers in all fields—politics, religion, education, entertainment, government, corporations—attempt to get into the consumer mental-waste processing in fierce competition for the short attention span there is. It is a war of propaganda in the fiercest, and a battle of human ingenuity at its most creative. But, for the consumer, it is a moment of the greatest peril to his sanity; and for his society, it begins an Era of Mind-Control such as it has never witnessed before, for the mind that daily processes trash is a trashed mind.

Naturally, in the Digital Era of Mental Trash, virtually all attention-getting objects in America end up being fraudulent schemes, untruths and plots for the Human Mental-Trash Receptacles: They must be quick, pleasing and without substance, to fit the empty receptacle of the American Mind that is always in the process of emptying itself. Under the circumstances, it can do no other.

To Humanity at large, Mental Trash represents hope forever unrealized, and perfect entertainment never found: So we continue our search in vain through more and more mental waste.

The mechanism by which the Digital Technology exists is perfectly fit for the Common Masses in America: It is easy to produce and distribute a massive quantity of objects that have neither shape nor meaning, perfect for the post-Industrial Americans who, in their solitary but affluent existence, crave to be *mentally* amused every moment. Mental Trash is there, with Consumer Capitalism eagerly responding to popular hunger for perpetual amusement, producing and supplying this inexhaustible new opioid in the fullest technological capacity that came with the Digital Revolution.

Mental Trash has reached its *absolute peak*, a routine state, in our Digital Era. The very nature of digital technology makes *permanence* impossible to maintain. In its mature stage, which we are approaching fast, *all things* are produced and exist only for a *moment's life* in Digital Form, with or without Snapchat. Images are produced in Digital Life only *to vanish as fast as they are produced and consumed,* and the Mental Trash Processing becomes a daily routine in America for its citizens who function as the industry's Mental-Trash Cans.

III.

In our Digital Era, what began in tiny bits in Humanity's early life now settles as our dominant consumption of daily energy and resources. With its dramatic dominance of our daily life with one another, now increasingly substituted by our moment's interest and amusement, our personal life becomes more *privatized* and our *society* further removed from our daily private consciousness. Although the digital network is world-wide and global, the very practice is solitary and unconnected, where it begins and ends in the private. When turned on, one enters the digital world privately; when turned off, one simply exits privately. Since it is not physically connected to anything, a person's entry and exist have no meaning to anyone else. So, by its nature, Digital Connection is a mirage that exists only in our imagination and as electronic impulses.

How much of our electronic impulses are produced and wasted without being actually seen or retained by a human being? If all the human beings on earth wrote letters of varying lengths all the time, to no one in particular, how many of those letters would get actually read by someone? Now, multiply the number of such letters by a million times, and you get the magnitude of Mental Trash. We can only guess. Continuing our guess, in Digital Mental Trash, the ratio of What is produced to What is actually consumed is perhaps *one million to one:* One Million produced and just One actually used by someone. The *ratio* of What is consumed and What is *retained* in the permanent system of human memory is perhaps *one billion to one*: In essence, Digital Mental Trash inevitably represents a vast, cosmic amount of *wasted* human resources in energy and creativity: In this mode of production and consumption in America's mental waste industry, destroying what goes unconsumed is a very large daily *industrial* process in itself. Virtually all *productive life* in America today is destined to be identical to *trashed life*, to vanish into the vast *emptiness* of Mental Trash processing. Producing and trashing, producing and trashing, is America's perpetual cycle of life and existence. This is the new American Way of Life: We live to *produce* trash, work to *consume* trash, compete to *throw away* more trash than others, and die on the heap of *unconsumed* trash, all this as an unending life cycle for all men, women and children. In this race, White Americans are head and shoulder above all others, and the world has envied them precisely for that reason.

Many White Americans have mentioned "anxiety" when interviewed by reporters who want to get a handle on what makes the Whites tick as Trump supporters. The anxiety they feel is quite contrary to their living reality which is relatively affluent, comfortable, and full of fantasy. But the feeling of anxiety persistently gnaws at them from within and on the subconscious level of life. Could this anxiety be accounted for by the large role of Mental Trash in their lives? Mental Trash comes from their entertainment and together it represents something quite shapeless and phantom-like. You can click on any image you want on your TV screen and computer screen, and click it off anytime you lose interest. But, this great power you demonstrate does not make you feel solid about your real power. As you control your digital world, which is meaningless and empty, with the mouse and the remote, you control nothing else in life. Surely, this self-contradiction must gnaw at you when you turn your Mental Trash off, and even when it is on at your command. Everything in Mental Trash is so. . . nothing, nothing but a flicker that is nothing but an electronic impulse. It comes and goes so fast and leaves nothing lingering that you might as well say it never existed. This is enough to keep you in permanent state of anxiety. The saying used to be, to describe an extremely ephemeral phenomenon, "here today, gone tomorrow." Mental Trash has become faster than that: It is now, *"here now, gone now."*

Why are the White Masses in Consumer Capitalism in the U.S. so prone to the Mental Trash affliction? The simplest and most-accurate answer is: The *absence of "society."* All of society's main function is to protect its citizens from all enemies, mental and physical. For the reasons of history and accident, the U.S. is not a "real" society and it never has been. At best, it has been called "the Nation of Strangers." All societies and nations have a "tribal" beginning that holds and unites the group together through its history and, if their survival is successful, marches into the modern world as a society and a nation. The U.S. does not have this origin: In fact, the closest thing which the U.S. resembles is a *country club* where people voluntarily become its members because they agree with its stated purpose (equality in freedom) and benefits (being *actually* equal in freedom). If this qualification were universally applied, it is doubtful how many present-day nations would qualify enough to have citizens at all.

By the quirks of frontier history, American society was created as an extension of "nature," a nation of "strangers," where it is everyman for himself. But, because of the freely-available *open land* (equivalent to money being equally available to all today) in the Golden Age of 19TH century America, a fortuitous phenomenon never seen before or since, this everyman-for-himself did *not* create a war-of-all-against-all "state of nature" in the New World. In it, while free and open, *equality in freedom (*or freedom in equality) prevailed because one's freedom to swing his arm rarely touched anyone close by. The U.S. was truly an "exception" where people did not *need a society* to protect themselves: With equality in freedom, both in land and in guns, they could protect themselves from each other. Although this system came to an end and a new System of Capital replaced the no-society frontier democracy and took its individual freedom away, and even through two World Wars and a great economic depression, the idea that people should take care of themselves held as an unwritten American lore.

In this vacuum of *society*, the Capitalists moved in, now bearing a gift called Mental Trash in their grand carnival named Consumer Capitalism, selling happiness and fulfillment. Its corporate mantra is "Give them what they want!" in response to the consumer mantra, "Give us what we want!" Against the nation's *best and brightest* working full steam for Consumer Capitalism, Mental Trash has thrived as never before. With neither the Government nor other Institutions offering to counterbalance the assault from the Mental Trash, the target masses in America are intellectually and humanly annihilated by the onslaught. In the combined assault from Capitalism, Selfish Nature, and Consumerism, White Americans have stood wholly unprotected for decades now, either by their community or by their own cumulated wisdom, trapped in their new role as the Mental Trash Can.

IV.

Why is the Internet so popular as to be the New Opium of our era as the medium through which we encounter and process mental waste? What makes it so addictive as to change our whole personality, character, and brain habits? Nicholas Carr, and many others, have noticed the changes in our thinking habits as we become addicted to the Internet and other things the computer does: We are not able to focus, especially concerning reading books, and concentration becomes more and more difficult, eventually becoming outright impossible. That much is well known and accepted as true.

Two questions are central to us: One, what makes the Internet (and other things that the computer does for us) so *addictive*, accounting for its popularity? Two, why is this addiction so *dangerous* to our mental health and well-being?

Answer to the first one: Its addictiveness comes from the *speed* with which it delivers what we want. Human survival requires many things: Food, knowledge, and war-making abilities, among other things. As our survival depends on food, knowledge, and war-making, in various orders, the speed in which these requirements are found, satisfied and obtained determines our survival or extinction, both individually and together. By nature, these requirements take time to materialize for us. Also by nature, we want them as fast as possible, and the faster, the better. For the lower social class, it is slower and takes longer.

Thus, the most distinct advantage of being *upper class* is the speed with which you get what you want: The higher your status or power, the faster you get what you want. While everyone goes through the customs and baggage checks at airport, the likes of Bill Gates or the Secretary of State never go through the lines and long waits. While you go around looking for a parking space at a military base, generals and colonels have their reserved special spaces. Everything is instant for them: For them, when they want it and when they get it is almost *simultaneous,* which means needs and satisfaction are together at the (almost) same time. This is the dream life of the Common People. In fact, the better than simultaneous is "anticipated," your satisfaction of needs being there waiting for you even *before* you expressed it. Good butlers and servants always anticipate their Masters' desires ahead of their materialization.

The Common Masses in America now have *their own* speedy satisfactions, in junk-food, in quick sex encounters, in drug-induced highs, and, now in our digital era, *the Internet* whose speedy delivery is its magic wand, or butlers and servants. For the commoners, the Internet delivers the upper-class privilege of *getting what they want when they want it.* It is so exhilarating that with the Internet, it is like being God on the Computer. The whole computer and Internet Industry's progress since its inception can be summed simply in *speed*: It has been getting *faster and faster* and the Commoners have become like upper-class and God in their thrill and magic power.

Critics like Carr now tell us that this new habit-forming Internet addiction creates behavior changes in us that resemble the symptoms of autism, unable to concentrate or connect to society. This leads us to the Second Question: Why is this addiction *so dangerous* to our health and wellbeing? If we all become like people with autism, what's wrong with that development?

After all, when *all* develop similar symptoms, then the symptoms will become normal behavior. When all are autistic, only the non-autistic normal people will become *abnormal*. When the whole society is made up of idiots and morons and imbeciles as a result of Internet addiction, then we all become *normal* idiots, morons and imbeciles: All your neighbors would be idiots, all your friends morons, and all your coworkers imbeciles, just like yourself. No issue there.

But there *is* an issue here with internet addiction: *Not all are internet-addicted.* Those who cause our internet-addiction are *themselves not Internet-Addicted.* Like drug dealers, they only *cause* our addiction, but stay *free* from it themselves. It is highly unlikely that Bill Gates, one of the culprits of our Internet-addiction, say, as an "enabler," *is* Internet-addicted himself; it is equally unlikely that he even spends that much time on the Internet, not any more than drug dealers being on drugs themselves.

It is highly unlikely that those who own Internet Servers are actually sitting in front of the computer and use their own Internet connections. (In fact, it is reported that the children of high computer gurus are sent to schools that forbid computer use. Nor are they permitted even moderate use of computers at home. It makes perfect sense: Why would they want to addict their own children to the Internet? On the email issues that dogged Hillary Clinton during the presidential election, the FBI's verdict was that she was "computer ignorant." But this digital ignorance, fatal for most working Americans, would hardly affect someone like her who can hire people to do all her digital work.). It is highly unlikely that the rich owners of McDonald's stock *eat* at McDonald's or that Coca Cola executives *drink* their own beverage. It is highly unlikely that the rich executives or stock owners at RJ Reynolds *smoke* the cigarettes, stuffed with enforcement chemicals, they sell to us. Just like the worker at a water-polluting corporation in the film *Erin Brokovich,* who refused to drink the water that her company had polluted, those who sell us the stuff do not consume what they sell to us, much less get *addicted* to it. They only addict *us*, the Commoners and Consumers of their products, but they themselves never touch their own stuff.

So the danger of internet-addiction is not that we all become addicts in America: It is that those who *cause* and *supply* the addiction stay sober, free of the addictive powers. They just make *us*, the dumb masses of America, addicts. Every day, Bill Gates and others like him devote their whole time and energy to make us, who are already Internet-crazy, *internet-crazier*: The secret is to make all of us Internet-crazy *without being* Internet-crazy *themselves*. Their model is the Drug Dealers who sell drugs to others but they themselves almost never take the drugs they sell.

What happens to us now, the Internet addicts and speed dependents? Like all addicts, we must *do* anything our addiction-suppliers command us to do to keep our addiction going: We become sitting ducks for their manipulation and control. This is where our *Mental Trash* begins and ends, and the fate of America hangs on the clicks of the Internet.

V.

Thus conceived in corporate profiteering and prospered in human yearnings for perpetual amusement, what began as an advanced but simple mechanism of exchanging information between institutions has now been transformed into a cesspool of corruption and depravity never before seen in history. What we now see on the Internet is virtually every conceivable product of human imagination that requires the highest order of ingenuity and creativity, just to be able to attract and hold someone's attention for a few precarious seconds. In the few seconds that are precariously open to persuasion, the Devil must make his pitch, to sell, sell and sell: Every human being on earth--from the Pope to the lowest of the Commoners who has access to this ubiquitous mechanism—feeds from this mental trough called the Internet.

Of course, the Internet is also the source of knowledge which is stored in great quantities on its simplified system. But its role as the source of knowledge varies for each nation. In most places where the Internet is allowed to prosper, the citizens' knowledge is supplemented by other channels of society, such as their collective history, tradition, folklore, class or religion or even government. It is rare that a society in the Old World relies exclusively on the Internet for its social wisdom and facts. In countries like Poland and Japan where Internet usage is fairly active, users are still burdened by their collective mores that remain strongly embedded in their everyday life, conscious and subconscious, which moderates their Internet use. However, it is practically the only source of wisdom and facts in America, especially with the emerging generations among Whites with no other social channels for their wisdom, facts and even manners. They are well versed in cliches, buzzwords, hashtags, and other idioms of the Internet but likely never heard of proverbs from their parents, like "one stitch in time saves nine" or other similar sayings as shortcuts to wisdom teaching. The digital Americans are perhaps the most savagely self-absorbed and socially-unconnected generation since the Romans at the Coliseum who select only those things their senses demand: Quick, easy and amusing, and naturally the basest of human passions and desires.

To illustrate this point of how base our Internet degeneration has become, here is Chauncey Devega, writing for *Salon*, reminding us of the "basest instincts" of Donald Trump as a presidential candidate: "During the Republican primaries, Donald Trump talked about the size of his penis, suggested that Marco Rubio urinated on himself during a debate, made allusions to menstruation, and implied that Mitt Romney would perform fellatio on him if so demanded." Now, no presidential candidate would ever behave this way unless he was gunning for the Internet generation's votes. It is virtually impossible to insult any American steeped in TV or Internet culture with debasing comments on the blogs. (On the other hand, a few actors and actresses committed suicide over the nasty blogs on the Internet in South Korea, a very digital-savvy society.) Trump played to their basest instincts and won; Clinton appealed to their best community instincts and lost.

The Internet, with its anonymity, is the most unvarnished display of humanity at its most naked self revelation. Almost exclusively as a forum for the common masses, the Internet is the haven of the anonymous crowds who come to reveal their most basic, primeval and private character without a hint of consciousness or shame. Like graffiti on the wall of a public restroom, you can leave all your pent-up anger or Jekyllian secrets on the electronic anonymity of the moment and exit. No social structure, no hierarchical ranking, no economic class matters in this land that's everywhere but does not really exist as a physical place. There everyone has a space and time to announce his existence and intentions to the world which is largely indifferent to both his existence and his announcement. It is the ultimate atomization of humanity in a post-industrial era, each with a name and password to unlock his kingdom granted by the new masters for a fee. In the crowded anonymity of the Internet, each nobody is allowed to be somebody of his imagination, and speak his mind to be nullified instantly by other minds who crowd the same place that ever expands into more emptiness to accommodate so much expanding nothingness.

The Internet is the microcosm of Humanity in Dante's Inferno, everybody trying to gain something from somebody else, lying, cheating, and screaming to get somebody else's attention to add a few more pennies to his account or to add a few more laughs to his daily share of fun and amusement. Until the emergence of the Internet, selling and buying were limited to the structure of physics governed by physical time and space. People went to the marketplace nearby, even a mall, to find what he wanted to buy. The merchants displayed their wares to the buyers nearby. The exchange was face to face and person to person in this physical world of trade, dominated by human needs and physical proximity.

The Internet has nullified this time and space concept of life by making it present everywhere and all the time. On every page of the Internet screen is the marketplace of perverse imagination, every human being crowding into the place to carve out his little presence. Politicians solicit votes here. Religious preach their Gods here. Philosophers of every stripe offer their thoughts here. Professors profess their knowledge here. Lonely hearts advertise themselves for love here. Merchants sell their wares, mostly immaterial, here. People with the lowest intellect can register themselves here with a name and password with equal aplomb. It is at once chaotic, bracing and hellish. If Hell is defined as a place of lost humanity, lacking even a smallest bit of human character, everyone shouting and snarling and gnashing the teeth, the Internet is just a perfect Hell on Earth. It is the most revolting, revealing representative of Humanity's self-depiction as greedy, selfish, deceptive beasts in the state of nature. This typical Internet devotee is the New Lord of the Internet Universe and of the Rings and of the Flies under whose fingertips a whole New World of Possibilities magically opens up, albeit only in his own Fantasy and Imagination. It is in the Internet World that, like the lounge in the Star Wars scenes where strange and grotesque characters congregate, the prevailing characters in Consumer Capitalism in America--like the Millennials, the Dumbest Generation, and the Trump-supporting Whites—congregate. It forms the microcosmic picture of a society at a certain historical and sociological stage of development for us to observe and describe.

Chapter Fourteen

The Lost Mind

After decades of Mental Trash and fantasy life in America, a great gift from Corporate America and White acquiescence, bills pile up on American Society. One of the most hopeless, disturbing and even frightening prospects for America is that Americans, especially White Americans, *cannot wake up or be taught about themselves or their society:* Americans have lost their minds. Mental Trash is so deeply engrained as America's intellectual and moral habits that the "American Mind" cannot realize what it has become—the Lost Mind—and the mind that is lost cannot recover itself. The so-called Millennials, the first computer-created generation, are the newest addition to the Lost Mind.

There used to be an advertisement about the importance of education that said, "A Mind is a Terrible Thing to Waste." But what *is* this thing called a 'Mind'? How do we *know* somebody has one or has wasted one? Of all the things, the Mind is perhaps the most difficult subject to discuss in America, simply because it is in America that we see a complete Destruction of the Human Mind that is unaware of its own destruction. You need a mind to discuss the mind. How can you discuss the mind where there is none with which to discuss it?

But, let us try by simplifying the answer in these two ways that involve our mind, *calculating* and *thinking*: If you are *calculating* as to what's best for you, just your self-interest, you are faced with certain options from you select your greatest value. Animals and insects, in common with businessmen and military planners, do this all the time as their main function. It is a technical and mechanical, but not human, process, like finding the quickest way to go from A to B, something you can relegate to a computer or a professional advisor. If you are deficient in this ability, you are deemed *ignorant.* In calculating cases, the decision is already imbedded in the options that you face, such as the route between A and B, profit calculus or military outcomes, not subject to your human decision-making.

If you are *thinking* as a "human being," you decisions involve other human beings, and the decisions you make take other human beings into consideration. Your thinking as a human being is, after all, a *moral* decision regarding "other people." You are making decisions because of them, for them, and about them—utilizing all the wisdom and ironic knowledge available--and this process is what we take as proof that your mind exists and you are making decisions through your mind and you are a thinking person. If you are deficient in this ability, and you are likely to have become a supporter of someone like Donald Trump, you are deemed *stupid* (although few would say this in your face), lacking in wisdom and irony.

In American society where the self is at the center of all decision-making, it is through calculating (for myself) that we arrive at most of what we decide, not thinking, which involves others (the opposite of the self). In America's system of Mental Trash consumption (choosing what we want), which puts the premium on self-interest, it is difficult, almost impossible, to think about other people in our decision-making.

It is perhaps only in America that we can live without other people and without our minds operating in our living process: American society requires, unlike anywhere else in the world, *no mind* from the members of society. Unthinking people are good for economic consumption and political salesmanship: They make good workers, consumers and voters. (Why would they play the "elevator music" in public places or plaster pleasant-but-meaningless paintings on public spaces? Basically to distract us. Distract us from what? From *thinking*.) Thus, when the person only calculates, and is unable to *think* with "other people" as the basis of his thinking, we conclude that the person, or his Social System, has wasted the mind, as it is a lost mind.

Now, here comes the difficult part of discussing the Mind in America: A mind that is already "wasted" is *not* a terrible thing because it is no longer a Mind, perhaps it is something similar to the response of Pavlov's dogs that respond to their conditioned stimulus. The advertisement about the wasted mind being a terrible thing was self-contradictory because, like a prevented suicide, a mind that is wasted doesn't know it is a wasted mind and is happy about its wasted state. Human beings do not waste their minds for nothing: To waste it, something *really good* must be offered to the mind-loser, like Faust making a pact with the Devil, in exchange for his mind to be wasted in return. For every lost mind, there is a good cause for the loss. Mental Trash is the good deal for most White people who exchanged their minds for it.

Anyone who wishes or hopes for a radical change in America, into whatever form, would have to overcome the two great barricades that the System of Capital has put up to protect itself. Why? One, Americans by and large *like* their consumer society and what they *consume in it*; they just want *more* of it. Two, Americans by and large *accept* their governing structure and its system as *legitimate and lawful*; they just want the government to work for *them*, not the others.

This observation seems to fly in the face of what we just witnessed in the 2016 political process, primaries and general elections, where Bernie Sanders and Donald Trump stood out as something new in America's politics: Sanders wanted Socialism and Trump wanted Fascism. Both are quite un-American in that they are outside the normal expectations of American politics, which is a combination of Liberalism and Capitalism into Neo-Liberal-Capitalism. Sanders caused quite a stir in the Democratic primaries; Trump did more than that, as he won the whole thing. The reader might ask: Are their movements not a sign, a very clear one more for Trump than Sanders, that they wanted a revolution against the existing American System?

Didn't Donald Trump's Fascism win over Corporate Capitalism (oddly represented by Hillary Clinton) with his radical revolt?

We can look at Bernie Sanders as a revolution against Capitalism if we consider raising Minimum Wage as a sign of defeating Capitalism, which it isn't. After all, Minimum Wage, however higher it goes, is still part of what Capitalism allows. Even if the Minimum Wage goes to a 100 dollars an hour, the difference would have to come from consumers, not the super-rich One Percent. Unless the One Percent becomes Minimum Wage earners, it is no revolution.

What Donald Trump accomplished is certainly more dramatic than Sanders' achievement, but the essence is the same. Because of the Trump shock and drama, thus appearing more persuasively revolutionary, it just takes a little more thinking to understand the true nature of Trump's win. Again, it's a lot more pomp and circumstance in Trump's win than substance, and we shall proceed with our thinking below. In short, Trump's victory formalized America's nationalist and racist heart, hitherto hidden under the Liberal-Capitalist cloak, now declared all over the world as America's open creed. Before Trump, America was somewhat aware of its historic legacy and tried to avoid outright shameful acts. After Trump, America is just shameless about its nationalist-racist intentions. With Trump, the U.S. has fallen into the open sewer and it is anybody's guess whether it will ever be able to smell good, and, more importantly, whether it will ever be *clean* again.

II.

One of the most common side-effects of Mental Trash is that it gives the ruled (White) masses a sense that they share in the power of governance, a feeling that they are ruling themselves. Often words like "democracy," "freedom of choice," "consumer preference" and other similar concepts are used to entice them into this type of what is essentially "imitation power." This imitation power, most effectively used in Mental Trash consumption as a method of the ruling class, is just now reaching its pinnacle among the consumers in the form of technological gadgetry and mass entertainment—notably in TV, computers, and smart-phones, all part of Mental Trash. These instruments increase the sense of personalized power for the consumer, all falsely and in imitation. Yet, at the same time that the masses get deeper into the lure and addictiveness of these media, they also increase their dependence on those that supply them with regularity and dependability: That is, the corporations that control them and the best and brightest that work as technicians for Corporate America that owns both *machines and people.*

It is not that the great masses of Americans are under the effective control of their corporate overlords, which has been a fact of life for nearly a century in America, that amazes those who observe. It is that, for the first time in the development of America as a nation, the masses of people--the proverbial White Masses who are most susceptible to this--are losing, or have already lost, their ability to live with their basic humanity and intelligence in this life of illusion. What they are beyond retrieving, perhaps, is their emotional and *ironic* ability to recognize their utter dependency on and addiction to the daily and hourly consumption of trivia after trivia, empty thrill after empty thrill, artificial laugh after laugh, that are recycled and resupplied all day, all year round. Slowly, their soul is being sapped into the corporate Mental Trash dump where it is transformed into profit accounts and controlling powers.

Ordinary White people who use these gadgets naturally think they own and control the TV, computers, and smartphones in their ready functions. What they do not realize is that they only own the metal-and-plastic frame of the machine, an empty shell, like an automobile without its engine and fuel. The real control belongs elsewhere. The metal-and-plastic "thing" is nothing without its *content,* like Frankenstein's corpse that has not been given its life. It is the content that makes TV a TV, a computer a computer, and a smart phone smart, and this content is (surprise) all controlled by the Corporations. The supremacy of the content, as opposed to the empty metal-and-plastic chunk, is easily demonstrated by the fact that the hardware is offered often free of charge as long the customer agrees to pay for the content.

Life in America today cannot be imagined without these gadgets, and the life of these gadgets cannot be imagined without their content. And, therefore, life in America today cannot be imagined without their life-saving dependence on the corporate suppliers of their daily content. All else is mere façade. Some day people may have to recite the "Lord's Prayer" that thanks Him for "our daily content" for our Mental Trash. The content is not just what makes the gadgets functional: It is also the content that fills our brains, shapes our minds, and tugs at our heart-strings. In short, what the corporations in America insert into our machines is what is being inserted into our brains, hearts and minds. It is everything we are. Not a click, not a tap, not a push, can be carried out on these machines without corporate permission and, more critically, without corporate intention. The White Masses in America, with or without Donald Trump in the White House, cannot live without it, and without corporate control over its inner life as well as its outer shell. And in this perspective, it is easy enough for us to realize that Trump's win was not a revolution, perhaps a great splash, but not a tsunami.

Just so that we know how our daily lifeline and our social-spiritual umbilical cord are all tied to Consumer Capitalism's supplier of our needs, just imagine the gun in the 19th century American West. Historians mention two factors that explain the political freedom and economic equality that prevailed in the hundred years or so following 1776: Open land and personal security. Open land gave every working man his reason for working hard and feeling secure with what he owned. The gun gave the Common Man his equality with everyone. Even an escaped slave was a free man if he had a gun. As the saying went, God did not make men equal: It was Colonel Colt, the inventor of the six-shooter, who did.

Now, to comprehend the corporate control of our daily lives with what fills our machines, do a little mental exercise in imagination: Imagine yourself being the Common Man with his gun in the 19th century, but *without the bullets*. Your personal security and freedom, your whole life, depend on the gun. Imagine that the *bullets* are tightly controlled by the corporate supplier, and cannot be obtained without a contract signed and payment made in perpetuity. Like your computer or cell-phone without its content, a gun without its bullets is nothing but a clump of metal in a certain shape. If the bullets being withheld were true--and thank God it was not in frontier life--those who controlled the bullets would have controlled America completely, as they do now with their content that fills our daily lives. This truly puts the Donald Trump Phenomenon in perspective. Surely, like a gun empty of its bullets still rustles up fear, all the sabre rattling at the White House by the nationalist and racist Cabinet and agencies could and would rattle up great fear especially among the Lesser Americans. But the bullets are held tightly by Corporate America.

Now, back to our time, we have our daily content, and we click, tap and push our gadgets, thanks to the payment we must religiously make. As these machines respond to our clicks, taps and pushes, we think they respond to *our command* as their Master and God. If the machines could laugh in irony, they would indeed laugh out loud. For they respond to their real Masters and Gods, not the imitation ones, who make the payment for the privilege of *acting* like their Masters and Gods. As long as our last payment to our Real Master and Real God is still good, the machines are commanded to respond to our clicks, taps and pushes. If only we could hear the machine's laughter.

III.

The generation most susceptible to Corporate America's mind control through Mental Trash is made up of the so-called "Millennials," a group that ranges from 18 to 40-something. They first emerged merely as the individual consumers of new technology, and then are now poised to become a significant part of America's future majority as the *avant- garde* of the White Masses. They are the full first-generation victims of Corporate America that is armed with the new technology of mind control.

Sometimes indistinguishable from, and certainly overlapping with, the "Dumbest Generation," the Millennials are simply the first fully-digitalized group that has come of age in our Computer Era. The Millennials are the emerging generation of digitally-conditioned Americans who represent the most advanced form of Corporate Americans, not surprisingly mostly White. They are the second of the two bookends that span the entire American history beginning in 1776. In this perspective, the Millennials are also the product of Corporate America's latest triumph in creating the most-controlled mind in American society to date.

As their group characteristics, the Millennials are perhaps the most self-absorbed generation in American (and by extension, Western) history since the citizens of Rome in their declining days. Instead of the Circus Maximus, Millennials have the Digital Maximus. Instead of the Coliseum, Millennials have the Social Media. Fine tuned to the here-and-now philosophy of the age, always on and connected to themselves and going nowhere, they are indifferent to anything political, public or historical: The modern-day "know-nothings," as a writer put it. Minute by minute, moment by moment, mood by mood, they feed on each other and are in turn fed by each other within their cohorts. Grown up with Wikipedia, Google and social media, they define their world and existence primarily within the flicks of the digital. They may show an interest, if their spirit moves, in some vaguely-conceived "civic" activities, such as demanding transparency from their municipal government or from their local businesses or volunteering for neighborhood events. But these flickers of interest are not collective or ideological, neither Jeffersonian nor Capitalist, in that they arise and fade on the whims of the moment or personal curiosity, largely unconnected to history or ideology, and therefore not sustainable as a movement. WikiLeaks, for example, perhaps the most "radical" of the Millennial byproducts, is essentially a site of sensationalism, soon to be forgotten, and never leads to any political-public action as a result. As one study on Millennnials concludes, they are "opting out" of their social reality.

In essence, Millennials are in perpetual pursuit of Narcissistic self-adulation, either in their own self-image or from each other. To them, the necessary distinction between knowledge and ignorance is relative and therefore meaningless, as is that between truth and falsehood, between past and future. They only recognize the distinction between "fun" and "not fun" or that between "interesting" and "not interesting." Thus, they are almost wholly dictated by the worst traits of contemporary culture: Personal whims and privatized moods.

Resembling the Hemingway-esque Lost Generation, described as "disoriented, wandering, directionless" (now "nameless" and "dumb") the Millennials are fast opting out of America digitally. Now threatening to become America's majority as fast the speed of digital spread, they are poised to become the New Puppets of Corporate America and its Consumer Technology, ushering in a host of new, some unthinkable, possibilities that are as ominous as they are unnerving. (Consensus is that Trump and Clinton split the Millennial vote, in itself an accomplishment for Trump). Looming as America's Digital Majority, what the Millennials could do, or not do, once they are fully integrated with the lost-minded White Majority, is mind-boggling as well.

IV.

The minds that are lost are also the minds that are crazy. As Americans have gone intellectually mindless, they have also gone psychologically insane. The price of Mental Trash is great and varied, but one of the greatest is the extent of the "crazy-ness" as the American Way of Life. Ever since the whole German nation went out of its mind for Hitler, no nation has ever seen so many "crazy" people among its population, affected variously by the madness-creating Mental Trash day after day, as in the U.S. today. To put in the simplest way possible, it is the death toll that we as a whole pay for the culture of Mental Trash. We are so crazy in America, according to the medication-taking statistics, that it is often said that a medium-sized city in America has more psychiatrists, the managers of our crazy society, than all of the nation of Japan. No other society uses psychological terms like "bipolarity" or "PTSD" as casually as if they are names for their pet dogs.

The size and the variety of the so-called "mental health" professionals in the U.S. are huge, and they are multiplying as the fastest growing profession in America. Just look at the list of those in the "mental-health" category who deal with "crazy" Americans: Aside from the traditional psychiatrists and psychoanalysts and psychologists and the specialties within each branch, therapists of all kinds flourish: Psychiatric nurses, clinical psychologists, clinical social workers, mental health counselors, psychiatric rehabilitation counselors, school psychologists, psychotherapists, occupational therapists, behavior analysts, substance abuse and behavioral disorders educators, psychiatric and mental health nurse practitioners, ADHD specialists, child psychologists, motivational speakers, etc., etc., etc.

Why are there so many "mental problems" that require help from so many "mental health" professionals? Why are there so many insane Americans, along with so many dumb Americans, in our midst? What in American life creates such *needs* for mind-adjustment? Why is our *mind* in such turmoil all the time and in so many ways? Is the vaunted "White anger" that elected Donald Trump part of this mental deterioration in America? Can Americans, White and non-white, really withstand Mental Trash pumped into their heads day and night and maintain their sanity?

In America today, virtually all of us face two very contradictory parts of life: One in which we dream and play, and the other in which we face reality and live. The first part, the "American Dream" for every American is to enjoy life, but to enjoy life we need to get what we want. To get what we want and enjoy life with it, we need *power over other people* so that we can get what we want (while others *cannot,* and their *inability* to get what *they* want makes *our* ability to get what *we* want possible). In America's own idea for fulfillment, no power, no fun.

The problem (and we can already see why we go crazy) is that, no matter how hard we try, the 99-percent of us, even the White Masses, would be in the position of the "cannot" crowd: Hence the 99-percent of Americans would need a lot of mental adjustment to reconcile with the fact that they are "failures."

This discrepancy between our Dream and Fantasy (which is to be part of the One-Percent with unlimited power and pleasure) and our Reality (which is to end up being part of the 99-percent nobodies) would need one of the two solutions: One, change the System so that it is not necessary for anyone to fail; and two, unable to do the first, make a "mental" adjustment with the help of the mental-health professionals. Mental Trash is a handy tool, along with "soma," the drug to pacify the mind, both real and in fiction, to work out the Second Solution.

The second solution for the Masses is quite cheap and abundant, as it is found in the around-the-clock supply of entertainment from Hollywood, Disneyland, Madison Avenue advertised Fantasy, Cell-phone technology, and so on, which gives them make-believe sense of ("imitation") power. While this Opium-like solution works most of the time, for most of American consumers as long as they can work, draw wages, and pay for their consumption. But even the deepest-addicted consumers sometimes wake up from their addiction and fantasy.

The 99-percent of failed Americans cannot simply live on the fantasy of entertainment opioids all the time, however wonderful the supply is from Hollywood and Disney and Madison Avenue. We cannot just live on fantasy without breaking down once in a while from our supply of entertainment and its addictive hold on our minds. Trained on a life based on individual consumption from early on, Americans have never learned to get their bearings of life from one another as neighbors, as citizens, and simply as fellow human beings. Remember, America has always been a nation of strangers, and more so in a Mental-Trash era. Each of us must handle our own survival and its stress and strain, individually and alone. When this breakdown occurs, which is more often than we know (by the sheer size and variety of mind-controllers in professions), the "mental-health" professionals are there to help us heal and go back to our routine of entertainment drugs.

Life in America, hence its occupational structure, seems to be divided into two main sectors: Those who *supply insanity*, and those who *fix insanity*. One part of American society gives us our illnesses and the other part of American society gives us our medicine, thus making America a perfect dystopia that is perfectly self-contained and self-correcting.

Why are there so few such "mental-health" professionals in other societies (and in fact, *none* in the Amish Community)? The answer is simple as it is just commonsense, in reverse of what was mentioned as the cause of America's mental troubles: In societies outside the U.S., their life is not so separated between *fantasy and reality, or is forced to be lived alternating between them*. In short, they live in either complete fantasy (perhaps like the North Koreans) or complete reality (like the Amish), not shuffling daily *between the two* like Americans. It is doubtful that, as harsh as their life was, any of the slaves in the American South went insane with their slave's condition. On the other hand, if they were forced to live their slave's life and freeman's life alternately, or unpredictably between the two, they *would* have gone crazy.

It is only in America that we have the very unpleasant task of living like lords in our fantasy world of Mental Trash but having to work like slaves in our real world of harsh economics and power. In our fantasy life, we are told, "You can do anything you want!" In our real life, "You can't do anything! You have no money, no power!" We alternate between these two extremes everyday, but rarely looking at both in an Ironic Whole: When we play in fantasy, we don't think about the reality of work and powerlessness; when we work, we endure the humiliation and enslavement of employment by fantasizing our play-life at the end of shift. Now, shifting between the two extreme opposites, that's enough psychological basis for insanity in American Life.

Between the Suppliers of Insanity (Corporate America) and the Fixers of Insanity ("mental health" professionals), we manage to live through another day. Most of the time, the front-liners, armed with their great supply of entertainment drugs, do their job of holding America together; sometimes, perhaps often, the frontline breaks down and the rear-liners, armed with the Prozacs and therapy, heal the battle-weary and restore America's routines again. It is America's Great Capitalist War of Profit and Consumption: The frontline is held by the Suppliers of Insanity (or fantasy) and the rearline is held by the Fixers of Insanity (psychotherapy and counseling). With the two sectors cooperating efficiently and effectively, America's so-called "mental health" is held together and staggers forward toward its unknown tomorrow.

It is a tenuous thread by which we can hang onto life. There are so many soldiers returning from the War on Terror that suffer from the Post Traumatic Stress Disorder (PTSD). Journalist Sebastian Junger writes in *National Geographic* (Feb. 2017) that PTSD afflicts over 20 percent of the American military personnel, as opposed to less than one percent among the Israeli military with similar battlefield duties. No wonder, the soldiers are caught between the extreme fantasy-like lifestyle on the one hand, where everything is rosy and wonderful, and the extremely harsh conditions of battlefield reality on the other, where their life hangs in balance. This extreme contrast, and contradiction, that American society creates for them, would be confusing enough to make anyone crazy! (But, not to worry, PTSD has created a nice cottage industry among the Pentagon contractors who profit from offering therapy and treatment for the afflicted.)

V.

Thus made Insane and childish, the White Masses have naturally become quite good at navel-gazing and mood-sensing about themselves. At the same time, fewer and fewer Americans remember that *they live and die in a society, according to the society's design.* To prove this trend on college campuses, the field of *psychology* has become quite popular; at the same time, the field of *sociology* has declined. For every 10 Psychology courses offered in the college classroom, about 3 Sociology courses are offered. This has been the trend since the end of the Vietnam War. America has forgotten about American Society!

Large issues of society are sexy no more: It's the personal mood, feeling, and pain that occupy the front and center of our daily consciousness. In short, the U.S. has become a Nation of Psychos. What accounts for this change in the fortunes of Psychology and Sociology, concerns for mood or society, which in turn reflect the larger historical trend in American society itself?

In our popular concept, Psychology is about us, ourselves, how we feel at this moment, our personal and emotional needs, and what others are feeling at the moment and why, but all individually, personally and privately. To this frame of mind, the so-called "society" is nothing but a repository of "psyches," moods and their swings in greater numbers: Politics is about voters' mood; the economy is about consumers' mood; religion is our spiritual mood. All kinds of mood combinations and permutations are analyzed, described, and explained in America as our national pastime.

Sociology, on the other hand, is about society, not ourselves or our mood swings but our neighborhoods, community, society and humanity at large. It includes us in every minute detail of its existence, but we do not include the society in our detailed life experience. It is a one-way existence: It controls everything we do or are, but we know or care nothing about it. In reality, the society is the here-and-now presence of all things that we inherit from our past (called history), our place in society (called social class), and our relations with other Americans (called human interactions).

Thus, our collective history together, our political-economic Power or lack of it, and our Everyday relationships with one another, *always interacting as a dynamic process, is what makes up our society and our own existence,* every moment and always. Abraham Lincoln once said, "No one can escape the judgment of History," but we might as well say today, "No one can escape the judgment of Society." It is the judgment of Society that makes some of us rich and powerful, many of us poor and powerless, some of us famous, many of us obscure, some of us legitimate and some of us criminal, some of us happy and some of us miserable, some of us live and some of us die, some things right and some things wrong, good and evil, everything.

What our society does to us, for us, or against us, is absolute and final, as there is no power greater than the society's power itself: Just think about its Laws, its courts and prisons, its judges and verdicts, its police and law enforcement, its military and government agencies, its Weapons of Mass Destruction, of the mind and the body, its media and schools, its professors and specialists, its congress and lawyers, all in the service of controlling its citizens, namely, us.

The only time this whole machinery of society collapses and is destroyed is through revolution, as in 1776 in America or in 1789 in France. But such revolutionary changes are rare and are becoming rarer because of the increasing psychological capacity of the governments to wage propaganda and control their citizens' minds and moods. In general, society is there long before we are born and will be there long after we are gone: Our so-called "individual," "personal," "private" lives are in reality nothing but living out of what society has assigned to us.

When we become rich and powerful, we tend to think that's all our own effort; when we become poor and powerless, we likewise think it's all our fault. This way of thinking itself is Historical: Our frontier experience of open land and free-and-equal existence in the 19th-century conditioned us to think along these individual-personal-private habits about ourselves. But, the truth is that every penny that Bill Gates owns is recognized as "Bill Gates' Property" simply our society's laws and powers that be allow it to be "Bill Gates' Property." If you lost of your job, and if you really cared to track down the Causes of your job loss, you might find them in the society's laws and powers that be that allowed it to happen: Neither "You are fired" can be uttered nor a "pink slip" can be issued to a worker unless our society allows it to be uttered or issued to a worker. In short, it is the U.S. System itself, not Bill Gates the Individual himself that creates his wealth and power.

Even the very idea that we are "workers," have "jobs," and "get paid," and all sorts of things related to our lives and deaths, are simply the workings of our society upon us. Not even death helps us escape society, as we have to be registered as "deceased" and our remains as well as our property must be legally disposed of as we die. The business of *society is nothing less than deadly*. All the major Institutions of Society, such as the Law and the military, education and religion, politics and economics, and those minor ones, like marriage and the family, have one single purpose in mind: Maintaining and expanding power by controlling the masses, mind and body.

It is perhaps this reason, the reason of comprehension, that most Americans do not want to think about their society or anything that requires thinking. Thinking about oneself is easy, but thinking about the *whole society*, a bunch of people unrelated to you other than in the abstract sense of "nation" or "society," is not easy and most people don't bother to think.

The need to think is preceded by the feeling about a social issue, something larger than oneself or one's mood swings. For Average White Americans, this cannot happen: The feeling is all about oneself, Me and Myself, My Moods, not about America as a whole, as a Nation of shared interest: It's Psychological America, its most unfettered selfishness at its normal, routine, daily preoccupation. With the world's best supply of entertainment and amusement, around the clock everywhere, it is impossible to have feelings about large "public" issues above and beyond oneself and one's narrowly-defined self-interest.

Add to this the inherited individualism acquired when America was a farming country where the individual was free, equal and rugged. In today's Corporate America, we depend on paychecks and daily entertainment to sustain ourselves, a pitiful lot, lonely and scared, yet are divided and conquered (as shown in the Trump Phenomenon) as "Mood Individuals" as if we still control our own destiny.

All this shows how great a system America's Capitalism truly is, as it controls all things American, mind, soul and body, even though half of them are sick and crazy. Its control of America is so deep, its origins so embedded in human nature, and our daily lives so intertwined with its power, that it is unfathomable that we could ever live in a world without Capitalism.

Chapter Fifteen

Capitalism Triumphant

Since the beginning of the last century, the world has seen three Great Ideologies rise to power and fame, two of them having faded from history, one still riding the crest of its power and fame: They are, chronologically, Communism in Russia, Nazism in Germany, and Capitalism in America. Nazism was destroyed when the Third Reich lost WWII; Communism self-destructed when the weight of its own internal contradiction was too much for the system to bear. Capitalism alone, among the great ideas that have once dominated the hearts and minds of their followers, stands as the main belief-system of the United States atop the world without a rival to match its economic and military power.

Among the great ideas that claimed fame in the twentieth century, Capitalism in the U.S. is unique in the way it commands love and loyalty from virtually all of its citizens. Even in the heyday of their existence, both Nazis and Communists had underground dissidents and insurgents and those who openly disagreed with the state ideology. No such thing exists in America: Not a single voice is heard in public that openly opposes Capitalism or resists what it offers. (Bernie Sanders' movement was not against Capitalism, just for a greater share of America's wealth for the 99 percent.)

In Germany, being a believer of National Socialism, a "Nazi," was a strong and strange experience because it did not fit the self-image of most Germans. The rise of Nazism, (National Socialism) was the revolutionary growth of a small band of political radicals led by Adolf Hitler. Becoming a Nazi required a process of indoctrination and membership. Being a member of the "National Socialist Party" made the person stand above and apart from the ordinary German citizens, with distinct uniforms, gestures and symbols. The Nazi party, even during the peak of its power and successful military ventures, at home and abroad, stood as something of an anomaly in German society. While supporting and even dying for the Third Reich, ordinary Germans and the Nazi members never quite melded as one nation. The Nazi members had to fight all the way, to be accepted by the Germans as a whole, even assigning Nazi officers to military units to make sure that the commanders followed Nazi ideology. Even at the peak of its membership, the Party was a small minority in German society. The Nazis, a small minority, and the German majority were not a match made in heaven, and often the ordinary Germans snickered about the "Nazis" behind their backs. Most Germans, at best, tolerated the weird Nazis.

In the Soviet Union, the Communists, themselves a new phenomenon in Russian history, suffered a similar minority status among the vast masses of the Russian population. The peasants, a great number in the population, had neither the heart nor the brain for the Marxist ideology of world history and human role in it. Obviously, it was an idea somewhat more sophisticated for the Russian masses than the Nazi Aryanism was to the Germans. Although the Soviets persisted in the claim that the Communist Party was a pan-national political representation of all Soviet citizens, the members of the Party remained apart from the general population of the Soviet Union. Like the Nazis in Germany, turning the Russian peasants into loyal and knowledgeable Communists was no small task. Like the Nazis in Germany, the vast majority of Russians and others in the network of the Soviet Socialist Republics, many of them joining the Union in chains, cared little about the strange, revolutionary ideology called Marxism or Communism, and less about making it their personal belief system. The Russians fought heroically to stop and later defeat the mighty German military, not as Communists, but as Russians, not as believers in the Communist Utopia, but as citizens of a nation that was invaded by a foreign power. It was plain Russian nationalism, more than the Soviet ideology of Marx and Lenin, that united the Russians. Again like the Nazis in Germany, the "Communists" were small in number and often alien to the great masses of Russian peasants. Just as nervous and suspicious as the Nazis about their minority status, the Soviets sent political Commissars (ideology officers) to watch the military, both in war and in peace, to make sure the commanders followed Communism.

How tenuous was the link between Nazism and Germany or between Communism and Russia! Quite in contrast to our view of Nazi Germany or Communist Russia—strong, iron-clad, unshakable bond between the Ideology and the Nation—both Nazism and Communism quickly vanished from view when their respective nations crumbled. After Germany's defeat in WWII, and Russia's implosion in the Cold War, both Nazism in Germany and Communism in Russia disappeared from their respective nations *as if they never really existed*! As if Nazism and Communism were a figment of our ideological-historical imagination that never existed in reality.

This brief backward glance at the strange rise and fall of the 20th century's two great ideologies--once so strong that they had unyielding visions of dominating the world--now gone, accentuates in our minds the only remaining Great Ideology of the Century, namely, American Capitalism. It is a revolutionary idea, quite like Nazism and Communism. It tells us that a man can own the whole world, controlling all the men and women in it as his "workers" or "employees," to do as he commands them to do. In Capitalism's undisguised philosophy, the strong rule and the weak obey, as Corey Robin said, even to the extent of what to think and when to pee, or as Jay Gould said, even to the extent of killing fellow workers on command.

This rise of Capitalist ideology is especially remarkable because its arrival at the end of the 19th century took place in America just when the U.S. had reached its peak, its un-Capitalistic majority enjoying political freedom and economic equality never seen in human history before. Those who made up the majority of property-owning independent entrepreneurs, controlling their own lives as well as their own national life, worked hard and kept what their hard work produced. If anyone told these American farmers and small businessmen that someday they would be hired hands, working for great owners of everything called Capitalists, they might have horse-whipped him as an insane nut.

If you lived in 19th-century U.S., you were a Common Man, who owned his own land and business, and bowing to no power on earth, free from bondage and secure in his own self-protection. To him, an average American, a member of the great majority of Americans, the idea of a strange thing called Capitalism—where one-percent controls 99-percent of Americans in absolute bondage--would have been the nightmare of the worst kind.

Today, the nutty and unthinkable nightmare is in America's hearts and minds as the most natural thing imaginable. Unlike the rise and fall of Nazism in Germany and Communism in Russia, American Capitalism is not a revolutionary ideology confined to a small group of fanatical followers. Without a thing called the "Capitalist Party," in the fashion of the Nazi Party or the Communist Party, Capitalism has virtually all of Americans as members of the non-existing "Capitalist Party." Virtually all Americans are born Capitalist and die Capitalist. Even at the peak of their prosperity, if you threw a stone on the German or Russian street from a roof-top, very likely it would *not* hit a Nazi in Germany or a Communist in Russia. Today, if you threw a stone on an American street, it is very certain that it would *not miss* hitting a Capitalist or a Capitalist wannabe! Unlike the Nazis or the Communists, who were a small minority within the nation, often struggling for recognition and respectability among the masses, the American Capitalist is Every American. Belief in Capitalism—often going by "free-enterprise system" or "market society" for easier comprehension, and "freedom of choice" or "consumer preference" on the individual comprehension of the idea—is held by virtually everyone in America, man or woman, child or adult, young or very old, rich or poor, white or black or in between, smart or stupid. Capitalism is so deeply held and so widely believed that even a child instantly recognizes that as "freedom" or "doing what you want and getting what you want," and so on. The idea of Capitalism is so secure in the American hearts and minds that it would hardly enter anyone's thought that we need a Nazi-like ideology officer or a Communist political Commissar to watch the military to make sure that Capitalism is entrenched properly in each soldier's heart and mind. Even if the nation of America disappeared tomorrow from the earth, the idea of Capitalism would remain in everyone's brain cells forever.

It is a common fact that the U.S. is the only advanced nation in the world that does not have a major leftist newspaper or magazine. Eric Alterman noted in his book, *Kabuki Democracy*, how utterly impossible for a president, especially a progressive one, in this case Obama, to create any "transformative" changes in America, meaning a change that would affect the very economic fabric of the nation. The touted Obamacare program, insuring poor Americans access to health care, was possible, observes Caroline Poplin of *McClatchy-Tribune New Service*, only with "as little disruption to corporate profit as possible." In short, Obamacare is a dishonest, at best, or fraudulent, at worst, deal for the masses. Perhaps it is so with the War on Terrorism, the War on Drugs, the War on Poverty, the War on.... Republicans come and go; Democrats come and go, and the Capitalist core remains the same. Many observers have also noted the startling homogeneity and conformity in a land teeming with technical innovations and revolutionary business concepts. But no fundamental deviations are allowed from the front-and-center foundations of Capitalism. Radical magazines like the *Nation, Mother Jones*, and other similar ones, must maintain a bureau in Washington and operate like one of the "mainstream" media outlets. As in the movies *Avatar, Michael Clayton, Erin Brokovich, Snowpiercer,* and many other such "class-themed" stories, the Good Guys always win in the end and comfort the 99-percent majority; the one-percent, on its part, for good measure, lodges weak but disingenuous complaints about Hollywood's allegedly "anti-corporate" biases, in the movies. These same movies cost hundreds of millions of dollars provided by the corporate investors.

Capitalism is so much part of America's unspoken premise that we rarely use the term "capitalism" anywhere in the lexicon of American consciousness or conversation, other than affirmatively. We are all Capitalists subconsciously and even unconsciously, which is in the deepest recesses of our minds and in our hearts, the kind that does not assert itself because there is no need to. Unlike its more fiercely-dynamic counterparts in Nazism and Communism that had to struggle to exist and to be loved by the masses, Capitalism sits in America's very bloodstream and social consciousness as if it is its natural birth right. Who would, indeed, not love the idea that promises that you can do anything you want to, with yourself, with others, with the world, if you have the power or money to do it? All you need to do with your life, it commands, is to be a winner at the game of power and money as your life's destiny and goal: Lie, steal or cheat if you must; or to do these better than your competitors, go to college.

The promises of Capitalism lure us and corrupt our souls, and why would they not? If the Capitalist System existed at the time of Shakespeare, we would have a Neil Simon who wrote all the Broadway hit plays, instead of a Shakespeare; if at the time of Beethoven, a John Williams who composed all the grand Hollywood movie music, instead of a Beethoven; if at the time of Michelangelo, he would be a popular portrait-painter for wealthy patrons; if at the time of Tolstoy, he would be writing all the New-York-Times-bestselling novels. By its own nature, and our own natural response to it, Capitalism would not allow anything else. In its system, all talented writers would be bestselling writers, all great composers would be composing for Hollywood, and all deep-thinking philosophers would be teaching at famous universities as untruthful professors—as they all do today in our Corporate America. Capitalism is absolute and final as America's System and Soul.

II.

Then, we have the band of Fascists led by Donald Trump that challenges this absolute Capitalist control of America. By the time this book goes to print, the excitement of Donald Trump has waned and the triumphant feeling that his supporters felt at the election is by now mired in criticisms and doubts. The groans and cries that may be heard from the Lesser Americans—the non-whites that the White Majority has trounced—may not be enough to sustain the great Trump Excitement. The *supply* of Mental Trash continues for the Great Capitalist System and the *consumption* of Mental Trash continues among the White Masses as selfishly, as childishly and as stupidly as before. It is as if the White Majority killed the other half of the working class for nothing. .

Why? Because America is controlled, not by political passions or powers, but by Corporate Capitalism which has controlled the American Nation ever since the beginning of the 20th century, first with material things and now with *Mental* Trash. Those who voted for Trump still get up in the morning to go to work under the same Master they did before Trump. The control of Corporate Capitalism has been deepened and legitimated in the last three decades of Neo-Liberal Capitalism, which expanded its control of Americans into the mental, psychological and political. Decades ago, it was relatively easy to point out where the actual evidence of corporate control was in America, as we could simply point to the factories, assembly-lines and smokestacks. Today, such things, including the famed "Rust Belt," have disappeared, as our consumption shifted to the non-material; indeed, if we were asked to point to the proof of corporate control in America, we would be somewhat puzzled as we must point to our minds that are the new victims of Corporate America.

What is a Corporation, which is the controlling tower of all things American, especially its minds? A corporation is an organization made up of many investors "chartered" to act for the benefit-profit of its investors. East India Company is one of the earliest and best-known such entities. Because of the very self-centered nature of all corporate intentions, the founding Fathers had a rather dim view of the corporate character and treated these for-profit corporate bodies with disdain for their very un-American motive in forming the corporation. As capitalism gradually took hold in late 19th century (as the term "Capitalism" was then just emerging in general usage), corporations came to be established as a "legal person" with all the rights and privileges of individual citizens. By the sheer *size advantage* that these super-sized "persons" enjoyed, they naturally began to dominate the American political-economic system.

So, what is a corporation today? In a nutshell, it is an *Economic Giant*, many times larger than the separate individual citizens, proportional to how many persons and their resources make up the corporation. Let's say a corporation has 1,000 employees and 1,000 shareholders who hold the company's stock. Now, we have a "legal person" who is actually made up 2,000 persons and their collective resources. That is an Economic Giant that an individual citizen or consumer, who remains a single person, cannot possibly match up against, either in wits or resources. As single individuals, we are always inferior in our dealings with these giant corporations (by definition, all corporations are *bigger* than us as individuals.) Why the government would not increase its regulatory watch over these corporations, say, 2,000 times, 20,000 times, or whatever their size requires, proportional to their sizes, more strongly than the single individual citizens is another topic. To illustrate: Even after the 2008 Wall Street meltdown, President Obama and Elizabeth Warren could not establish a federal watchdog agency, with real teeth, to regulate Wall Street banks. Angry and disappointed, Warren ran for the Senate and was elected, leaving a saga behind her of the great corporate powers even the U.S. government cannot match.

By their nature, commercial corporations are armed to the teeth: Every single element in their human, material, technical, and organizational resources enlisted to the maximum degree for the sole purpose of making a profit, at first selling goods and services, and now selling images of no practical value, such as Mental Trash, brainwashing the consumer. The consuming public, as citizens in a nation of strangers, at the same time, is made up of *unorganized* single individuals: In much of their consuming life, whatever it is they are consuming, it is likely a solitary act. By nature, consuming is done alone, even when the consumer is at a stadium with 100,000 other spectators. Two consumers looking for good shoes to buy may exchange information and cooperate with each other to locate the best buy. But, two consumers looking for a good entertaining event go their separate ways. So, a corporation is made up of many people, pooling their resources, so that one corporation is as strong as *many people rolled into one.* A consumer in America, especially a White consumer, is a loner, by his own habits of consumption as well as by the historical development in technology and propaganda that shapes his consumer behavior. For reasons that are unique to the White Masses in America, White Americans are solitary wolves, intensely devoted to their consumer enjoyment unconnected to other Americans.

There is no competition between the solitary consumer and giant corporations. The consumer must consume whatever the corporation sells. In the American economic (and the compliant political sub-) system, it is the corporation that sets the rules of all things economic, including what to be demanded and who is to supply it and how the two factors shall meet in the consumer's mind and pocketbook. Against this corporate Goliath, the Consumer-Davids stand no chance: The consumer-Davids are always cheated, always outsmarted, always disfranchised, always brainwashed, and always dumbed down by their Corporate Goliath. An organization, relentlessly pursuing its profit, with all the resources of thousands of brains, is just too much for the lone consumer who predictably remain childish, selfish and stupid with his "freedom of choice."

Consumers never defeat corporations; only corporations defeat corporations. Kodak, the film giant, lost out at the marketplace, not because the consumers destroyed the corporation, but because the digital industry, the upstart image technology, simply made its products more appealing to the consumers.

In other nations, as it was during 19th century America itself, such corporate advantage in size and avarice, its very nature, is well recognized and their governments use their vast and deep leverage of power to control this predatory corporate nature to protect their citizens. But in America's "Corporate Capitalism," the government works basically as the handmaid of the corporation through the various legal channels of employment revolving doors, lobbying, legislative favors for special interests, and so on, that are the ongoing facts of life. So, in America, neither the government nor the citizens (nor God, as Capitalism is obviously thriving) can prevent the corporations from exercising their multiplied power.

American consumers still control the vast number of *votes*, figuratively 99 percent of them. But, thanks to the intense Mental Trash pumped into them by Corporate America, they are now split right down the middle between Trump Whites and anti-Trump non-whites—against each other. They remain utterly divided and unorganized with their political power wasted upon each other, not aiming at Corporate Capitalism that laughs all the way to the bank everyday. By voting for Trump, not Sanders or Clinton, the White Majority directed their anxiety and wrath at the Lesser Americans, the easier target, not Corporate America who had destroyed their brains and hearts with Mental Trash and their jobs with "microchips and automation," as economist Thomas Friedman diagnosed. Thus, divided and conquered, American consumers are ruled by the few well-organized corporations much easier than the 500-million Indians by a mere handful of the British colonial rulers.

Contrary to their propaganda messages and images, the very character of corporations breeds dishonesty and inhumanity. In Jeffersonian America, people rarely expected to receive rewards in life many times *larger* than the labor they put into it. It would be unthinkable that a man who works 50-acre farmland would somehow expect 500-acre harvest for his labor's reward. In today's Corporate America, the idea is to create Maximum Rewards (say, 100 times larger than the labor we put into it) for Minimum Efforts. In our conventional definition and expectation, "corporate profit" must be many times larger than our labor's just reward. But the problem with Corporate Capitalism is this: If we expect the "100-times-larger rewards" for our average effort, where do we expect the 100-times-larger rewards to come from? The dishonest and inhuman character of Corporate Capitalism is inevitable because its "profit," its "return on investment," must come from the Victims of the System; and the System cannot do otherwise for its business.

Capitalism has its own simple logic, whose power of simplicity is superior to all known theologies and philosophies: *To increase profit, you do everything you can toward that end.* It is the same logic that the military uses confronting its enemy: You do anything to defeat the enemy. In war and capitalism, *all is fair* and *all is accepted.* (Both in Capitalism and in war, there are "rules" to follow, but winning takes care of most of these rules.) If you are a capitalist, *what else* can you *do* other than pursue your profit to the end of the world?

When you hire an employee, it is logical that you try to get the most labor out of him by making him work, work, and work some more; you pay him the least you can get away with; when he can no longer perform, you replace him with someone more productive. When you sell something, you try to get the best price out of your ware. If nobody wants to buy it, advertise it or lower the price; if there is no competition, try the highest possible price on your product; if you are threatened by competition, do everything to destroy your competition.

You try to get the best legal advantage possible over your competition and over the buyer; if necessary, you bribe, you cheat, you steal, you lie with the Law-makers and government officials; you are a "businessman" and in the U.S. that justifies everything and anything.

The *Logic of Capitalism* is simple: *Make more profit than anybody else; do it the cheapest way possible.* In capitalism, there is no such thing as country, love, God or conscience; profit justifies and explains *all things* in it; as a capitalist, you must win or you do not exist and you do not deserve to exist. You fail and you die.

Thus, the System of Capital has the clearest, simplest, and easiest logic of human decision-making to follow that has ever been invented. Once you have decided on the path of Capitalism, the marching orders have been given: Get the most profit you can, in any way you can. Because of the simplicity of the concept and execution, its closest cousin are Militarism and Fascism in their theory and method. In Militarism, military battle and capitalist strategy are exactly the same: Win and conquer. In Fascism, both ideologies thrive in pursuit of power: The strong rule the weak. With Trump's introduction of Fascism to complement the existing Militarism, all three systems are quite thriving in America today. Between the old power of Capitalism and the new power of Fascism, the Military smartly stays neutral. If and when a friction develops between Capitalism and Fascism, as we anticipate it, the Military might not be able to maintain its neutrality.

The trouble with the Logic of Capitalism is that it is *self-destructive*. If everyone followed the Capitalist Logic, we could not possibly *live in society* as human beings and as members of humanity at large: We would have to *return to NATURE* as savage animals. (In the U.S., this has already happened). Even though it is self-destructive to humanity and community, in the meantime, Capitalism is a darn appealing system because it gives us everything our heart desires. It is like *drug addiction*: We all know it is bad and will kill us, but in the meantime, the Drug Effect is irresistible.

While the Logic of Capitalism is the strongest force of nature ever known to man, the human beings themselves remain quite illogical about their own fate under Capitalism. They may be aware that Capitalism will eventually kill them all; but they are too weak of will or too stupid of wisdom to be able to do much about it. To match the Logic of Capitalism, which is the strongest force ever encountered by man (Witness: It has destroyed Jesus, Thomas Jefferson, Adam Smith, and Karl Marx), man needs something equally mighty to save himself from Capitalism. Alas, Humanity is with neither the will nor the wisdom to survive the Capitalist onslaught. In every contest, Capitalism wins and Humanity loses, and this one-sided battle will continue seemingly forever. Well, unless either the Nuclear Holocaust or the Environmental Ending comes before Capitalism's self-destruction.

In our cultural life, Corporate America provides us, Whites and non-whites, a steady supply of daily Mental Trash as our pleasures, from ballgames to movies, from social connections to information, from potato chips to electronic games, for its profit. The supply is so unbroken, the quality so irresistible, that we, consumers, are completely dependent on it and cannot possibly live without its steady supply in our daily life.

"Good" societies, such as Scandinavian ones, recognizing the natural threat that corporations pose, by their sheer size and resource advantage, on their civil community and citizen welfare, make sure that one-sided relations between corporations and citizens do not naturally favor the former. In Scandinavia and Japan, for example, corporations must operate within the tightly-binding imperatives of community, society and humanity. Neither the government nor the citizenry--with heavy taxation as well as frequent public outrage at corporate wrongdoing—allows the corporations to run rampant with their gigantic size and influence.

In America, such countervailing influences on corporate tyranny do not exist because Corporate Capitalism controls both the American citizens as well as their government. (How and why that government-corporation collusion, such as the infamous "government-Monsanto revolving door," occurs is discussed in Chapter 18.)

III.

To understand what makes Capitalism's One-Percent so powerful and formidable, in essence dwarfing the new Trumpian Fascism, is to recognize the fact that Corporate America has become our New God, theologically and literally. Capitalism did not replace God as America's new deity: It simply made God a Servant of Capitalism. If you doubt it, just notice a popular book entitled *JESUS, CEO*, which argues that Jesus is a great model for corporate CEOs. Free copies of this book are distributed freely at churches! (This book follows another book that says Pope John Paul II is also a great model for corporate CEOs. Before that, another book claimed that Attila the Hun was a great CEO model, thus listing Jesus, the Pope, and Attila the Hun as three ideal-type CEO models!)

In this confusion of Mammon with God, we have made Capitalism our new God in America, which resembles Satan more than God. How have we done this? Let's consider the general attributes of God that we are traditionally taught to be unique characteristics of the Divine One: *All powerful, all knowing, all good, all eternal, and being everywhere.* Unsurprisingly, these attributes of God are now what we attribute to Corporate America. When we think of "All Powerful," we are likely to think about Corporate America, not God. Here are the ways we have made God irrelevant in America.

I. It is *ALL POWERFUL*: No opposition, political or otherwise, is allowed, Trumpian Fascism notwithstanding. No resistance to its offerings is allowed. Capitalism as the ideology of Corporate America is unquestioned, other than as harmless electoral topics in the media, themselves owned and run by Corporate America, mostly for comic relief and sometimes as false self-criticism. ("End of Capitalism?" *TIME* magazine once asked during a critical self-examination. Its own conclusion: No.) It is total in its degree of control and totalitarian in its mode of delivery and, hence, absolute in its power. In the grand footsteps of such predecessors as Rome and The Third Reich, Corporate America is all powerful, as God. No one in America is allowed to oppose the Capitalist System to resist what the System offers by way of our daily Mental Trash.

II. It is *ALL KNOWING*: Corporate America knows everything about White America, but not vice versa, and all the studies about you are being used against you and for Corporate America's own benefit. It is safe to assume that all it knows about you and White America—through your records, scientific researches, professional studies—will always be used *against* you. It controls all the channels of knowledge so that you learn only what it wants you to learn; it collects and stores all the information it wants to know about you and all that you do—all your yearnings and cravings--none of which is for *your* own wellbeing. It knows what you dream about, what you fear, what you are likely to do tomorrow. Remember, it is your new God.

III. It is *ALL GOOD*: Like the Lord God of Old, the images of Corporate America are etched in our minds as All Good. Images are important only when substance is non-existent, and the images of Goodness are essential to the survival and prosperity of Corporate America. All things that come to our minds about corporations in America are that they are good; they create jobs for us and serve our consumer needs. Because it controls all the channels and bits of information about anything, White America knows about Corporate America only by what it gives out through the media, in the classroom, in folklore and success stories, all of which are Good, just like our God Almighty. Anyone who disagrees with, is critical of, or opposes the Corporate System risks harsh and unforgiving punishment from the Almighty Corporate America. Individuals who stand up to the corporate powers in America in one form or another--in the long run of things--do not win. (Remember, how Donald Trump skirted the topic of "capitalism" and "wealth" altogether during his campaign?)

IV. It is *EVERYWHRE* at once: Like the Big Brother cameras, the long arm of Corporate America is omnipresent; wherever there is a person, a mind or a dollar to be found and owned, around the clock, to seduce, to control or to destroy all in its path. White America can neither escape nor ignore its omnipresent shadow that is everywhere, on the street, in our minds, in our stomachs, occupying all of our senses and thoughts, when we are awake and when we are asleep. Only death can escape its omnipresence.

V. It is *ALL ETERNAL*: Corporate America and its capitalism have trumped all its competitors—Abraham, Buddha, Jesus, Mohammed, Jefferson, Smith, Marx, Thoreau, to name the famous few—as History's Triumphant Winner. Some quick thinkers are so impressed with the triumph of Corporate America that they have declared that history as we have known it has ended, with "Neo-Liberal Capitalism" as the sole winner.

VI. It is *LOVED BY ALL*: Corporate America has trumped even God in one respect: Unlike God, who has had to endure atheists and agnostics in His Reign, the New God is loved by all. In American Corporate Capitalism, there is plenty to love by all: There are over 1,000 channels on an average TV set, over 1,500 magazines on the shelf, over 5.000 breakfast cereals to choose from, a new movie produced each day, billions of websites to browse on the computer and smartphones, available to all, from age 2 to death. As our New God, Corporate America turns our living rooms into dying rooms where we, once we enter it, become dead to the world, but come alive to pay our visit to the New God. This much love from humanity even the old Almighty could not have imagined getting.

Subordinating the traditional God to its more worldly purpose is a monumental power of control. And Corporate America has been busy, wielding its mighty power, mightier than God's to expand its power and wealth through Consumer Capitalism, giving people *what they want*.

What does Trump's win mean in this picture of Capitalism as our New God in America? Probably in the media, some noise. In substantive measure of economic-political reality? Nothing. Capitalism rules.

How does Capitalism, more specifically the American kind, Consumer Capitalism, rule Americans, body and soul, so completely? What has Corporate America with its all-reaching Consumer Capitalism, giving people what they want, done with its mighty power? What does this getting- all-you-want type of society *do* to people when they are continually subjected to it? Logically and naturally, it creates *addiction* among the consumers, mostly White consumers, with its products, mostly in entertainment and distraction in a system called "Give-them-what-they-want." Just imagine what kind an adult a child would become if he was given everything he demanded as he was growing up.

IV.

WHEN YOU ALWAYS GET WHAT YOU WANT, YOU BECOME FIRST *ADDICTED* TO IT AND THEN *ENSLAVED* TO ITS REGULAR SUPPLY, MOSTLY WITHOUT YOUR KNOWING ABOUT IT.

Of all the products that Consumer Capitalism regularly supplies, which most White Americans have been consuming in the last three decades, we have given the all-inclusive name *MENTAL TRASH*. Since it is the defining determinant of America's addiction and enslavement, we need to know more about addiction and its enslaving effects.

A few Americans, especially Whites, know or sense in their daily routine life that they may be *addicted* to some form of activities, mostly related to entertainment. They may casually say, "I'm addicted to sugar and fat." But oddly, or maybe not oddly, they never say, "I'm *enslaved* to sugar and fat." What is the difference between addiction and enslavement, and why are we willing to admit to one but not to other?

Addiction is a psychological, personal state of being, an experience we can recognize in our daily life: After all, many of us know that we are addicted to sugar and fat. Somehow we feel that we can kick the "bad habit" and that possibility encourage us to freely admit that we are addicted to this or that. Addiction, as debilitating as it is, is a condition we created in our lives ourselves, we reason, and, therefore, we can kick it out of our lives at will.

But, virtually none of us is aware, much less willing to admit, that we are *enslaved* by entertainment, now mostly in digital form disguised as "communication," "information," or "social media." If we admitted to a state of enslavement to these things, we would have to admit that, by its powerful control of our mind and body, the enslavement shatters our sense of reality in which we feel we are in control. It is a catastrophic contradiction of everything we know to be true: In this contrary reality, what we enjoy as "communication" is actually "mis-communication," "information" is actually "mis-information" and "social media" is actually "anti-social media." In this realization, "freedom" becomes slavery and "lifestyle" is made up of the chains that bind and deliver us to bondage.

Recognizing our bondage to entertainment, which we can neither escape nor resist when it persistently dominates our lives, requires more than alert personal or psychological smarts: It requires a penetrating, and quite difficult, understanding of our entire S*ocial System* in its many institutional aspects, such as its history, politics, economics, culture, both hidden and visible. In most societies run by power elites, the truth is hidden and only the platitudes, for general public consumption, are visibly available to public view. In America, because of its peculiar lack of community and history, we arrive at "consensus" largely by the method of persuasion, which is to say, by propaganda. This makes any public recognition of social facts, such as the evil deeds of the System, extremely difficult and mostly impossible. As a result, by and large, we as Americans remain quite ignorant of the whole institutional web of power and influence that passes as "normal" and "routine." Just ask this question: How many of us think of our employment as enslavement?

What is enslavement? Its legality aside, *enslavement is a situation where one must do what one's master tells him to do.* All of us in America live by two daily commands from our masters: WORK AND BE ENTERTAINED.

Addiction, unlike enslavement, reduces everything to a state of personal experience and psychological talk; it is in our daily conversations, problems and remedies, perhaps in counseling, perhaps in therapy, or perhaps in more consumption.

Enslavement, on the other hand, is a hard reality of Power—institutional, legal, ideological, educational, military, intellectual, even religious forces that bind and control us, according to the design of those who own the Power. What form it takes, whether Feudal or Contractual, is irrelevant as the result is just the same on the enslaved. But, because such forces of control exist in the name of "the Constitution," "the Law," "legitimacy," "moral right," that is all good and American, it never occurs to us that all such wonderful-sounding word-devices are actually the shackles that the Power uses to enslave us to their idea of how *our* lives should be lived. It never occurs to us, under such advanced persuasion technique, that life in America—especially in our daily working to life to pay for our Consumer Life—is a cruel, forced life of servitude from which no one escapes. It is enslavement in the most classic sense of the word.

We would sooner recognize the Chinese foot-binding of women, to prevent their escape from bondage, as cruel enslavement than the fact that Consumer Capitalism in America is just as cruel, and inescapable, an enslavement. Like all those who live the lives of the enslaved by a Power and a System that they cannot oppose or resist, America's Consumer Enslavement also has the consumers' *minds* enslaved as well by the will of the master who controls and shapes the way the enslaved consumers *think*. With all the instruments of persuasion—all sorts of advertisements, media propaganda, classroom mis-education, by America's Best and Brightest—you don't need Auschwitz or Gulags. Just give them anything they want ("Neo-Liberalism"), and they will invariably ask for the stuff that would slowly kill their bodies and minds. There is no greater proof than the election of Donald Trump to Presidency that this has been working out as perfectly as Consumer Capitalism intended it for decades (although Trump was not Capitalism's choice as discussed in Chapter 12).

Thus, the American-style consumer enslavement manufactures (or brainwashes) not only the individual sensory pleasure itself, mostly in the immediate images, words, events, mostly in the form of Mental Trash; but also how the enslaved *feel and think* in the abstract intellectual issues of Good, Freedom, Justice, America, Happiness, Knowledge, and so on, all in the way their minds are shaped and fulfilled by their Consumer Capitalism. A man who enjoys "reality TV" is not just enjoying the image or story development in front of him, but also, mostly unbeknownst to him, inevitably internalizes all the accompanying ideas the "reality TV" represents as Good, Free, Justice, America, Happiness and Knowledge in his mind's reality.

This process of mind control—or Mind Destruction—affects all American consumers, but most severely the White Americans who are its most ardent victims. The White Trump-voter, after the election, is still in the same society and individual position as before, still under the Master he has always served as an economic slave. The only difference, as he wakes up in the "Trump Administration," is the vague psychological satisfaction he now enjoys that White America is now kicking the Lesser humanity--the Muslim, Hispanic, black and female minorities, and weaker international partners and adversaries as they are already down. Aside from that, nothing will change substantially. They will work just as before, spending all that hard-earned wage on his entertainment addiction, namely, Mental Trash, that keeps him in his unchangeable economic enslavement. Well, he feels he is better off under the new leader to his liking: He has other slaves to lord over. That's about all that Capitalist America will grant the child-leader with a loaded gun and his 5-year-old Child Crusaders who continue to wallow in the hazy twilight of Mental Trash. In the contest for power, America's Capitalism will always be one step ahead of Trump's Fascism.

Chapter Sixteen

Capitalism Eternal

The question has puzzled a few observers during the rise of Donald Trump: Does Trump's Revolution approve Capitalism or reject it? Trump has not said much about what he thinks of Capitalism itself; nor have his storm-troopers said much by way of their loud grievances and clear demands what they really think of Capitalism. Curiously in this silence, we must assume that, since they are not loudly or clearly rejecting the Economic System in power, while loudly and clearly rejecting the Political System, they approve Capitalism. While it is puzzling that they rejected America's *status quo* without rejecting the very foundations of its power base, the Capitalism System, while being thoroughly victimized by its Consumer Capitalism, and its Mental Trash addiction, we have to marvel at the wonders of Capitalist Success in America. Consumer Capitalism destroyed White intelligence and corrupted White humanity, but the White Masses still love it! What is the secret of Capitalism's enduring success?

Reiteration seems in order to clarify this puzzle. Capitalism teaches all Americans, White and non-white, indeed all human beings within its reach, to avoid work, by becoming rich and making other people do the work for them. This Capitalist Theory of Reward, while never an open official doctrine of Capitalist Philosophy, describes nevertheless the vicious and inhuman nature of American society that has become a *savage nation* both with each other and with the world. But, it also explains Capitalism's innate popularity in America and elsewhere. Never mind that the chances of the Masses succeeding in transforming the Theory into Reality is close to Zero.

Human history has been a battle over labor, which is required so that, as living beings, we must provide food for survival, and, later, when food is enough, we pursue comfort and, in its most advanced form, pleasure: Thus survival, comfort, and pleasure form the basis of human life which begins and ends with labor. The success and popularity of Capitalism is actually located in the very nature of our tendency to avoid labor.

We could say Human History is really a History of Labor, who does it for whom and why. Naturally two camps have developed over the issue of labor, or who should labor and for whom, in short, our battle over labor. In order to unlock the secrets of Capitalism, we are well served by presenting this History of Labor below:

SCHOOL I: LABOR IS TO BE AVOIDED. According to this school, labor is a bad thing as contrary to Human Nature, and we should avoid it by making somebody else do the work for us.

SCHOOL II: LABOR IS TO BE EMBRACED. According to this school, labor is a good thing, for theological as well as philosophical reasons, and we should embrace and enjoy it in harmony with Human Nature and with one another.

First, the school that argues that labor should be avoided and we should make somebody else do it by all means:

Human labor is bad and should be avoided as much as possible; it should be performed only by the lowliest and weakest of society. The strongest, most successful in the war of all against all, own the victor's share of human wealth produced by the defeated and conquered. Historically, this side is represented by the great powers like Roman Imperialism, German Nazism, and now America's own Capitalism. Today, this simple philosophy of Capitalism has an enormous advantage over its opponents (such as Christianity) in capturing the human heart, especially in the U.S. where simplicity is the cardinal virtue in persuasion. Just compare the formulas for the two systems of thought, Capitalism and Christianity:

Capitalism appeals to our self-interest. It says whatever is Good for Me is the definition of Good . It is always

Me = Me = Me = Me. . .

The universal appeal of Capitalism is that one never has to go outside of himself to understand the whole philosophy of Capitalism. It is basically the philosophy of human beings at their simplest and most natural. It is so simple and so natural that no formal instruction is even needed to turn a human being into a believer in Capitalism: "Just Do What is Good for You" is enough. Even a five-year-old at a short summer camp can easily grasp the basic philosophy of Capitalism.

Now, the school that advocates that Labor is good for society and humanity and should be performed gladly and earnestly:

Unlike the simple and natural appeal of Capitalist self-centered labor-avoidance, this labor-is-good philosophy is something of a hard-sell that requires a repeated instruction, sometimes lasting one's whole lifetime to learn.

The Labor Theory of Christianity, as Capitalism's Chief Adversary, is a bit complicated because, in order to understand it, one must go outside of oneself, to move toward or grasp something that is not oneself : For example, we must leave what is beneficial to ourselves (or, "deny yourself") to do good for others, often called "neighbors" or "brothers." To be a Christian and love labor, we must believe that we should love others as we love ourselves. This is quite the opposite of the easy self-loving instruction that Capitalism teaches us, to define others through ourselves; Christianity tells us to define ourselves through others. Since we are born with no inborn connections with other human beings, we stand to each other as strangers. Animals are endowed with genetics that tie them together into one group, but for human beings it is not easy to think of other people as importantly as ourselves. Capitalism teaches us the concept of Myself as the center of all things, which requires no thinking at all: We are born, live and die with Myself that never leaves Me, Me and Me. Christianity says love others; Capitalism says love yourself and use other people's labor for your benefit.

This is a distinct disadvantage for Christianity because, unlike Capitalism, it must ask people to go to the next higher level of thinking about themselves: For example, it says we live through our Brothers and Neighbors, and our Brothers and Neighbors live through me. To write it as a formula, it comes out like this:

Me = Brothers = Me = Brothers. . .

Now, this formula complicates life because what makes up Me must include what is not Me, namely, other human beings: Using this simple formula, Christianity says laboring for Me is the same as laboring for my Brothers and Neighbors. The essence of Christian teachings, we are taught, is that all labor is *shared labor*.

When these two contradictory forces of human thought fight over our souls, Capitalism is more likely to win because of its virtue in appealing to our simple self-interest: Moving from Me to Me and back to Me requires no leap of ironic imagination—the lifeblood of wisdom and intelligence—or developing new insights; it is merely a repetition of Myself, Myself, Myself, and more of Myself. The teachings of Capitalism can be summed up easily in a child (or even an idiot with no human intelligence) repeating himself every day, Me, Me, Me, Me.

It is hardly any wonder that 99 percent of humanity, living or dead, have been occupied with this simplicity of temptation—first with religion and now with Capitalist Temptation of no-labor promise—and succumbing to the temptation of letting other people do the work for you. On the other hand, connecting Myself to a stranger as my brother requires a great leap of ironic imagination, wisdom and insight. In it, we must answer the baffling question: Why should this Stranger be part of Myself, and Myself part of the Stranger, and why should I labor for this stranger just as gladly as I should do it for

Myself and Myself alone? Or, as Abel famously asked God: "Am I my brother's keeper?"

To most people, the answer is not forthcoming. Because of the enormous difficulty of finding a suitable answer to this question—intellectual, spiritual, practical—most of humanity most of the time give up and go with the first formula, that Myself is Myself. Why should I be my brother's keeper? Even Jesus did not offer any plausible explanations as to *why* we should love one another and share our labor; He merely left a Commandment of Love: "Love one another as I have loved you." Indeed, if a child asked his parents why we should love one another and share with each other the fruit of our labor, the parents would find it quite difficult to explain to the child's, and very probably to their own, satisfaction without referring to Jesus' authority in the Bible. Philosophically, we can find answers in our transition from "nature" where everyman is for himself to "society" where all are brothers, the idea is more abstract than convincing. This difficulty is compounded in America, where the Self is strong and most answers to life's vexing questions are not embedded in assumed tradition or collective consciousness. With the frontier backdrop that created the "rugged" individualism, "society" never really had a chance to be part of America's subconscious. It is natural then that most Americans brainwashed in Capitalism for generations would think nothing of using other people's labor and avoid having to labor themselves.

II.

Historically, this Capitalist theory of labor avoidance is what sustained the kings and lords, most prominently through the Roman Empire and the Nazi Reich, with the idea that conquerors like the Romans and the Germans could avoid labor by making the conquered slaves do the work.

In the 20th and 21st centuries, the Capitalists (especially the U.S. variety) are the inheritors of the powers of Romans and Nazis, with the idea that the reward of success in Capitalism entitles them to avoid having to work by making the not-so-successful (perhaps the 99 percent) do the work for them. Romans, Nazis and Capitalists unite in the simple and natural idea that the powerful should command the labor and energy of the powerless . In this sense, Capitalism is just as appealing in its simplicity to the Capitalists as Roman Imperialism appealed to the Romans and German Nazism appealed to the Germans. But, unlike the Romans and Nazis, the membership in American Capitalism is wide-open and, in theory, any one can be a Capitalist and avoid labor: There lies the unique advantage of American Capitalism in conquering all its idea competitors, like Christianity, that have tried to appeal to the Masses and failed.

In contrast to Capitalism, Christianity teaches us that human labor is God's gift and commandment to humanity and should be performed gladly and its reward should be shared equally among those who labor and toil. In the ideas of Western democracy, from which the New World inherited its own democratic-republican liberty and equality, it is through labor shared that humans define community, peace and brotherhood, as well as political and economic justice, often called "the Golden Rule."

The battle between human nature and society over labor, fought by all the combatants on both sides, has ended and America's winner-take-all Capitalism is now the sole winner among the world religions and philosophies that initially shaped America:

The Talented Few make up the top One Percent in America as the core of its Capitalism that embodies the idea of success essentially in avoiding labor and making somebody else do the work. With this pool of talent in pacifying the hungers and cravings of the labor-laden masses, they also control the hearts and minds of those who long to escape their labor and toil.

That Capitalism stands virtually alone as the world's most powerful idea testifies to its historic triumph over all its enemies, domestic or foreign. Sociologist Todd Gitlin agrees with this assessment of history, when he says that the triumph of American Capitalism is "the latest in a long succession of bidders for global unification. It succeeds the Latin imposed by the Roman Empire and the Catholic Church, and Marxist Leninism (tried by the Soviets)." America's Capitalism licked 'em all! (Italics supplied).

In the war over labor--to work or not to work—Capitalism vanquished all pro-labor ideas and triumphed over all its foes. Littered among the dead in the hands of Capitalism are history's once-great ideas that stood in its way in America and elsewhere:

1. Judaism: Judaic idea of the Garden of Eden and the first "perfect" society of men.
2. Christianity: Christian idea of love as prelude to heaven on earth.
3. Jeffersonianism: Thomas Jefferson's idea for egalitarian-utopian America.
4. Smithianism: Adam Smith's political economy for the wealth of all, not just few.
5. Marxism: Karl Marx's "workers paradise" in socialism and shared labor.

In our struggle against the burden of labor and desire to give it to somebody else, these are what we might call the "Five Great Ideas"—now vanquished by American Capitalism, complete and whole--that have affected mankind more than any other ideas, prior to Capitalism. They are, as systems of ideas called "ideology," listed in order of their appearance in history, as reminders to us again, how Capitalism conquered them all. These ideas, once powerful and famous have been vanquished by Capitalism, which whispers into our ears today, as they did in the beginning of human history in the guise of the Devil at the Garden of Eden, "You don't have to work if you become rich; you can let somebody else do the work for you! You can have it all!"

In essence, the basic impetus of Capitalism is at the core of Human Nature: To the extent that you accumulate Capital, you accumulate Power, and, proportional to the Power you have accumulated, you can pretty much dictate your terms over other human beings. This is the reason we would rather be the Nazi than the Jew, rich than poor, and, ultimately, evil than good. Among the terms we want to dictate is the term of "no work" as we can dictate somebody else to do the work for us. Rich people dictate and poor people obey.

It is the fact of life that there are rich people and poor people in America. The few rich (perhaps one-percent) have enough money and power to live a life of their own choice, and the many poor (perhaps 99-percent) have to do all the work that the rich people don't want to do. It's Masters and Slaves all over again, now in a slightly altered and window-dressed form. The poor are not exactly in chains or live in huts, but the legal contracts that bind them are just as tough, or tougher, for them to break as the chains for the real slaves. Just to make the rich-poor picture clearer, we raise a what-if question:

What if *sex* were just hard labor for men, same as working on the farm or at a factory? Men would fight wars to avoid it, enslave other men to do it for them, and hire contract employees today to do the dirty work for them. (The words "sex slave" would have a very different meaning then.) There would be all sorts of propaganda machinery to make the sex work not so revolting so that the lower-class men don't avert it as much.

Naturally, no upper-class person would want to perform it. All sexual acts would be performed by slaves, employees and enlistees. All upper-class children would be produced by lower-class men who must work for the upper-class. All their labor contracts might include their "sex service" clause so that the working class employees cannot avoid performing it for their employers. Like the casualties of war, many lower-class men would die while performing sex for the upper-class men, and the survivors would bitter-ly complain about their lot in having to perform sex acts for the rich men. Some revolutionaries would talk about the Declaration of Human Rights, which include *not* to have to perform the sex work for the rich. Marie Antoi-nette may be deliberately misquoted as having said a very disgusting thing, like "let them have sex!" when the peasants were gathered outside the palace.

Sex would be simply detested labor as any other forms of labor. The rich people, desperate to continue their bloodlines for money inheritance and power maintenance, would force the Government to enact a Sex Draft which declares that all men at their 18th birthday must register at the local Sex Draft

Board. Of course, some men may dodge the draft by running away to Canada or Mexico where they are free from the sex labor. The Media will have stories of men who got caught and brought back to their special Sex Labor Detention Center where the rich people would get their pick of the litter to have them perform the sex work for them. . .

What if *eating* were just hard labor for men, same as working on the farm or at a factory? Men would fight wars *not to have to eat;* would work hard to make other men do the eating. . . Good thing that sex and food are universally loved by men so that the upper-class men gladly perform the work for both. But, whatever else that are detested by the rich, poor men must perform in their stead, as slaves, employees, and enlistees, who live and die doing the chores that the rich avoid.

In spite of what the labor-loving Christians and Socialists say, Capitalism is unbeatable : It is human nature at its simplest and most natural . No one, not even Jesus of Nazareth, has been able to beat its temptation in America. Donald Trump's America is its latest testament of its success.

III.

If you are one of the political radicals, perhaps of the left-leaning variety, the news is not good: The revolution that you hope and expect, to overthrow the Capitalist System, is not going to happen.

Ten reasons suffice:

First, the ancient regimes, in the American Colonies, in Russia, in France, and so on where the Massive Revolution took place, had no technology or psychology that modern regimes possess and were easier to amass a critical amount of primitive energy for people. Such historical events have made the Historians think that a revolution may be a common occurrence that is possible even today: It happened just once, at the end of Feudalism and at the threshold of the Modern World, no more.

Second, modern humans are systematically brainwashed into massive obedience and submission, from early on with their public education system with the ideas of "legitimate government," "public administration," "equality of opportunity," and so on, that reify their reality into permanence and acceptance.

Third, the modern systems are too complex to be subject to the simple primordial passions of man for change. Today, there are too many arguments and counter-arguments, too many relativistic positions, too many philosophers and believers of their own private and professional worlds to have a common agreement.

Fourth, today, the military is too powerful: One company can subdue the whole crowd; one division can wipe out the whole country's citizens. Naturally, many juntas have taken place in third-world countries, military men taking over the government, but only one, that of South Korea, has turned into a successful democratic transformation.

Fifth, today, the development of "the Professional Class," the best and brightest in society, are so separated and compartmentalized into their own professional careers, protocols and interests, basically status quo and economically conservative, that they are mostly change-resistant in the system. Unlike their earlier counterparts in America, France, Russia or China, modern intellectuals do not sympathize with the Common Man but side with the ruling class that hires their professional talent. You cannot start a revolution without the professional class—those people who deal with ideas in society, your mind-leader—on your side: Years of formal education completely *institutionalize* their minds by their respective professional schools. By the time they matriculate from their training, not only are they well skilled in their respective professional trades, but they have also become mental lackeys and believe in their institutions, all against the Common Masses.

Sixth, today, with the advent of the Digital Gadgetry and Social Network Services, the powerless masses have false notions of power, a feeling that they are also empowered with Public Forums, and this Imitation Power pacifies their passion and diverts their festering anger, for which they have legitimate outlets.

Seventh, today, there is the advanced system of mind-control in psychotherapy, mood-altering drugs, numerous self-help-type resolutions, etc., that do not require a public channel of expression.

Eighth, with the advent of various means of entertainment, all year long and 24-hours daily, to distract the human mind and dissipate the angry feeling; the yearly calendar, especially in the U.S., is nothing but a series of Events and Happenings that follow one after the other, giving the mind no respite from such continuous amusement in dramatic public spectacles.

Ninth, today, the reaches of Psychology-Psychiatry have become so extensive, wide-ranging and powerful that the psychological-psychiatric profession virtually controls all feelings-related and interpersonal thoughts and behaviors, including political radicalism. Not unlike the Soviet psychiatrists in the bygone era, the so-called American "mental health professional" is basically a tool of the Power-Holding Class and is used to control people's minds toward Obedience and Submission to the system and false daily Happiness.

Tenth, today, the Law-enforcement system in the U.S. is frighteningly effective and efficient, especially fortified following September-Eleven. Virtually anything goes in the name of National Security, and the public, so institutionalized with fear of Terrorism and so intimidated by the Law's show of power, is willing to accept any degree of law-enforcement.

Day after day, with ever-improving technology and psychology, the ship of the U.S. sails its predetermined course: Let the lawmakers make their laws for the rich; let the judges bang their gavels on legal pronouncements; let the professors teach their truth in the classrooms; let the preachers and priests preach and promise their heavens; let the media entertain the masses with their popular programs; let the politicians make their voters feel their political power; and let the masses scream and holler in ecstasy over their daily, hourly fantasy. Nothing will change.

These are the reasons why our misery will continue into all eternity in America. As Dante told those who entered Inferno, we say: You Americans, *ABANDON ALL HOPE!* If nothing will change to alter the substance and structure of American society for a long time to come, what is the System that's in place that will not be budged? In other words, what rules America now and later? The answer is American Consumer Capitalism. Not even the Trumpian Revolution can touch it.

Chapter Seventeen

How Money Buys the Law

As the dominance of Capitalism in all facets of American life is obvious, we need to highlight the connection between Law and Money to make it more emphatically clear. It is natural that a Capitalist (literally "money-based") society even law-making is part of the money process. Actually, it is money's most central function as money made at the marketplace must be augmented by money stolen legally. The Law is what controls citizens' thoughts and public behaving and this great power comes under the institution that controls the *source* of power. In Saudi Arabia's theocratic society, religious precepts make up the power that makes the Law. In America, a "Capitalist Society," it is natural that money is the power that passes the Law. In short, thinking and behaving in America are the works of the Law that works for the Money System, namely, Capitalism. What, then, is the actual process by which money ends up *buying* the Law in America?

In the State of Nature before Humanity moved forward to form a society (or a commonwealth), power was ordinarily obtained by the Laws of Nature, that is, by brute strength. After we moved to establish a social system, brute strength became less useful. The new method of power-acquisition, the *bloodline*, somewhat between brute strength and the modern system yet to come, was adopted. The bloodline concept was merged into a broader basis of legitimate power called Feudalism or simply Tradition. Saudi Arabia is a Feudal Society, and England is a society based largely on Tradition.

The modern system (sometimes called the "Rational System" among social scientists) is based neither on brute strength nor on bloodline: Rather, it is based on *calculus*, hence the idea of "rationality," as in rational calculus. The U.S. is generally regarded as the most-rational and -calculus-based Social System in the world today. In virtually every decision-made in America, few of us ever think about God or Tradition or Neighbors: We simply ask ourselves, What's the best for me? That is rational calculus.

When we think of "rational" ways of doing things, we think of "calculating" the pros and cons; when we think of "calculating" to arrive at the best decision, we think of "rationally" weighing options and alternatives, not affected by either emotion or tradition. Whether it is based on brute strength, bloodline, or modern rational calculus, once power is established, it becomes "legitimate" power. Legitimacy is *not* possible without power, and no power is ever illegitimate. Once in society, not in nature, all of legitimate power is expressed in the Law, whether made in Tradition or in Rational Calculus. In Saudi Arabia, the Law is made by Feudal Tradition more than anything; in England, by a combination of Tradition and Rational Calculus. In the U.S., it is *all rational calculus* that makes the Law.

It is no coincidence that the most Rationally-Calculating society is also the most money-based society in the System of Capital: In short, the U.S. has the world's *simplest calculus system based on money*. (If we think Donald Trump is a very simplistic person, in all of his thinking and behaving, it is because he has always devoted his whole life to one thing and one thing only, money, the simplest thing in the world to understand and play with.) In America virtually all of the society's vexing problems are either based on money or solved by money: Either we take away money to punish, or we add money to reward and solve issues. We could almost say, 99 percent of Americas daily calculus is done in money, for money, and about money, directly and indirectly.

The Law-as-Legislation (law-making) runs America in the sense that Tradition-as-Law runs Saudi Arabia and England. Since the Law is everything that rules America, and, unlike the Saudis or English who rely on Tradition quite a bit, all laws are made by rational calculus in America. As all things in society are decided on rational calculus, it is logical that all Laws themselves are made by rational calculus in America.

All Rational Calculus in America is based on *numbers*, either in the number of *votes* or in the number of *dollars*. For most of its history, the U.S. had the number of Votes outdoing the number of Dollars. Especially in the 19th-century, the U.S. was all votes as there were relatively few dollars floating around: America was a *political society*, and virtually all the Laws were made as *political decisions* of the American Majority, enough to worry a French visitor about the "Tyranny of the Majority."

Today, with the astronomical amount of wealth to go around, dollars have taken over votes and the tyranny of the majority is about the majority of Dollars, not votes. The Votes, not completely gone from the scene, hang around to add a little background to the Power that the Dollar takes and keeps, but once in a while, upset the election predictions to surprise and disrupt the dollar-proceedings. In essence, all calculus in the Dollars (and vote-counting, when it occurs, is mostly a side-show to make the Dollar look good and legitimate). We tend to think it was the Vote that elected Donald Trump, but after going through the existence of Mental Trash in our midst and understanding how it has destroyed White Americans, we now know that it was the Dollar that elected Trump.

Now, we are ready to see how the dollar makes the law in America: A law-maker, either in the Senate or in the House, is about to decide on a law. As all decisions go, the law-maker can go *one way or the other*. If he decides one way, Group A gets all the benefit of the law. If it goes the other way, Group B gets all the benefit. Let's say Group A is represented by a Corporation like Monsanto; and Group B by some individual farmers. Monsanto pours money, by way of lobbying, into the Process of law-making. (In a money-based society, all money is legitimate and can be used according to the owner's wishes, which includes getting their favorite law-makers re-elected. This is in essence what the U.S. Supreme Court ruled recently). Group B, being poor, spends little or no money on the law-making process. The law-maker starts his rational calculating: It is between 10-million dollars from Group A and zero-dollars from Group B. We can ask, as an innocent child would, is there anything like the "legislator's conscience" on the part of the Law-maker? By and large, No, because we are talking about a "Rational-Calculating" modern system where only cold calculus, not tradition, not conscience, no feelings of any kind, is in operation. The Law-maker rationally calculates as all Americans rationally calculate in every decision they make (other than finding a marriage partner, whose decision fails half the time maybe because it is *not* based on rational calculus).

So, in these circumstances, what is the most likely decision that the Law-maker can make upon his rational calculus? Naturally, and in the most-"American Way" possible, Monsanto, of Group A, gets the decision: The law passes to benefit Monsanto.

To put it in the simplest way possible, this is why and how money makes-buys the Law in America. Now, the innocent among us might remain incredulous: Is the law-making process in America *that crass* and *that callous*, as to sell it to the highest bidder, they might ask? Not surprisingly, the answer is, Yes, aside from some procedural and window-dressing wrinkles to be added, that's basically how it is done. The "complexity" of passing a bill in Congress is the complexity of the bidding, similar amounts of money being bandied about that makes the decision making somewhat complex among similar sources of influence, not the complexity of conflicting moral decisions. The rule is: *You could pass any law in America, say, giving Hitler America's Medal of Freedom posthumously, if you had enough money to lobby the law-makers!*

Some people, especially on the Left of the political spectrum, get mad that the U.S. Congress is wholly bought and operated by the corporations and the Super Rich. Why would it *not be*? Just think: They are the ones who have all the dollars you need to lobby the law-makers; in matters of money, perhaps not a single law passes the Congress that favors the poor. The U.S. is a "capitalist" (money-based) society where rational calculus *is* about the only way we make decisions; you want something done, spend money and it will get done. All power is embodied in the Law. So *money, calculus*, and *the law* come together, so inevitably, so logically, and so naturally, to form their unholy alliance.

If you are still unconvinced how so blatantly money buys laws in America, let us take a look at the Big Picture to restate what is obvious: In a money-based society, all things are measured, exchanged, and judged by money units, including morality, beauty, truth, justice and life itself. Money is both Legal (legitimate) and Good (holy) in America. It is logical that money buys laws too, perhaps not directly at the marketplace, but indirectly through the lobbying money and the Political Process of Legislation. Why is this Logical? Because all laws, ultimately, are laws of money that determine how power is distributed in America and the way power is distributed is the way wealth is distributed since in America power and wealth are identical. (In Russia and China, they are also identical, but in the Opposite Way of America: There, *power buys wealth.* In America, wealth buys power). So, in America, every law-making act is a contest between different sizes of money, and normally whoever (or whatever) spends more money wins the law: Virtually all Acts that pass at the U.S. Congress are the Win for the larger-sized money. To argue, or believe, that this doesn't exist in America is to argue, or believe, that money doesn't exist in America. We say money makes the world go around, and that world certainly includes the law-making world. All of America's moral precepts, political process, and public knowledge proceed from this principle of money which is universally recognized as true, just and democratic. There is nothing strange or untoward about it if we begin with our *money-based system of society* in America, which is called "Capitalism." Considering the way America's social system follows the Capitalist System, America's *silence* about money buying laws is nothing strange. It is the way it should be.

II.

One question rarely raised concerning money, since money commands unquestioned legal and moral authority in America, is this: What *is* money and how does it affect Humanity? By way of searching for the answers to the above, consider these possibilities that money creates in our social life: If "freedom" has to be paid for with money, it is no longer freedom, but *slavery*. If "love" has to be paid for with money, it is *prostitution*. If "justice" has to be paid for with money, it is *corruption*. If "good" has to be paid for with money, it is *evil*. What else can they be?

And most disturbing of all: Just think that the United States of America is a society that is absolutely, single-mindedly, and relentlessly devoted to one goal, and one goal only: To corrupt every American within its borders, and if possible, everyone on the globe, so that *they all think well of money and money-based life!* If you doubt this wisdom, just see who is sitting in the White House!

In fact, there is no such thing as an American Mind that is not created, like the creature of Dr. Frankenstein, by the best and brightest workers who work for Corporate America. When an American cries or laughs, very likely he cries or laughs because Dr. Frankenstein supplied him something to cry or laugh about, through a mass medium like a TV screen, a classroom, a computer program, a story, a movie, a billboard, a newspaper headline, a magazine cover, some tool somewhere invented and run by the One-Percent and its best and brightest professionals.

What Americans eat, think, choose, act, relate or dream and define, concrete and vague, all the things and ideas that make up the so-called American Mind, as we have seen earlier, is being slowly but surely shaped by such institutions at the service of the One Percent and its money. In fact, the One-Percent itself is *defined* by money and nothing else. When a teacher teaches her students, when a worker dreams of doing something for the weekend, when a legislator votes on his agenda, when a corporate chief makes his next move, when a writer pens his words and ideas, when a child fantasizes about his future. . . the long shadow of money is cast across all thoughts, feelings, plans—indeed, everything in America—that is done or contemplated. Never in the history of humanity is the thought process of virtually everyone—we mean, literally everyone—hatched under the mechanisms that serve the One-Percent and its money. The power of the Corporate America is everywhere, like the air we breathe, but it is, like the air itself, invisible and unrecognizable.

A man who picks up a DVD for the evening would never think--not once--that his action to purchase the movie and decision to spend the evening with it, rather than something else of his choice, is actually the cumulative effect of a long series of campaigns carried out ceaselessly by the One-Percent and its money. He has no idea that his money, his purchase, his time and so on--all the decisions related to the event--were created out of nothing, almost like the act of God, that materialized only because the money willed it to materialize. Nor does he recognize that all things that exist in his mind exist simply because the One Percent who controls corporations willed them to exist. Nor does he understand that his whole existence--along with the existence of the rest of the 99-percent masses, White or non-white—is the creation of his New God, the One Percent and its money of his society, who signals his brain to activate on the next cycle of events. Nor does he realize that, when this signal is absent because he is late on payment, his brain remains essentially empty. Just imagine what the word "consciousness" or "awareness" means to an average American.

Indeed, the air we breathe is so omnipresent that it is difficult for the public, White and non-white, to get a clear view of the air itself. When there is so much to enjoy for the masses everywhere—cheap movies and beer, entertaining TV and computers around the clock, easy sex and easier social interactions, thrilling games and events all year round--the Monsanto-government collusion, and all others that corrupt and sell out America, fades into boredom and insignificance. The hidden order of the day for the 99 percent is: *Don't bite the hand that feeds you, and, the trough is big enough for everyone!*

Corporate Capitalism in the U.S. has effectively transformed the American majority into sleepy non-beings—including the otherwise-noisy Triumpian storm-troopers--who live with the Devil of their choice that demands their souls and die with the newest toys in their arms. There is no way the American Masses can counter the power of the Capitalist System when that System controls the minds of the Masses through government, entertainment, education, media, propaganda, psychology, the Law, and anything else that can be enlisted in the mind-game by the power of money. There are no institutions in America that are friends of the 99-percent: Not the U.S. Supreme Court, not the Bank of America, not the National Football League, not the American Red Cross, not Harvard University, not the Armed Forces, not the Catholic Church, not Disney World. . . . . All of them are either the tools of the top One Percent or in cahoots with them, to benefit in their own institutional power games. To put it crudely (as gentility goes nowhere with the sleepy non-beings in America): The Capitalist System has everybody in America, especially the White Masses, *by the balls!*

Aside from sporadic and scattered reactions, there is no sizable citizen anger or visible reaction to this Corporate dominance of American life. Even the stormtroopers in the Trump camp have said nothing about how Corporations control all of America, including its government; they are just satisfied with controlling the Lesser Americans while they themselves are controlled by Corporate America. Now, we ask: *Why is there no citizen anger or reaction, even from the Trumpian Revolutionaries ?*

The first truth about Corporate America is that, in the absence of force, in voluntary democracy, Corporations take what citizen-consumers give them. "Corporate Evil" is possible only when citizen-consumers *allow* Corporations to succeed with their means and goals. In other words, Corporate Evil is not possible without Dumb Citizens. But, ironically, it is the Corporation that makes American citizens dumb!

Corporations succeed because we, as individuals, citizens and consumers, share the same goal with corporations: Expanding our power over others. As private individuals, we aim to expand our power over others on an individual scale. We consume what corporations offer only because we wish to achieve our own individual goals of power expansion on an individual level. In short, we are no better off morally than Corporate America: In fact, we *are* Corporate America. Both Corporations and Individual Americans want the same thing and pursue the same thing. They are fellow travelers, not adversaries. Corporations succeed on a larger scale of things because of their larger resources. We, as individual citizens, are happy to take the breadcrumbs in our small institutional roles.

In an ideal civil society, we create Government because we do not trust ourselves, as citizens and as corporations, to be good to one another on our own. When our individual power is greater than somebody else's, we tend to bully him into submission. We institute government, larger than all of the individuals put together, to prevent this from happening. But in the process of Capitalist Development where money corrupts this purpose of government, the Government becomes "corporatized," as part of Corporate America rather than as its *counterpart*. It now bullies weak individual citizens in behalf of the real bullies, the corporations. Typical to this development, Trump's government is presently constituted to bully the Lesser Americans, not to protect them from the bigger bullies, such as White America and its Corporations.

The government in the U.S. allows Corporations to expand their powers at the expense of its consumer-citizens. At the same time, it also allows the citizens to expand their individual powers over other citizen-individuals in a mini-Capitalist battleground, such as the dramatic case of Trumpian Whites over non-whites. The government does this by allowing corporations to operate in society as if they are in the "state-of-nature" power contest and expansion.

The government is also a depository of careers, and as bureaucratic careerists pursuing their individual reward, serving corporate and government positions interchangeably, the officials serve Corporate America over the civic society. In American governing philosophy for a "natural society," power is justified only with minimum interference from civic society. The only victims are the masses who are powerless. Even with their massive voting power, they can only whimper, not roar, in a Capitalist System. The Trumpian rebels, their intelligence and humanity destroyed by Mental Trash, alternately whimper at their Corporate Master and snarl at the Lesser American brethren.

Corporations exist to expand their power by making money, destroying jobs as easily as creating jobs, all depending on what gives them their maximum profit. Individuals do the same, for their own power expansion (maximum profit), being evil as easily as being gppd to one another, just as easily as do the corporations. Corporate evil is just larger because of their scale of operation.

Are there any victims produced when government regulators are in cozy relations with the corporations that they are supposed to *regulate*? Yes: The American Public, Whites *and* non-whites, which is at the moment divided between Whites who are indifferent and non-whites who are powerless. That non-white victimization is greater than that for Whites does not really alter the nature of victimization.

III.

How does Corporate America keep the public believing, by and large, that the System is just and fair? The false public belief is accomplished by the function of the Law--from the U.S. Constitution to Municipal Rules--that has American citizens believe that American is governed by the rule of Law. When Americans see the Law in action in its popular image--the black-robed, legalese-speaking judges and the mysterious workings of the Law under the judges' gavels--they are generally awed by the supreme myths of how justice is upheld in America.

To represent this corporate system, in upholding its morality and justice in our public image, none is better than the U.S. Supreme Court where all the baffling questions of the Law get settled by the greatest repository of wisdom in the land. Also, at the same time, the U.S. Supreme Court is the *best* and *most effective* of all American Institutions for the final and absolute judgment of all things, and, therefore, most susceptible to corruption among all institutionalized agencies of society. Not subject to elections or recalls, the judges at the Supreme Court enjoy immunity from citizen control more majestically than any other such agencies of society. With its imposing building and nine well-dressed judges (laughingly called "Justices,"), the U.S. Supreme Court represents the Constitutional interpretations of the U.S. and its words are final in the legal authority of America (subject to overturning only by another, perhaps equally-corrupt, institutional body, the U.S. Congress).

When a candidate is selected to become one of the Justices at the Supreme Court, interested parties do not ask whether the candidate is qualified but whether he-she is "conservative" or "liberal," whether he-she is likely to vote this way or that on a given case. When a Justice says Yes or No on an issue, it is the fact of the vote that is of interest to the public, not whether it is a "just" yes or "just" no. To those on the Right, who prefer a Yes on an issue, they would rather have an "unjust Yes," than a "just No." The Opposite goes for those on the Left. If the nine Dummies said Yes, the Right would be just as happy; if the nine Dummies said No, the Left would be just as happy.

The U.S. Supreme Court is thus non-sense of the first order and represents one of the finest propaganda effects and image managements for Law and Order in America. To understand this strange phenomenon and unravel this legal mystery, let's backtrack.

The U.S. Supreme Court makes "decisions," like all other institutions empowered to do so, by choosing one side or the other between two contending parties. What they do is to say which party is right and which party is wrong, or something of that sort. Their decisions could be about something as mundane as marriages and something as serious as murder and the death penalty.

In most cases and by right, the parties in dispute are entitled to a jury trial. The Jury, made up of different numbers up to 12, is summoned to make the decisions on each case. Naturally, some cases are trivial and some are life-and-death. The typical Jury consists of those citizens in all walks of life—housewives, janitors, doctors, professors, white-collar workers, blue-collar workers, unemployed, black, white, old, young, whoever draws the number. In short, the Jury is the cross section of America, nothing special or unusual in education, gender, appearance, intelligence, weight, height, skin color, whatsoever.

These totally non-descript compositions of the agency of the law, once sworn in, are asked to make decisions on all cases, including life and death matters. Whatever they decide in a case, their vote is absolute and final and cannot be held accountable for their vote. There is no higher authority of the law. Their biases and prejudices make up the substance of America's judgment and they are accepted as the ultimate verdict as if from God Himself. A Jury is the microcosm of America at any given time. In a small size and sample, it represents all the biases and prejudices, and therefore everything about America, in its body. It is the same body that elects the President, Congress, and all the governors and mayors of the nation in ultimate authority and legitimacy. The Jury is the final repository of all that is America and American Thought and American Action.

Now, let's shift our attention to the U.S. Supreme Court. There, we have Nine permanent members of decision making. Why do we have these Nine Justices as our permanent jury members? It is impossible for a Jury to come to a wrongful verdict and make other errors of judgment, but we have no complaints about the Jury System itself. Why are we having the nine permanent members sitting there at the U.S. Supreme Court? Why are we not having a Jury, summoned for each case or session, at the Supreme Court to render its verdict?

Now, people would argue that the cases decided at the Supreme Court are "important," "significant," having an "impact on the nation," and so on. But the latest case argued and decided at the Supreme Court is something concerning gay marriages. Is this more important, significant, etc., than life and death? Other cases that come to the Court are no more or less important than gay marriages. But which cases are more important is just a matter of subjective opinion. The nine Justices are a permanent fixture, their biases and prejudices eventually materializing as *votes*. Their knowledge, their wisdom, their experience, whatever, merely end up being a vote, and a vote is a vote whether it is rendered by a Supreme Court justice or by a hobo, and it is the vote that the contesting party watches as they watch any jury decision.

It so happens that the justices rarely change their life-time habits of bias and prejudice. And that is the reason why the parties and presidents who appoint them go through some serious thinking. What they are looking for, when they choose a new justice, is not knowledge, wisdom or experience, but a sure vote, to be cast according to the expectations of the sponsor. Justice X votes on issues exactly as expected; so does Justice Y, and so does Justice Z. They basically have to die or get incapacitated to be replaced by another fixed vote. So, ultimately, there is no difference in the play of bias and prejudice whether it is the Justice or the hobo off the street. (In fact, a hobo's ironic wisdom and knowledge might be more beneficial to the average citizens). But, why is this supreme Court mystery harmful to the Republic?

This simple Yes-or-No vote, no different from any average citizen jury's, is harmful because of its propaganda effect, making the citizens think that there is something mighty wise and mighty mysterious going on there, and some mighty omnipotent minds are at work at the U.S. Supreme Court to insure our justice, truth and the American way. In our public image, the nine Justices are the High Priests of Wisdom, and King Solomon reincarnated in our midst to deliver the Ultimate in Justice. But the nine Justices are no such things. They are just part of the Government made up of political infighting and personal biases and prejudices, each political party struggling to put *their* biases and prejudices in the Supreme Court.

It's like the Emperor's new clothes, which is nothing at all: What's going on at an average session of the U.S. Supreme Court is nothing but the Justices casting their tried-and-true known vote, according to their party politics and lifetime's habit of love and hate. Certainly nothing to do with their knowledge or wisdom of the fate of the Republic or its justice administration. They are just old men and women of known judicial records, Liberal or Conservative, that their political patrons support and push. There is not a single Justice at the U.S. Supreme Court, as we contemplate the matter right now, who is deliberating the case according to his Constitutional Wisdom, Knowledge, or Fate of the Republic, not according to his lifetime's bias and prejudice and payback to the system that has put him or her in his place today.

Which is total hooey! The Republic would certainly be no worse off to be decided by a randomly-selected Jury of Common Citizens. Why, they vote and elect all Congressional members and the President of the U.S. and virtually everybody else! Why can't these citizens, selected as a Jury of the Commons, sit in the U.S. Supreme Court?

What kind of Important Cases eventually do end up at the U.S. Supreme Court for its decision, to see if there is any justification for the Supreme Court?

The Associated Press says recently, "Big Issues Still Awaiting Supreme Court Rulings," before the Justices can enjoy the summer breaks looming ahead. What are those "Big Issues," according to the news outlet? It lists the following Big Issues confronting the nine Justices before their summer recess:

1. CONTRACEPTIVE COVERAGE: Should corporate employers be allowed not to pay insurance premiums on their employees contraception health plans? Maybe, maybe not.
2. ABORTION CLINIC BUFFER ZONES: Should abortion clinics have buffer zones keeping protesters away? Maybe, maybe not.
3. CELLPHONE SEARCHES: Should the police be allowed to search cellphones without a warrant? Maybe, maybe not.
4. TV ON THE INTERNET: Should Internet operators be allowed to broadcast TV programs to digital outlets? Maybe, maybe not.
5. GREENHOUSE GASES: Some industry groups assert that the EPA overstepped in its environmental enforcement; are they correct? Maybe, maybe not.
6. UNION FEES: Should unions be allowed to collect fees from the workers who object? Maybe, maybe not.
7. SECURITIES FRAUD: Should investors be deterred from class-action suits against Halliburton? Maybe, maybe not.
8. "FALSE" CAMPAIGN CLAIMS: Should the state police be allowed to police campaign promises over the First Amendment rights? Maybe, maybe not.

These are some of the so-called "Big Issues" that confront the Justices at the U.S. Supreme Court. We need to ask: What makes them "Big Issues"? We notice that none of the issues has national implications, nor does any determine the fate of America. All of the issues have two sides, the plaintiff and the defendant. These are issues that have two sides, which means one side will win, and the other side will lose. It is *not* a Hitler vs. The Free World, or a Joan of Arc vs. The Church. As far as the American Nation goes, it matters little or nothing whoever wins or loses. They are some of the issues that ordinary juries all over America deal with all the time: They happen to end up in the Supreme Court only because the loser wouldn't give up, *not* because it is a big issue. These are issues any ordinary citizens of America can deliberate and on which they can cast their "yes" or "no" vote. Both sides have already made their arguments and all the reasons have already been stated by both sides. There is nothing to be done except say Yes or No. If Yes, then the Plaintiff will provide the reasons for its win; if no, the Defendant will.

It is what is fashionably called a "no brainer" when there is no intellectual or moral challenge to one's conclusion or decision: Any conclusion or decision will do. The very fact that the case has gone all the way to the Supreme Court proves that it is *not important*, except to the persons, groups and lawyers involved. Truly important decisions, like Hitler vs. The Free World or Joan of Arc vs. The Church, are not decided by the court, any court: It is decided by a power above and beyond the court, say, by the King, or his Star Chamber, or his Army, or whatever that holds the Great Power of All.

The cases that go to the Supreme Court are some political-financial issues over which both sides disagree. They require neither Solomons nor Great Legal Scholarship. The judges are called "Justices," the place is called "Supreme Court," and they dress and talk in a peculiar way, all of which just covers up the Ordinariness of their Business. It is just a Constitutional-Legal Game that the U.S. happens to play seriously. Just like the World Cup, however, even nothing becomes something if played seriously enough long enough: This is the very Principle on which all government propagandists depend.

Just like the World Cup, many Americans don't pay any attention to the "Big Issues" of the "Supreme" court, nor to its "Justices." Anything that has two sides arguing is just a game. The last time a Big Issue was decided, it took 60-million lives (nearly 1-million of them American), and the U.S. Supreme Court Justices were neither Supreme nor Just in that Big Issue. In fact, they had nothing to do with the Big Event that we call World War II.

Chapter Eighteen

The Ten Reminders

As we come to the end of our quest here, let's list the ten ways in which the triumph of Capitalism can be most commonly experienced and observed, reminders of what we all continually face in America.

I. *WHAT WE EAT*: The majority eat what the One Percent feeds them (thanks to Monsanto, in great part) that slowly kills them with fat, sugar, and salt, and all the processing, to which the majority is wholly beholden and addicted. This addiction is so thorough that, for the first time in the nation's history, the Lesser Americans—especially the poorer Black and Hispanic population--are not going to live as long as their parent generation. There is no place the 99-percent, White and non-white, can turn to find inexpensive healthy food for their families because the so-called "food industry" controls all of the shelves at grocery stores and also our taste-buds, aided a good deal by the government regulators at FDA, DOA and EPA who are in cahoots with the food corporations. Americans, whether White or non-white, are being fattened up for a slow death as the gigantic agri-business determines what we eat and think about eating. The Food Industry (yes, literarily an *industry*) recognizes that what happens at the brain must go through the stomach, and they are right: The American Masses think with their stomach. We are what we eat, and what we eat is largely controlled by the food factories of the agri-industry. The government, the only regulator that can help us, is no help because it is run by those dispatched from the food industry, like Monsanto.

II. *ENTERTAINMENT:* The majority eat another kind of food fed by the one-percent: They are addicted and enslaved, quite literally, by the around-the-clock spectacles of Mental Trash in entertainment and distraction concocted and supplied by America's best and brightest, turning every living room into a dying room of their soul and intelligence. The world has never seen anything of this order since the days of the Roman Circus. With this, the human heart and thinking ability of the majority--so visible and remarkable in 1776 and in the fight against Hitler--are now asleep in the haze of the New Opium of entertainment supplied by the Best and Brightest. The Masses work and endure the humiliation and dehumanization of their employment, just to ensure the continuing supply of this New Opium that occupies all of their non-working hours. To the delight of the rulers, entertainment slowly dumbs down the majority and kills off their social alertness, leaving them selfish with themselves but obedient with their ruling masters, happy all the time, like the population in *Brave New World* euphoric on *Soma*.

III. *CORPORATE TRAINING:* The American Masses, White and non-white, are educated, publicly and privately, on all levels, from kindergarten to graduate school, to become the docile but efficient workers for Corporate America. All the arts and sciences they learn are the arts and sciences of how to enrich the corporate overlords. From Harvard to on-line schools, the majority compete to see who can serve their new masters better and more loyally, necessarily against the interest of their fellow 99-percent. Some of them learn how to manage people as Human Resource Managers and Efficiency Experts. A "good education" in America does not mean creating a good mind or intellect produced by studying human history or its accumulated wisdom in irony, but a training that would open the door to a lifetime's employment in the corporate world. The "liberal arts" education does not liberate anyone, but merely delivers the graduate into a chain of job contracts and obedience to power. All teachers and professors are merely the overseers of slave plantations, making sure that their pupils and students learn the proper ways of compliance (with "marketable skills" and degrees) in corporate life. In the process, all so-called "radical" minds are weeded out as dysfunctional and anti-Capitalist.

IV. *ECONOMIC POWER:* The Capitalist elite controls America's political and economic power, neutralizing the former with the latter. The majority that used to "tyrannize" American political power--as De Tocqueville saw in 19th-century America--is now the voting machine for Donald Trump to get their boots on the necks of the Lesser Americans. Today's U.S. is the only democratic nation in the world where the 99-percent masses are divided against each other. The Bill Gateses of America go to bed comfortably and in peace, knowing that there is no danger of mass revolt against their wealth. In their eyes, the 99-percent, Whites against non-whites, are well tamed by training and education and made obedient to their economic masters with the regular supply of entertainment opium. The political majority, like the Trump voters, can make noise and fuss about this or that issue at election time, but it is all for the show. Its noise has no substantial power and its fuss is merely those of disgruntled consumers and children; and the logic of consumption makes "consumers" and "children" one and the same—both choosing what their capricious hearts demand.

V. *THE LAW:* The control of the majority by the One Percent is carried out in various ways and aspects of American life, but foremost, in the play of the Law. The Law—how it is made, enforced and privatized, all legally and legitimately—is the secret wand of Power in America. Other nations have their collective tradition, Crown, religion, tribal mythology or history to tame the wild hearts in their citizens; the U.S. has none of those, only the Law. But the Law is controlled by the Corporate elite who controls the law-makers with its great power and influence of lobbying, which is the power and influence of money. *TIME* magazine ran a cover story entitled *"The Best Laws Money Can Buy"* (May 12, 2010) that in a typical year, the lobbyists spent 3.5 billion dollars on the law-makers; and that is over 6.5 million dollars *per law-maker*. In a "capitalist" (which means "money-based") society, there is nothing stronger or more powerful than money. In a logical sequence of cause and effect, American money controls the American Law: Money makes and enforces the Law. From the Supreme Court judge to the beat cop, it is implicitly and often explicitly understood that all law business is money business, as the Law is money and money is the Law. The One Percent has all the money (often imaginary money) and the 99 percent, White and non-white, none; and the One Percent has its hand on the power lever in America, all legitimately and constitutionally, as did the Nazis and Communists in their own time. But unlike the latter two, the American version is universally loved and supported by those who are controlled by it.

Naturally, all the power, and its control, that Corporate America has over the 99 per cent is vested in the Law in America. When a rich person is charged with a wrongdoing he generally protests, crying out, "I've not done anything *illegal!*" while a poor person is likely to protest, "I've not done anything *wrong!*" The rich person relies on the "goodness" of the Law, to be friendly to him and to be on his side, and in this expectation he is not disappointed. The poor must rely on the "moral good," perhaps thinking that some higher justice, will prevail, which is seldom. The poor may have Divine Law and Justice on their side, and for that they tend to pray fervently. But the rich have the real law on their side—the Law, Courts, Law-Enforcement, the Military, Prisons—and there is no contest.

The Law, unlike what most Americans think of it as a fair instrument of justice, is thus a great shield that protects the rich with all the legitimacy that is symbolized and substantiated. Once you are rich and the Law is on your side, you are virtually home free in American justice that is built of money, by money and for money. This conditionality and temporality of the Law — that the rich and the Law are mutually connected and that this is so only so long as the present laws hold true--can be better understood in the following hypothetical process: If we had another 1776-like change in America, the comfort and peace of mind that pervades the rich today would evaporate instantly in the revolutionary change; there would be a new Constitution where money influence is no more; the rich, say, the Bill Gateses, would be charged with a crime, perhaps "Crimes against Humanity," for defrauding and dehumanizing the masses in America, destroying community, society and humanity in America with false claims and temptations; there would be public hangings of the rich, now poor and powerless, to warn the world: The United States is back to the way it is supposed to be, a nation of the people, by the people and for the people. Of course, to make sure this fantasy never comes about, Consumer Capitalism does everything to keep the consumers, especially White, stupid, self-centered, childish, only thinking about what is in their private hearts and no more, never forming anything like the 1776-style social consciousness. Shall we call this *legal* "mind control"?

VI. *MIND-CONTROL:* Along with the education and the Law, Corporate America controls the 99-percent where it really counts: At their mental level. This mind control is carried out daily by none other than the mass media and its Mental Trash arsenal. Using the instruments of entertainment and commentaries, the media teach the consumer majority, around the clock without pause or stop, the beauty, the logic, the fantasy of the "American System," which naturally favors the rich one-percent and idiotizes the 99-percent. The "Lifestyles of the Rich and Famous" is shown to the delight of the masses but never the "Lifestyles of the Poor and Wretched." (This subtle propaganda technique was a favorite weapon of mind-control among the Nazis in the Third Reich.) No one understands the logic of a wasted mind better than the ruling class whose ultimate goal is *to waste all minds in America.* Consumer Capitalism wants all minds wasted to idiocy. In fact, the main function of the Media is to create Wasted Minds, as a quintessential American Brand of minds, to make everyone intellectually empty and socially disjointed, and very successfully so. The total effect of a popular TV program may be measured in the high Nielsen Ratings, but every number in the Nielsen Ratings is actually the Number of the Wasted Minds (We should actually call it the Nielsen Wasted-Minds Ratings). All media programs compete to see who can garner up the greatest number of Wasted Minds. The Super Bowl and the Oscar Night are among the top contenders.

VII. *LABOR AND TOIL:* The earlier Americans, the absolute majority of them, believed in labor for all, and what their labor created became their own private property. What their labor created was what they owned. This Work Ethic also created America's Golden Age of freedom and equality for the majority. Labor was God's gift to man if it was to be shared by all, and this was supported by Jesus, Jefferson, Smith and anyone else whose ideas were enlightened. In their time, benefits came from their own labor and enterprise they owned themselves. Today, profits come from *capital* and naturally only *capitalists* benefit from it. The majority, the once entrepreneurs and owners of their livelihood, is chained to their jobs and paychecks to pay for their debt-based consumption, always goaded to spend way more than their income. They labor and toil basically to pay for the debt they owe to the one-percent, while hating their labor and desperately wanting to escape their toil. Corporate America, in cooperation with the government and social institutions, encourages the 99-percent majority, White and non-white, to spend themselves to death, and then work themselves to death, to pay for their debt. The new philosophy of work in America is that it is bad if you have to do it, and good if you can make somebody else do it. Hence, the new ethos is that the poor suckers work themselves to death, while the One Percent plays, calling it "the American Dream." The end-result: The majority in America exists only to provide labor and toil so that the One Percent can play around the clock.

VIII. *PSYCHOLOGY AND ANGER MANAGED:* In 1776, the majority got angry and revolted against their government and its overlords, risking their own deaths and ruins. Today, the White Majority risked ridicule and scorn of the world by getting angry against their Lesser American brethren, not their Corporate Master. By voting for Donald Trump, they barked up the wrong tree entirely. Their real enemy is Corporate America that turns them into idiots and children, not the Lesser American minority that does all the dirty work for them and endures all sorts of discrimination in a racist society. Authentic public anger is an emotion that is fast disappearing from the American majority's political arsenal and emotional staple. In place of public anger--which may galvanize and channel private depressions and frustrations into healthy social consciousness—the System encourages consumer complaining and voter dissatisfaction: For the former we visit the Better Business Bureau, and for the latter, we write to our Congressmen or look for a Messiah. There is something wrong with a person who is angry, the consensus goes. With all the affluence, entertainment, pleasure of every known kind, why would anyone in America get angry? Well, the White Majority finally got angry, but only to make themselves the Joke of the Century and America the Fascist Nation of the 21st century. The only people who still get angry authentically are blacks over civil-rights issues and with yet-untamed anger at injustice. For good measure, Corporate America, with its best-and-brightest professional workers, has created something called "anger management." All public anger is resolved into happiness and contentment once this management process is applied to the angry emotion or, God-forbid, the cause. With numerous other psychological-psychiatric-therapeutic means of resolution at its disposal, anger has become a "mental" issue, to be avoided by all means in America.

IX. *TECHNOLOGY AND FANTASY:* There is another chain that binds the 99-percent majority, whether White or non-white, in America: That is, the chains of Hi-Technology. With the invention of the computing machine, and its most widespread consumer product, the cell-phone, the 1776 idea of man in control of his own tools has become a myth with the 99 percent, now spearheaded by the Millennials, who, now, are the servants of their own technological machines. As Henry David Thoreau said, they have become "the tools of their tools." Tools and low-tech machines used to serve people; now people serve the amusing machines, as their daily activities, human thoughts and social connections are dictated by the machines. But, as noted, the machines are mere metal-and-plastic clumps of things whose true owners are the owners of Corporate America, who can make the contraptions come alive only upon payment from the Masses. Of all the mind-controlling tools, the computing machine is perhaps the most efficient: It creates a world of instant fantasy and dreams just at the fingertips of the users, usually the consuming majority, who feel they are Kings and Masters with those machines and their *imitation* power. It is hard to imagine that those in the top One Percent members bury their faces in the cell-phone. They need no fantasy or dreams to feed themselves: The *real world* is under their fingertips and the human beings who obey them are the *real people*, not screen figures. Only the dummies in the 99 percent, especially White Americans, tap their way into fantasyland, thinking they are Kings and Masters of the little mechanical Genie.

X. *LIBERTY AND FREEDOM:* And, then, as the final nail in the coffin of the 99-percent in America, they have turned on each other in the magic of "freedom." They fight one another with guns in their homes, locks on the door, and lawsuits in courtrooms, all for their individual freedom. And finally, the White Majority declared war on the Lesser Half of America with nationalism and racism, brute force and naked power. The word the 1776 generation favored was "liberty," not freedom. Liberty means people are united against the enemy of liberty, generally tyranny, which threatens the life and happiness of all members of society. For liberty, they were united as brothers and citizens, and fought and died together. Freedom is wholly opposite of liberty: It means *my* freedom, *my* own right to do whatever *I* want, nothing to do with anyone else's freedom or right. Hence, my own freedom always comes into conflict with somebody else's freedom, and we rush to our individual fortresses with guns, locks and lawsuits. While liberty unites us, freedom thus turns everyone against everyone else, in general suspicion of neighbor against neighbor, brother against brother, stranger against stranger, and finally White Americans against non-white Americans. But for the White Majority, freedom is a great thing, as in "consumer freedom," "free choice," "free-enterprise," and "Make America Great Again," so on. They have no idea that for freedom of selfish pursuits, they have destroyed the liberty for all citizens, and will eventually destroy themselves: They are just too corrupted by Corporate America's Mental Trash and mind-control to realize that their real enemy is elsewhere.

In American reality, thus, it is not that difficult for a small minority, especially armed with modern technology and sophisticated psychology, to rule the masses once their weakness is figured out. History has shown, time and again prior to the American case, the many examples of colonialism where this sort of administration is so easily carried out. Hitler is said to have admired the British efficiency in its rule of vastly-populated India. "Let's learn from the English," Hitler is recorded to have said in his famous Table Talk, as the German model for control over the Slavs, "who, with two hundred and fifty thousand men in all, including fifty thousand soldiers, govern four hundred million Indians."

Today, Donald Trump's America is a gigantic step backward to the days of Europe between two World Wars where brute power and naked Fascist ideology was rising, shamelessly and massively. Trump's win is more than the deterioration of the 1776 idealism in America; it is about the nature of humanity witnessed all over the world since time immemorial—the 99 percent of all humanity, living and dead—that is being dramatically acted out on the Trumpian stage, to show us how easily so few can control so many.

Bibliography

Arendt, Hannah. 1963. *The Origins of Totalitarianism*. New York: Meridian Books.

Bauerlein, Mark. 2008. *The Dumbest Generation: How the Digital Age Stupefies Young Americans and Jeopardizes Our Future*. New York, NY: Jeremy P. Tarcher/Penguin.

Boorstin, Daniel. 1973. *The Americans*. Vol. I-III. New York: Vintage.

Bryce, James. 1995. *The American Commonwealth. 2 volumes*. Indianapolis: Liberty Fund.

Carr, Nicholas. 2010. *The Shallows: What the Internet is doing to our Brains*. New York: W.W. Norton.

Cherry, Conrad. *God's New Israel*. 1999. Chapel Hill, NC: University of North Carolina Press.

C.B. MacPherson. 1961. *The Political Theory of Possessive Individualism*. NY: Oxford University Press.

De Tocqueville, Alexis. 2001. *Democracy in America*. Edited and abridged by Richard D. Heffner. NY: New American Library.

Ekirch, Arthur. 1973. *The Decline of American Liberalism*. NY: Atheneum.

Gilbert, Gustave. 1947. *The Nuremberg Diary*. New York: Farrar, Straus, and Company.

Hacker, Andrew. 1992. *Two Nations: Black and White, Separate, Hostile, Unequl*. NY: Scribner.

Hochschild, Arlie. 2003. *The Managed Heart*. Berkeley, CA: University of California Press.

Huer, Jon. 1977. *The Dead End*. Dubuque, IW: Kendall-Hunt.

————. 1991. *The Wages of Sin*. NY: Praeger Publishers.

————. 2010. *American Paradise*. Lanham, MD: University Press of America.

————. 2010. *Auschwitz, USA*. Lanham, MD. Rowman & Littlefield.

————. 2012. *Call From The Cave*. Lanham, MD: Hamilton Books.

————. 2015. *Labor Avoidance*. Lanham, MD: Rowman & Littlefield.

Locke, John. 1997. Woolhouse, Roger, ed., An Essay Concerning Human Understanding. New York: Penguin Books.

Martineau, Harriet. *1837. Society in America; 3 volumes*. London: Saunders and Otley (reissued by Cambridge University Press in 2009).

McLuhan, Marshall. 1964. *Understanding Media: The Extension of Man*. London: Routledge.

Mills, C. Wright. 1951. *White Collar*. NY: Oxford University Press.

Postman, Neil. 1985. *Amusing Ourselves to Death*. NY: Penguin, USA.

Potter, David. 1954. *People of Plenty*. Chicago, IL: Chicago University Press.

Riesman, David. 1962. *The Lonely Crowd*. New Haven, CT: Yale University Press.

Roberts, Paul. 2015. *The Impulse Society: America in the Age of Instant Gratification*. 2015. NY: Bloomsbury Publishing.

Shirer, William L. 1960. *The Rise and Fall of the Third Reich*. NY: Simon and Schuster.

Smith, Adam. 2010. *The Wealth of Nations*. London: Simon & Brown.

Stone, Oliver, and Peter Kuznick. 2012. *The Untold History of the United States*. NY: Gallery Books.

Veblen, Thorstein.1994. *The Theory of the Leisure Class: An Economic Study of Institutions*. NY: Penguin Books.

Weber, Max. 1958. *The Protestant Ethic and the Spirit of Capitalism*. NY: Charles Scribner's & Son.

———. 1964. *Theory of Social and Economic Organization*. Tr. by Talcott Parsons. NY: Free Press.

Zipf, George Kingsley. 1972. *Human Behavior and the Principle of Least Effort*. NY: Hafner Publishing Co.

Index

Altman, Eric, 46, 144

American social character, 95–104;
Americans as victims of consumption,
96; and Thomas Jefferson, 101;
character studies, 95; shaped by
entertainment, 96; understanding
Trump via social character, 96

American Society, 18; and advertising
expenditure, 19; and American
Exceptionalism, 27; and computer time,
19; and consumption as American Way
of Life, 113; and drug-taking, 20; and
frontier history, 123, 133, 143; and
mass entertainment, 115; and its "two
sides", 34; and its economic system, 36;
and lawyers, 20; and lost mind in,
129–140; and obesity, 20; and prison
inmates, 18; and solitary life, 35; and
the War on Terror, 20, 138; and wealth
gap, 20; and work hating, 19, 34; as
creator of Donald Trump, 32; as
economic society, 64, 68; as political
society (19th century), 168; as first
"natural" society, 18; as a savage
nation, 22, 35; as superpower, 25; as
"untried civilization", 27; dominance of
capitalism in, 70

Bauerlein, Mark, 31
Best and Brightest, xi, 36, 51, 55, 97

calculating and thinking, 129–130;
calculating defined, 129; thinking
defined, 130

Camp Humphreys, ix, x

"Capitalist Party", 143

Churchill, Winston, 21

Circus Maximus, 134

Civil War (American), 8

Classic Liberalism, 4, 68

consumer capitalism, ix, xii, 6, 11, 12, 21,
34, 36; and Dumbest Generation, 56;
and mass society, 76, 91–92;
controlling consumers, 152; cultural
garbage and, ix, xi; supplier of mental
needs, 133

consumer addiction (and enslavement),
152–155

control by capitalism, 179–185; in what we
eat, 179; through schooling, 180; via
economic power, 180; with mind
control, 182; with use of psychology,
183

Corporate America (capitalism), xi, 36, 48,
80; and "Capitalist Party", 143; and
Chinese opium addicts, 92; and
dispersed control by, 145; and
Founding Fathers, 54; and government,
173; and institutional corruption, 172;
and legitimacy, 54; and liberal society,
37; and Trump's Fascism, 39, 63–73;
and its conflict with Fascism, 63, 71,

72; as all eternal, 151; as all good, 151; as all knowing, 151; as all powerful, 150; as everywhere, 151; as loved by all, 152; as New God in America, 150–152; as spread in U.S., 144; as supplier of insanity in America, 137, 145; as supplier of Mental Trash, 149–150; as owners of machines and people, 131, 133; compared to Nazism and Communism, 141–144; consumer defined, 146–147; corporation defined, 146, 148; dishonesty of, 148; how money buys laws, 167–174; how capitalism controls America, 179–185; logic of, 149, 157, 173; similarities with Fascism, 64; similarities with citizens, 172–173; state of nature and, 149

Darwinism, 69
Dante (of Divine Comedy), 165
David and Goliath (in U.S. system), 147
democracy, 52–53; and Electoral College, 54; and totalitarianism, 53; and Tyranny of Majority (de Tocqueville), 54, 78, 80, 168; democracy in America, 53, 143
Digital Revolution, 21, 92; and the Dumbest Generation, 32, 55, 82; Carr, Nicholas (of the Shallows), 117, 125; Internet as new opium, 124, 126–128
Dolan, Cardinal (of New York), 13

Enlightenment, 14, 26
entertainment in America, 37, 93; as capitalism's control, 179; as childish fantasy, 39; as everywhere always on, 172

Feudalism, 81, 82

Garden of Eden, 47

Hacker, Andrew, 12

Internet, 124–128; addiction to, 124, 126–128; and factor of anonymity, 127; Bill Gates and, 125–126; critique of, 126–128; mind control by, 126; nullification of time and space, 128;

South Korea and, 127; speed and, 124–125; White anxiety and, 122

Jay Gould quote, 82, 83

King Lear, 44

labor (and capitalism), 157–163; avoidance of, 160; Christianity and, 159–160, 161; how capitalism prevailed, 161–162; rich and poor in America, 162; Romans and Nazis and, 160; "sex slaves" and, 162–163; Talented Few and, 161; Two Schools of Labor, 158–160
law and law-making (in America), 167–174; and U.S. Supreme Court, 174–178; and controlling America, 181; defined, 167; functions of (in America), 174; logic of money and power, 170; rational system of, 167–168; through history, 167
liberty and freedom (contrasted), 184
Lindbergh, Charles, 3–4, 5, 6
lost mind, 129–140; and "others", 130; and Common Man, 133; and false power, 132; and insanity, 135–138; and PTSD, 135, 138; causes of, 130; difficulty of regaining, 130, 132

McCarthy Communist Scare, 8, 88
McLuhan, Marshall, ix
Medal of Freedom (for Hitler), 169
Mental Trash, xii, 115–128; and Mental-Trash Receptacle, 117; and consequences of, 119; and digital culture, 120–122; and "here now, gone now", 122; and Internet, 126–128; and living room as "dying room", 119; and mental health professionals, 129, 135, 137; and "nation of strangers", 122–123; and reality as relative, 119; and speed of service, 124–125; and White Americans, 123; anxiety as caused by, 122; as center of consumer capitalism, 128; as dumbing down America, 95; as impossible to quit, 116; as ruling method, 131; as ubiquitous, 117; as wasted entertainment, 118; defined, 116, 117

Millennials, x, 134–135, 183
minimum wage, 131
Monsanto, 78, 169
Moore, Michael, 11
"Moral Immunity" (Donald Trump),
   41–48; and Child with Loaded Gun, 43;
   and living with lies, 48; and presidential
   power, 45; and Trump's moral beliefs,
   45; defined, 41; God's, 43; Hitler's, 42;
   of Pied Piper, 43; Trump's, 42, 43, 44;
   Trump as sociopath, 46
Moranto, Robert, 8
Morrow, Lance, 31
Mother Jones, 11, 144
Muskie, Ed, 42

Nation magazine, 11, 46, 144
national character, 33
Nazis (and Hitler), xii, 5, 16, 21, 25, 26,
   42, 54, 58, 141; being a Nazi in
   Germany, 141, 142, 143
Ninety-Nine Percent, 81, 83, 141

One Percent, 13, 69, 81, 90, 93; as
   powerful controller of society, 150

psychology and sociology, 138–140; and
   individual, 139; and social institutions,
   140; "Bill Gates' Property", 139;
   functions of society, 139, 140;
   Lincoln's quote on history, 139;
   popularity of psychology, 138, 140;
   unpopularity of sociology, 138–140
Postman, Neil, 31
privatization (of White America), xii

Reich, Robert, 11
revolution (impossibility of), 163–165
Revolutionary War (American), 8
Rockefeller, Nelson, 42

Sanders, Bernie, 131
Scandinavia (as good society), 150
Snapchat, x
social consciousness, 101–103
Soviet Union (and Communism), 142, 143
speed (of service) and social class,
   124–125
Super Bowl, 2, 89; Vince Lombardi and, 2

Supreme Court (of U.S.), 174–178

Trump, Donald, x; and American
   intellectuals, 1, 15–18, 23, 51–52; and
   capitalism, 67, 157; and climate change,
   86; and Clinton (Hillary), 9, 13, 131;
   and consumer capitalism, 2; and
   division in America, 29–30, 31; and
   fake news, 2; and George W. Bush, 2,
   9; and Henry David Thoreau, 3; and his
   "moral immunity", 41–48; and
   Hollywood portrayal of Whites, 29; and
   how he won presidency, 105–113; and
   Jesus Christ, 3, 47, 163; and Lesser
   Americans, 38, 45, 75, 86, 133, 145,
   155; and Military Establishment, 45;
   and national character, 32; and
   nationalism and racism, 11, 12, 26; and
   non-whites, 11, 14, 89, 147; and "one
   America", 11, 12, 14; and other
   candidates, 10; and Russia, 2; and
   "Teflon President", 41; and world
   trends, 103–104; and WWIII, 42, 44; as
   American Fascist, 28, 65–67, 89, 131,
   145; as Child with a Loaded Gun, 6, 31,
   35; as caged in the White House,
   86–88; as demagogue, 85–93; as
   emperor with no clothes, 26; as *Enfant
   Terrible*, 43, 44; as entertainer, 49; as a
   man-child, 42; as amoral, 45–46; as
   ideologically ambiguous, 67, 78–80; as
   Messiah (and Savior), 5, 6; as the most
   disputed president, xi; as made in the
   USA, xii, 4; as product of
   entertainment, 115; as quintessential
   American, 1, 12, 48, 85–86; as
   secondary to capitalism, 152; as Tabula
   Rasa, 45; between capitalism and
   fascism, 63–73, 70; compared to Putin
   and Xi, 45; media attacks against,
   75–77; Patty Dwyer and, x; Trump's
   America and Lincoln's America, 31;
   "Trump Whites", x, 3, 6, 10, 21, 22, 30,
   37, 38, 43, 50–52, 146; "Trumpian
   Revolutionaries", 172
TV watching in U.S., 19

voting as hypnosis, 7–8

WATS (White American Trump Supporters), 99, 102, 146
WANTS (White American Not Trump Supporters), 99, 100, 102
"White anger", 36, 57–62; and white privileges, 59–60; causes of white anger, 61; question of, 57; America as White Society, 61

Yankee horse traders, x